The New Criminal Justice

Criminal justice in the United States is in the midst of momentous changes: an era of low crime rates not seen since the 1960s, and a variety of budget crunches also exerting profound impacts on the system. This is the first book available to chronicle these changes and suggest a new, emerging model to the criminal justice system, emphasizing:

- collaboration across agencies previously viewed as relatively autonomous
- a focus on local problems and local solutions rather than a widely shared understanding of crime or broad application of similar interventions
- a deep commitment to research that guides problem assessment and policy formulation and intervention
- ideal for use in graduate as well as undergraduate capstone courses.

John M. Klofas is Professor of Criminal Justice, Chairperson of the Department of Criminal Justice at Rochester Institute of Technology, and Director of the Center for Public Safety Initiatives (CPSI).

Natalie Kroovand Hipple is a Research Specialist at the School of Criminal Justice at Michigan State University.

Edmund F. McGarrell is Director and Professor of the School of Criminal Justice at Michigan State University.

CRIMINOLOGY AND JUSTICE STUDIES SERIES

Edited by **Chester Britt**, Northeastern University, **Shaun L. Gabbidon**, Penn State Harrisburg, and **Nancy Rodriguez**, Arizona State University

Criminology and Justice Studies offers works that make both intellectual and stylistic innovations in the study of crime and criminal justice. The goal of the series is to publish works that model the best scholarship and thinking in the criminology and criminal justice field today, but in a style which connects that scholarship to a wider audience including advanced undergraduates, graduate students, and the general public. The works in this series help fill the gap between academic monographs and encyclopedic textbooks by making innovative scholarship accessible to a large audience without the superficiality of many texts.

BOOKS IN THE SERIES

Published
Biosocial Criminology: New Directions in Theory and Research edited by Anthony Walsh and Kevin M. Beaver
Community Policing in America by Jeremy M. Wilson
Criminal Justice Theory edited by David E. Duffee and Edward R. Maguire
Criminological Perspectives on Race and Crime by Shaun L. Gabbidon
Lifers by John Irwin
Race, Law and American Society: 1607 to Present by Gloria J. Browne-Marshall
Today's White Collar Crime by Hank J. Brightman
White Collar Crime: An Opportunity Perspective by Michael Benson and Sally Simpson

Forthcoming
Crime and the Lifecourse by Michael Benson and Alex Piquero
Criminological Perspectives on Race and Crime, Second Edition by Shaun L. Gabbidon
The Policing of Terrorism by Mathieu Deflem
Structural Equations Modeling for Criminology and Criminal Justice by George Higgins

Also of interest from Routledge
Racist America: Roots, Current Realities, and Future Reparations, Second Edition by Joe R. Feagin
GIS and Spatial Analysis for the Social Sciences by Robert Nash Parker and Emily K. Asencio
Regression Analysis for the Social Sciences by Rachel A. Gordon
Operation Gatekeeper and Beyond: The War on Illegals and the Remaking of the U.S.–Mexico Boundary by Joseph Nevins

The New Criminal Justice

American Communities and the Changing World of Crime Control

Edited by

John Klofas
Rochester Institute of Technology

Natalie Kroovand Hipple
Michigan State University

Edmund McGarrell
Michigan State University

Routledge
Taylor & Francis Group

NEW YORK AND LONDON

First published 2010
by Routledge
270 Madison Avenue, New York, NY 10016

Simultaneously published in the UK
by Routledge
2 Park Square, Milton Park, Abingdon, Oxon OX14 4RN

Routledge is an imprint of the Taylor & Francis Group, an informa business

© 2010 Taylor & Francis

Typeset in Sabon by Prepress Projects Ltd, Perth, UK
Printed and bound in the United States of America on acid-free paper by Edwards Brothers, Inc.

Library of Congress Cataloging in Publication Data

Klofas, John.

The new criminal justice : American communities and the changing world of crime control / John Klofas, Natalie Kroovand Hipple, Edmund McGarrell.

p. cm. — (Criminology and justice studies series)

ISBN 978-0-415-99722-5 (hardback) — ISBN 978-0-415-99728-7 (pbk.) — ISBN 978-0-203-86016-8 (e-book) 1. Criminal justice, Administration of—United States. 2. Crime prevention—United States. 3. Law enforcement—United States. I. Hipple, Natalie Kroovand. II. McGarrell, Edmund F., 1956– III. Title.

HV9950.K55 2010

364.973—dc22

2009030958

ISBN10: 0-415-99722-4 (hbk)
ISBN10: 0-415-99728-3 (pbk)
ISBN10: 0-203-86016-0 (ebk)

ISBN13: 978-0-415-99722-5 (hbk)
ISBN13: 978-0-415-99728-7 (pbk)
ISBN13: 978-0-203-86016-8 (ebk)

CONTENTS

SECTION I: THE CHANGING WORLD OF CRIMINAL JUSTICE

JOHN M. KLOFAS, NATALIE KROOVAND HIPPLE, AND EDMUND F. MCGARRELL

This chapter outlines the book by describing the New Criminal Justice and how it is different than the Systems Model of Criminal Justice. This new approach is characterized by collaborative arrangements of powerful coalitions at the local level driven by locally relevant research and organized to reduce violent crime.

JOHN M. KLOFAS

The President's Commission's chart of the criminal justice system has not only been its most recognized addition to the field but has also served important goals by describing the system, allowing simulation, and helping identify the consequences of change. With similar purpose in mind, this chapter seeks to provide a graphical model of the New Criminal Justice. The diagram adds the essential features of the new model and includes a "fuzzy logic" approach.

EDMUND F. MCGARRELL

Project Safe Neighborhoods embodies the core elements of the New Criminal Justice. This chapter describes Project Safe Neighborhoods and how it built on successful programs such as Boston Ceasefire and Project Exile. It lays the foundation for Chapters 4–7.

SECTION II: THE NEW CRIMINAL JUSTICE IN PRACTICE

SECTION III: NEW KNOWLEDGE FOR NEW PRACTICE IN CRIMINAL JUSTICE

SECTION IV: WHERE DO WE GO FROM HERE?

FIGURES

TABLES

SERIES EDITOR FOREWORD

Criminology and Justice Studies offers works that make both intellectual and stylistic innovations in the study of crime and criminal justice. The goal of the series is to publish works that model the best scholarship and thinking in the field today, but in a style that connects that scholarship to a wider audience including advanced undergraduates and graduate students. The works in the series help fill the gap between academic monographs and encyclopedic textbooks by making innovative scholarship accessible to a large audience without the superficiality of many texts.

The New Criminal Justice presents an insightful look into the function and activities of the criminal justice system. Whereas the systems model of criminal justice has dominated our understanding of the justice system for years, the authors of this text present a different perspective, the New Criminal Justice model, which creatively characterizes our current criminal justice system. The New Criminal Justice model comprises collaborative arrangements of powerful coalitions at the local level driven by locally relevant research and organized to reduce violent crime. By outlining the essential features of this new model including a "fuzzy logic" approach, "action research," and concrete examples such as Project Safe Neighborhoods, Boston Ceasefire, and Project Exile that exemplify the core elements of the New Criminal Justice, the authors present a comprehensive and creative new perspective to the study of the justice system. The New Criminal Justice model as outlined by the authors has important implications for the teaching of criminal justice and research of the justice system. This book will make readers reconsider theories of criminal justice and criminology, encourage analysis of criminal justice problems across communities within the context of specific social and political environments, and ultimately, provide a new perspective for understating crime reduction efforts in America.

Nancy Rodriguez
Shaun Gabbidon
Chester Britt
Series Editors

FOREWORD

John Klofas, Natalie Hipple, and Ed McGarrell have compiled an excellent volume, far more than just a collection of chapters. Like many edited books, there are outstanding contributions, with important findings and policy statements. Unlike most edited books, however, this volume highlights one of the most important new themes in criminal justice in the past decade. It is not an overstatement to say that this book lays out the model for the New Criminal Justice. For those who only paid attention to life course criminology, hierarchical linear modeling, or macro-level theory for the past decade, you missed the emergence of this important, new way of dealing with crime problems. The New Criminal Justice is evidence based, practice oriented, and theoretically driven. The New Criminal Justice has research in the beginning, the middle, and the end of the model. In fact, there really is no end to research in this model, or shouldn't be, as it should be a loop that reinvents itself.

Sparked by high rates of violence in the 1990s and the frustration of the public, elected officials and criminal justice leaders, a new criminal justice emerged around the turn of the century. This movement, not yet fully institutionalized, is based on five key principles: (1) data-driven approaches to guide the development, implementation and assessment of interventions, (2) staying focused on short-term problems, (3) a strategic focus on interventions, (4) a conceptual model of what caused the problem and how to address it, and (5) an integrated functionality across systems, persons, roles, and ranks. This paradigm shift in the practice of criminal justice and criminal justice research has its roots in problem-solving approaches to crime, though it extends much further. At the federal level, initiatives such as the Strategic Approaches to Community Safety Initiative (SACSI) and Project Safe Neighborhoods (PSN) did a great deal to push the paradigm shift ahead. These initiatives provided funding, leadership, training, and a methodology by which political jurisdictions, agencies, and communities could focus on problems of criminal justice in manageable ways. At the local level, the leadership of police chiefs in New York, Los Angeles, Chicago, and Boston through initiatives such as COMPSTAT, the Boston Gun Project, and CAPS were important for engaging local law enforcement leaders. I had the opportunity to observe the leadership of the three editors of this volume firsthand, as a participant in both SACSI and PSN. When these initiatives began, I had worked with criminal justice and elected officials in St. Louis for nearly a quarter of a century. Despite the city's reputation (and ranking) as one of the most violent cities in America, the four officials most integral to addressing the violence problem had never met on a regular basis. It is hard to fathom that the Police Chief, Prosecutor, U.S. Attorney, and Mayor in a city with rates of violence eight to ten times as high as national rates did not meet regularly to address the problem of violence. First SACSI and then PSN brought these four individuals together on a monthly basis to review data, discuss trends, review approaches, and recommend changes in policy and practice. This is a practice that continues today, some ten years and several personnel changes later.

The chapters that follow describe SACSI, PSN and other related interventions in considerable detail. It is not my intention to review the content of the book in this foreword. Instead I intend to discuss some of the processes that led to the emergence of such approaches, their strengths, their dark side(s), and what the future might hold. At its core this approach cautions against quick fixes, promotes institutional change, and pushes the role of research to what is often an uncomfortable level for many researchers and practitioners. There is no more uneasy feeling for a researcher than to be put on the spot in a meeting by a police chief, probation head, or lead prosecutor to tell the group what to do.

It is important to put the New Criminal Justice in a broader context. In the evolution of American criminal justice, there have been several significant watershed events, commissions, or practices. The 1931 Wickersham Commission helped transform criminal justice from the grasp of local politics and a lack of professional orientation to a different track. At about the same time, the first Uniform Crime Reports were published in 1930, and in the following year the FBI took over their collection, publication, and dissemination, bringing some greater uniformity to data that had the potential to be used for decision making, policy assessment, and planning. Following World War II, a number of leaders emerged in criminal justice, promoting the value of education for criminal justice employees, particularly the police. August Vollmer was particularly important to this movement. The role of the 1967 President's Commission is highlighted in this volume, and played a substantial role in moving the practice of criminal justice forward from its traditional "practice as usual" military model into one that had the potential for the use of data, science, and policy assessment. I emphasize the word "potential" here, because a number of key factors were not present at that time to ease the transition to a more scientific practice of criminal justice. Most notable among the missing parts was the ability to process data and information in real time (or nearly real time) with the widespread availability of computers and relatively straightforward software. The COPS office led and funded the inclusion of laptop computers in patrol cars. The use of COMPSTAT in New York City, and now across the country, made police decision making confront the reality of their own data, a change key to the emergence of the New Criminal Justice.

These changes laid the groundwork for the New Criminal Justice described by the editors of this volume. One of the key factors that eased the transition to the New Criminal Justice was the inclusion of research as part of the role of criminal justice practitioners. Indeed, the role of research, be it in the collection of new data, the use of new techniques of analysis, or larger technical capabilities, and the "embedding" of researchers in criminal justice agencies are key features for each of these dramatic changes in the practice of criminal justice. Today, it is not uncommon to hear police chiefs and probation heads talk about research produced by their own departments. Indeed, in a presentation made to the 2009 Bureau of Justice Statistics, the police chief of St. Louis (Dr. Dan Isom) presented a sophisticated time series analysis of the relationship between burglaries and copper prices. It seems the chief had discovered that, when copper prices spiked, thefts of plumbing and gutters from houses increased as well. The use of such data, analysis, and creative thinking is something that holds out hope that the New Criminal Justice is not simply the intervention "du jour," made popular by Pied Piper–like descriptions from outsiders, but instead represents an institutionalization of a new way to approaching, defining, and analyzing problems.

A key inspiration for the New Criminal Justice described and advocated by the editors came from the work in Project Safe Neighborhoods. PSN was administered through the US Justice Department by the 94 US Attorney's offices (though one declined to participate). Thus in a way, PSN represented 93 different experiments, as PSN was described as a process, not a model to be implemented according to a well-defined blueprint. Some of those experiments were quite successful, and this book does an excellent job explaining those successful experiments. But, in any large distribution, events tend to resemble a normal distribution, and there were about as many failures as there were successes, and of course, the largest group in the middle that achieved modest successes. We don't talk about failure enough. The "successful" interventions are held up as models to be emulated, often independent of the context in which the models were implemented. But the failures hold just as much for us to learn from, and in many cases more than the successes. After all, a solid process and outcome evaluation that shows a program failed should lead us to avoid using that intervention in the future. It is also the case that failed interventions can provide insights for successful implementations. One of the legacies of the New Criminal Justice, as practiced by Klofas, Hipple, and McGarrell is the documentation of the process of creating change in criminal justice. Their work shows that this process is much like watching sausage being made: it often has a messy side to it.

But there are cautions to be raised about this New Criminal Justice. For those of us trained in the 1970s, Herbert Packer's influential book, *The Limits of the Criminal Sanction*, was a key in shaping our orientation to the way that the criminal justice system works. Packer contrasted the due process model with the crime control model. The former described the processing of cases in the due process model as resembling an obstacle course, whereas the crime control model exhibited the efficiency of an assembly line. The former produced justice, the latter outcomes. The emphasis on improving the working of the system in the New Criminal Justice clearly looks like an assembly line. Indeed, one of the more prominent PSN sites regarded changing the system as its primary task, believing that the deterrence message would not be credible because offenders understood that the system seldom worked in the ways its leaders said it would. So, in identifying the potential dark sides of the New Criminal Justice, there is a concern that the tilt toward efficiency will further trample the rights of the accused, or produce increases in the disparity of arrest and sentencing. That can be tempered by an increase in precision in the application of the criminal sanction. We shall see how that works out. A second dark side is what might be termed "research imperialism," a belief that research always has the answers. Often our answers are right if they are limited to a specific context at a particular point in time and executed by a specific set of actors. The reaction to research that is wrong or premature may lead to a rejection of the larger research enterprise. A third and related concern is overgeneralizing and overselling the results of research. Some interventions – the Boston Gun Project comes quickly to mind – become oversold and over-replicated with little concern for the actual context, components, or impact of the initial proposal. A fourth concern is something that researchers excel at, waiting to draw conclusions and offer advice until all the data are in and all of the analysis has been collected; for many researchers this never happens. There is also a final concern about the New Criminal Justice. It emerged at a time when rates of violent crime were already falling. But what happens when the rates go back up? Will mayors, police chiefs, probation heads, and others who are accountable for crime rates so willingly receive outsiders, collaborate, and be investing in their crime analysis units, rather than more cops on the beat?

These concerns pale in light of the remarkable contributions to date made by the New Criminal Justice. Klofas, Hipple, and McGarrell were crusaders in the effort to spread the word about creating partnerships, embedding research into practice, and using data to drive decisions. They were joined by Lois Mock, formerly of the National Institute of Justice, a tireless advocate of the role of research and researchers in decision making in criminal justice. Lois' efforts are proof that one person can make a difference.

The key lessons of the New Criminal Justice are to keep a sharp focus on the problem at hand, be strategic in planning interventions, use data to guide decisions and assess the future of interventions, and use broad-based partnerships to address crime problems. These are not new in and of themselves, but in combination they do represent a new approach, the new criminal justice. The financial challenges faced by cities, states, and the federal government have upped the ante for smart criminal justice. The editors of this volume provide important lessons – what to do and what not to do – for those whose task it is to ensure safe communities. The individuals and agencies whose task that is will be wise to pay careful attention to the processes documented in this volume. If they don't pay attention to the lessons described here, it will be at their own peril.

Scott H. Decker, Ph.D..
Phoenix, Arizona

PREFACE

The origins of this volume can probably be traced to a point at which a number of seemingly disconnected paths happened to cross. Not the least of those paths is represented by the editors themselves. Before the work that helped build the foundation for this book we knew each other but not well. But it was not just our coming together that seems to have mattered. The ideas we shared seemed to have common roots. In our own teaching experiences we each began to notice a tendency to stray from what seemed to be the doctrinal foundations of our field.

Although our introductory texts marched us and our students through the criminal justice system from the police, through the courts, and then on to corrections, we each found ourselves increasingly distracted along the way. The number of exceptions to the direct path seemed to grow with each course we taught. Drug courts emerged but seemed to be neither fish nor fowl. Prosecutors did not seek to prove guilt and defense attorneys did not claim innocence. Community policing had thrust officers into new roles. In corrections a myriad of alternatives to incarceration blurred the lines of punishment and treatment. When it came to juvenile justice it seemed still harder to identify the typical pathways that cases traveled.

Other experiences also drew us away from a more traditional view of the criminal justice system. We each knew progressive police chiefs who were not content to continue to do the same old things as they saw problems of violence rise in their communities. Some prosecutors too seemed to be searching for new roles in the fight against crime. And when we looked behind those officials it was common to see community members trying to organize to address violence in their neighborhoods.

The three of our paths crossed when it also became clear that there were new roles for researchers in this growing response to crime and violence. Researchers were not to be relegated to after-the-fact evaluations or to independent tests of esoteric hypotheses. There was to be a role for them in strategic planning with their local criminal justice systems.

Many of our experiences contrasted sharply with the most common portrayal of the criminal justice system. Over 40 years after its release, the 1967 report of the President's Commission on Law Enforcement and the Administration of Justice remains an influential document. No part has been more influential than the diagram of the criminal justice system presented in the Commission's report on technology as directed by Dr. Alfred Blumstein. We have all learned and taught the way that criminal justice works as presented in that graphic. The classic model has been one of largely predictable movement of serious cases through the system, feedback loops, and the use of systems theory to predict the impact of change.

As Blumstein has noted, however, recent heightened concern with crime, particularly violent crime, is now changing the criminal justice system. For the editors of this volume those changes became most evident in our close work with two major projects supported by the National Institute of Justice (NIJ). The first project, known as Strategic Approaches to Community Safety Initiative (SACSI), supported researchers to participate in problem solving in criminal justice in ten cities. In the second project, Project Safe Neighborhoods (PSN), the problem-solving approach was expanded to cover nearly every federal judicial district in the country, at least with respect to violent gun-, gang-, and drug-related crime.

These programs showed the potential and the great power of the new shape that criminal justice was taking. In the New Criminal Justice the focus is on addressing crime at the local level. National models have given way to localized analyses and innovations. Coalitions of agencies work together as partners, pooling their resources and powers to address crime, rather than as the loosely linked organizations suggested in the earlier model. Finally, the New Criminal Justice relies heavily on research and capable researchers to help direct its strategies. For the editors of this volume the uneasiness of teaching a seemingly incomplete model and the experiences across a broad spectrum of local communities suggested the need to re-examine basic assumptions about how criminal justice works. The collective experience has convinced us that, with little attention from the public, and little examination within the field of criminal justice, a new and different model of criminal justice is continuing to emerge.

The book divides the discussion of this model into four main sections. The first section lays the theoretical and conceptual groundwork for later descriptions of the practice of criminal justice in communities across the country. In it we describe the origins of the New Criminal Justice and its current shape. We suggest that the concept of fuzzy logic may help understand how different communities may view crime and respond to it differently. Section II describes in detail the elements of the New Criminal Justice and presents cases studies of the application of the model to crime reduction problems. Section III describes the new role of research in criminal justice. After tracing the involvement of NIJ in supporting this research, a series of chapters by accomplished action researchers reports on the strengths and potential hazards of undertaking a role in this type of strategic planning. The final section of the book addresses what has been learned from the experiences with the New Criminal Justice under Project Safe Neighborhoods. In the last chapter we return to what first attracted our attention to this subject. Here we tackle more directly how the New Criminal Justice might address the teaching issues with which we opened this preface.

In the paragraphs above we trace the ideas that led to the creation of this volume. We are grateful to the reviewers of the volume who saw enough in early drafts to be interested but also saw the need for greater explanation and organization. We are also grateful to the many colleagues who participated with us in the experiments in criminal justice that formed the foundation of this book. Practitioners and researchers in well over 100 communities around the country provided the path that is ultimately described in these chapters. With some of them we shared a great deal of time and energy. For their contributions we are particularly grateful to Scott Decker, Jack McDevitt, and Tim Bynum. We are, of course, very grateful to the authors who allowed us to use their work in this book. One of those stands out in particular. Lois Mock, senior social scientist—now retired from NIJ—not only provided a valuable chapter on action research but also was an important contributor to the overall effort represented here and it was her guiding hand during her long career which assured that research would be preserved as a critical feature of Project Safe Neighborhoods. Lois was succeeded at NIJ by Phelan Wyrick and subsequently by Louis Tuthill, both of whom have demonstrated a similar commitment to advancing action research and evidence-based practice to address gun crime.

Lois, Phelan, and Louis worked with an outstanding team at the NIJ, the Bureau of Justice Assistance, and a number of offices at the Department of Justice who supported not only our research on Project Safe Neighborhoods but also the integration of research into Project Safe Neighborhoods task forces throughout the country.

We must also acknowledge the U.S. Attorneys, Assistant U.S. Attorneys, Law Enforcement Coordinators, chiefs of police, sheriffs, SASCI Coordinators, local prosecutors, police officers, crime analysts, community members, researchers, and all of those individuals on the ground and in the trenches creating the New Criminal Justice in their jurisdictions. Without your support and gracious cooperation, our research would not have been possible.

We are also thankful for the support of our families and friends during the time it took to complete this project. They not only suffered with us through the lengthy writing and editing process but also supported us through the frequent travel needed to document the work being carried out around the country. Finally, a book would be of little value without its readers. We are thus thankful to all those who spend time with these pages and we hope that you will provide us with your thoughts on what we see as a significant change in the field of criminal justice.

John M. Klofas
Natalie Kroovand Hipple
Edmund F. McGarrell

SECTION 1

The Changing World of Criminal Justice

It is nearly impossible to overstate the importance of President Johnson's Crime Commission and its 1967 report. Although other organizations had examined the processes of criminal justice before, the Commission provided the most sweeping and influential analysis of the Nation's response to crime. At its center was the concept of a system of agencies and offices in linear formation passing cases on from one to another, each with its own mission and each providing some check and balance on those that come before it. This book opens with the recognition of the power of the Commission's work, especially as it developed the description and the diagram of the criminal justice system presented in the report of the task force on technology. The first chapter argues that the Commission's thinking represented as close to an intellectual revolution as has been seen in criminal justice. It remains a powerful influence on our thinking, but significant changes have also occurred.

Chapter 1 of this volume presents the core of critical ideas for the book. It argues that the view of the criminal justice system as a linear model in which cases move forward across semi-autonomous agencies does not fully capture the criminal justice process today. Instead, interest in problem solving in general and crime reduction in particular has required us to consider a more complex and more powerful model of criminal justice. The emerging model emphasizes: (1) collaboration across agencies previously viewed as relatively autonomous, (2) a focus on local problems and local solutions rather than a widely shared understanding of crime or broad application of similar interventions, and (3) finally a deep commitment to research, which guides problem assessment and policy formulation and intervention.

Chapter 2 takes on the task that proved so important to the President's Commission, the ability to describe in detail and to portray the operations of the criminal justice process. One goal of the Commission was to present a model of the way that cases are processed so that the impact of changes in the number or types of cases, or in the ways decisions were made, could be modeled and used to understand and predict probable outcomes. The well-known diagram of the criminal justice system was intended to serve as a living portrait of how that system worked and how changes in any part of it might affect changes in its other parts.

The chapter addresses the question of how case processing may be viewed differently when we recognize the increased significance of the three elements of agency collaboration, local focus and reliance of research. To those factors we also introduce a somewhat new and different tool to assist in describing criminal justice. Fuzzy logic has been used by systems analysts to allow their models to incorporate degrees of ambiguity in decision-making processes. In our case we allow for consideration of different degrees of severity of crimes or degrees of certainty about guilt or innocence or degrees to which sanctions might be thought of as therapeutic or punitive. The combination of these elements allows us to consider three different aspects of the criminal justice system including: (1) the community process by which the resources for addressing crime are assembled differently across communities, (2) the process by which behavior comes to be regarded as of greater or lesser concern to community members, and (3) ways in which communities can respond to that behavior. The principles of this model also indicate that, at each step, surveillance of offenders and potential offenders influences decision making through a feedback process. Considering the three characteristics of the New Criminal Justice and applying "fuzzy logic" focuses attention on substantially different aspects of case processing than in the original Commission approach.

Chapter 3 provides an outline of the implementation of many of the ideas discussed in the first two chapters. It reviews Project Safe Neighborhoods, a program that we will visit again in subsequent chapters. The project provided a national model of the process of strategic problem solving aimed at a reduction in violent crime and particularly a reduction in gun crimes. With support through United States Attorneys' Offices, local criminal justice systems, working with trained researchers, collaborated in a process of problem identification, specification, and intervention. The project's core characteristics included accountability or a focus on real crime reduction, partnerships in criminal justice, outreach to communities, and significant training focused on strategic planning. As later chapters will show, these elements could be combined in ways to produce many different programs based on local needs, but together they resulted in an often novel and cohesive approach to local crime problems.

DISCUSSION QUESTIONS

1 The first section of this book may be its most challenging. The reader is asked to consider with a new eye something that has become very familiar. The President's Commission view of criminal justice has been a powerful way of organizing what we know in the field. Can you now reconsider the criminal justice system and see how our language of crime and the response to it matches the Commission model? How does our current lexicon handle things such as forfeiture cases that are not moved forward through the system? Think of drug courts that offer treatment alternatives to sanctions but which may themselves require extensive jail stays. How are these courts like or unlike other criminal proceedings?

2 The core ideas of collaboration across the criminal justice system, local focus, and use of research suggest only the broadest elements related to understanding and processing criminal offenses. They do not, in and of themselves, promise positive outcomes such as lower crime and fairer outcomes. Consider how these elements may work together to improve these sorts of outcomes and how they might also contribute to problems. What kind of safeguards might help minimize the potential problems you see?

3 These chapters suggest that criminal justice is becoming organized in new ways and around new core ideas. It is suggested that the classic model of criminal justice is changing. What are the implications of this for those who work in criminal justice? What new knowledge or skills do you think will be useful under this new approach to crime and crime control?

CHAPTER 1

The New Criminal Justice

John M. Klofas, Natalie Kroovand Hipplo, and Edmund F. McGarrell

In his classic work, *The Structure of Scientific Revolutions*, Thomas Kuhn argued that "normal science" plods along based upon principles on which there is general agreement in a particular discipline or field of science (1970). Change occurs by revolution when those key principles are disconfirmed by research. The resulting crisis spawns new theories. They then go on to guide a new era of "puzzle solving" science that is propelled toward its next revolution when accepted doctrine will once again be rejected through research. For Kuhn, that is the path of progress in the sciences.

Rarely has change in American criminal justice been described in terms of revolution. More commonly change in this field has been described using more modest terms, usually by invoking the language of organizational change or knowledge utilization rather than the language of revolution (see Stojkovic et al., 2008; Havelock, 1979). Among the common descriptions, change in criminal justice has often been seen as the result of rational planning (see Hudzik and Cordner, 1983). From an alternative view, reforms have sometimes been driven by the coercive power of the courts (Ekland-Olson and Martin, 1988). Through the sixties, the Supreme Court under Earl Warren was often seen as moving criminal justice to the left, whereas later Courts have been viewed as reaching different results in their compromises of conflicting liberal and conservative ideologies. Scholars have argued that struggles over these ideological positions dominate policy making in the field of criminal justice (see Cullen and Gilbert, 1982). And too, change may result from technological innovation. The influence of the squad car or radios or even 9-1-1 systems comes to mind (Gaines et al., 2003). On the other hand, change in criminal justice has sometimes been viewed as the barely perceptible reflection of incremental steps driven by a wide range of marginally potent influences (see Schafer, 2004).

REVOLUTION AND THE 1967 PRESIDENT'S COMMISSION

If one were to seek to understand change in criminal justice in the United States as revolutionary the only event in recent history that might qualify for investigation would be the publication of the 1967 President's Crime Commission report, *The Challenge of Crime in a Free Society* (1967a) and its companion volumes, although there is certainly no consensus on this point. Arguably the Commission report presented a number of ideas that represented significant departures from the past. The task force report on crime and its impact brought attention to victimization issues and the measurement of crime (Reiss, 1994). Kelling and Coles (1996, p. 46) argue that the Commission's support for decriminalizing drunkenness had a significant influence. The report on juvenile delinquency and youth crime pushed an agenda of diversion and deinstitutionalization (Pisciotta, 1994). The report on science and technology has been credited with having significant influences on the development of forensics and information systems (Blumstein, 1994). Despite these claims, however, none of these effects would seem to rise to the level of revolutionary in either their description or their impact. In fact, a 25-year retrospective look at the impact of the 1967 President's Commission report concludes that analyses of its effects "should caution us about expecting too much in the way of long-term effects of blue-ribbon crime commissions" (Conley, 1994, p. xiii).

To consider only the Commission's specific recommendations, though, may miss the forest for the trees. The President's Commission did take one position that seems to be taken largely for granted today, but which arguably rose to the level of revolutionary at the time. That position has been so widely accepted that few seemed able to imagine that a different paradigm once shaped thinking about criminal justice or that a new paradigm could emerge. Specifically, the President's Commission provided, if not the first, certainly the strongest endorsement of the idea that the agencies of criminal justice comprised a "system" (see Walker, 1978). With analytic roots in the understanding of biological and mechanical systems, the criminal justice system was seen as moving cases forward from one agency to the next, almost always in one direction but having some built-in feedback and self-regulating mechanisms. The Commission noted "the criminal process . . . is not a hodgepodge of random actions. It is rather a continuum—an orderly progression of events . . . A study of the system must begin by examining it as a whole" (p. 7). Although the Commission notes that lower serious offenses might be handled differently, and that there were local differences, it presented a unified overall design. The depiction of this "Systems Model" was translated into an iconic diagram that has been reprinted in nearly every criminal justice textbook since it first appeared in the President's Commission's summary report.

Still, agreement has not been universal. Kelling and Coles (1996) provided one critique of viewing criminal justice as a system, particularly with reference to the police role. They note that the system model, which placed police at the front end of the structure, had the effect of narrowing the expected role of the police nearly exclusively to law enforcement. Lost was the view of the police as a provider of a wide range of general services while functioning as a branch of local government. Police departments, which were once seen as primarily local institutions, now were to be viewed as reflecting a set of common national interests and bureaucratic procedures. They were recognized as the front end of a largely linear system through which people, or more to the point cases, moved. Under the system model, the loosely coupled agencies of criminal justice pursued their own separate missions, one after another, and, in doing so, provided some checks and balances on one another. It is a model of clarity of purpose and rationality of process.

Of course, the extent to which the operation of the system ever truly reflected the ideal type suggested by its model could be debated. Certainly, critics found the inefficiencies worthy of note. What the Crime Commission described as a "system" was soon described as an "informal system" or even a "non-system" and other models were invoked to describe it, among them, for example, the model of wedding cake (see Walker, 1988) whose virtue was to recognize differences in case treatment according to the significance of the underlying offense.

Despite these re-examinations one should not underestimate the power of the system paradigm. Even today, the tendency is to see police, courts and corrections as having largely separate missions linked by the unidirectional movement of cases across them.

Criminal justice systems in different jurisdictions, including the state level or federal level, are also seen largely as only loosely coupled with local agencies. In this view criminal justice is examined as a process in which inputs from one part are exported to the next in a sequence moving from police to courts to corrections. The process is described with a language using concepts of case flow and outcome. Even most of its critics accept the basic systems perspective, but complain of its fragmentation and inefficiencies. They often support reforms to streamline or otherwise improve system efficiency.

There are also other indicators of the potency of this paradigm in criminal justice. Some have found virtue in what others have lamented as fragmentation. In maintaining that creating a more monolithic system merits caution, Kevin Wright (2004) has argued that the existing complex system has several advantages. First, in its current state, the system allows its loosely connected member agencies to reflect diversity in ideas about justice. Some interests, he argues, can reflect such goals as incapacitation and retribution, whereas others represent interests in reintegration and community supervision. Second, the lack of integration across the system allows adaptation to special problems. Wright notes that corrections can moderate, but not fully reverse, harsh sentences resulting from periodic public outcries. Finally, he argues that the inconsistencies and irregularities across the system serve as a check on state power (see also Forst, 1977).

Even its strongest critics, then, appear to have adopted the basic premise of the President's Commission. But today there is also reason to question that premise. Although perhaps not so dramatic as the crises that Kuhn argues undermine scientific paradigms (1970, p. 66), there are changes in criminal justice that remain mostly ignored, but which may portend even more significant change in the near future.

THE NEW CRIMINAL JUSTICE

The fundamental argument of this chapter is that observation today will permit description of a different model of criminal justice from that described by the President's Commission in 1967. In this new model, the organizations of criminal justice no longer operate in a sequence, connected through the handoff of criminal suspects or cases. Instead, in many jurisdictions across the country representatives of the principle components of the criminal justice system interact directly and regularly. They gather to pool their powers and their resources to address crime problems. Most often, the singular goal is the reduction of violent crime. In pursuit of that, police and prosecutors prioritize targets of investigation and prosecution, parole and probation add special search and seizure powers to the mix, and jails and prisons are tapped for intelligence information. Federal and local authorities negotiate prosecution based on who has the greatest likelihood of conviction and the potential for the most serious sanction. The New Criminal Justice is a model of cooperation and collaborative problem solving that bears only limited resemblance to the system depicted by the 1967 President's Commission. At least in some places across the country today the once semi-autonomous agencies of justice are now a conglomeration negotiating and pursuing a common goal.

THE ORIGINS OF THE NEW CRIMINAL JUSTICE

It may not have been a revolutionary disconfirming of deeply held principles that changed criminal justice, but faith in several experiments did certainly assist.

In Richmond, Virginia, and later in Rochester, New York, federal prosecutors, concerned over violence in their communities, sought more effective ways to deal with the specific problem of gun violence. They compared local and federal gun laws to understand differences in procedural requirements and severity of sentences. They developed what became known as "Project Exile," in which local and federal prosecutors routinely reviewed gun cases together to decide which avenue of prosecution to pursue (Richman, 2001). A media campaign delivered a message of grim deterrence to those who would violate gun laws. The media message threatened long sentences of exile in far-from-home federal prisons. A key part of Project Exile was regular meetings of key decision makers from across the local criminal justice system. The advisory boards represented a common interest in improving prosecution in gun crimes and a pooling of resources in pursuit of that goal.

While Project Exile was developing, an equally significant intervention was occurring in Boston. The Boston Gun Project also focused on gun crime and particularly firearm-related deaths of young people. The project was directed by David Kennedy, Anne Piehl, and Anthony Braga (1996) of the Kennedy School of Government at Harvard University and was supported by the National Institute of Justice. An inter-agency working group was formed to study the nature of Boston's youth violence problems. The group included the Boston Police Department, the U.S. Attorney's Office, the County Probation and Prosecutor's Offices, local representatives from the Bureau of Alcohol, Tobacco, Firearms, and Explosives and an organization of street outreach workers. The group developed a "lever pulling" strategy with which any available means, such as probation or parole violations, warrants, and even cold cases, were used against targeted street gang members who became the focus of attention because of their continued involvement in violence (Kennedy, 1997, see McGarrell et al., 2006). The police worked closely with prosecutors and probation officers to enforce laws and conditions of supervision and to incarcerate members of gangs when the gang was known to have been involved in violence. What became known as "Operation Ceasefire" was designed also to inform other gang members of this crackdown and its potential application to them should they engage in serious violence. Gang members were brought together to be confronted by a new level of cooperation across the criminal justice system and to hear the threat of coordinated enforcement and enhanced sanctions that would result from further violence.

Operation Ceasefire was credited with bringing about a sudden and dramatic decline in youth violence in Boston. It was associated with a 63 percent decrease in youth homicide, a 32 percent decrease in shots fired in the target areas and a 24 percent decrease in gun-related assaults (Kennedy et al., 2001). Apart from developing the model of "focused deterrence," the program is known for the successful coordination of the inter-agency planning group and the addition of researchers to the strategic planning process. The model has been adopted in numerous localities around the country (see McDevitt et al., 2006).

The lessons of the Boston Ceasefire Program led to another set of experimental interventions that were supported through the National Institute of Justice. Five cities received support under a project named Strategic Approaches to Community Safety Initiatives (SACSI). One year later, five additional cities became part of the SACSI program (Dalton, 2003). In a seemingly unexamined shuffle of traditional organizational relationships, U.S. Attorneys applied for the selection of cities within their districts to participate in the program. The direct funding was used primarily for the purpose of supporting researchers. These researchers would then work with task forces and members from across local criminal justice agencies, organized by the U.S. Attorney, to analyze and develop interventions to address some local violent crime problem. The strategic planning task forces brought together the leaders of a wide array of local, state, and federal criminal justice agencies all working on a local crime problem. The members' responsibilities were to meet regularly, and to plan, implement, and evaluate local anti-crime interventions. A national assessment found that the participation of cities in SACSI has established a new set of robust inter-organizational relationships and demonstrated evidence of reduced violent crime (Roehl et al., 2008).

When a new presidential administration began to develop its domestic agenda, the experiences of Project Exile, the Boston Project, and SACSI were fresh in the minds of career Department of Justice staffers. They were therefore available to influence the Bush administration's flagship approach to crime control strategy, what became known as Project Safe Neighborhoods (PSN).

PSN has been focused on the problem of local gun crime in the United States (Project Safe Neighborhoods, 2001). Many descriptions of PSN emphasize review of gun offenses by local and federal prosecutors and the selection of federal prosecution for cases when that route promises the highest likelihood of conviction and the harshest sanctions (see Decker and McDevitt, 2006). PSN, which provides funding to all federal judicial districts, has been viewed by some, at least partially, as a nationwide version of Project Exile.

It seems more appropriate to describe the program as "nationwide" rather than "national" because of its focus on local crime and the coordination of local agencies. The situation is quite different from what might be described as the federalization of some crimes, for example drug offenses. The control of national and international drug distribution has been central to a national drug control policy. The largely local nature of violence and gun markets has meant that a national market focus has not been nearly as prominent a feature of PSN.

There are also other key elements of the PSN program that build on the earlier collaborative efforts. The federal districts have assembled PSN task forces composed of the leaders of local and state agencies and the local branches of federal agencies. All districts have engaged the assistance of research partners to work with the task forces to plan anti-gun crime strategies. In descriptions of four PSN-related model crime strategies, for example, each intervention is based on a task force combining the various strengths and powers of criminal justice agencies to work together using data and analysis to intervene to reduce violent crime.

PSN has thus helped to distribute across the nation a structure that is in many ways different from the structure of criminal justice described by the 1967 President's Commission. There are also other examples of adoption of this new model. In New York state, for example, the state's criminal justice planning agency has tied substantial funding to a requirement that local criminal justice systems organize multi-jurisdictional planning groups and incorporate increasingly sophisticated crime analysis. The state of Massachusetts has modeled a ten-city program after the SACSI model, the state of North Carolina is implementing a very similar model, and collaborative approaches have recently been extended under the U.S. Justice Department's comprehensive anti-gang initiative in twelve cities.

In jurisdictions across the country, then, regular meetings occur that would be unexpected under the Systems Model that has so often been used to describe the criminal justice process. At those meetings, prosecutors, police from different levels of government, and other leaders of criminal justice agencies routinely select targets for their investigations together, devise effective operations, and collectively choose case-processing strategies. They coordinate their plans for enforcement, adjudication, and sanctions to reflect a commonly shared sense of purpose. They study their problems together and evaluate their collective efforts. Their actions, it can be argued, reflect a radical if not revolutionary change in criminal justice.

CHARACTERISTICS OF THE NEW CRIMINAL JUSTICE

Just as Kuhn describes the paradigm shifts that distinguish scientific eras it is possible to describe the characteristics of the New Criminal Justice in contrast with the organizing principles of early models. Below are three efforts to distinguish the present from the past and to consider the potential implications of these differences.

Expanded Power

Perhaps the most obvious feature of the New Criminal Justice is the greatly expanded investigative, enforcement, and prosecutorial powers of criminal justice coalitions. One might describe these new structural arrangements as strategic, but first and foremost they are powerful.

Under the Systems Model promulgated by the President's Commission, at least in its ideal type, the agencies of criminal justice exercise their power more or less in linear fashion, one after another. Their cumulative effect may reflect addition or subtraction at each step in a process. For example, parole release decisions may increase or mitigate the harshness of punishment resulting from a highly charged public trial (Petersilia, 1999). Likewise, grand jury review and plea agreements can reflect tensions and conflicts in the system and can allow for individualized justice independent of the arrest decision (Neubauer, 2004). Under the New Criminal Justice the collaboration across agencies also produces what might be regarded as a multiplicative effect in which the powers available to investigate, prosecute, and punish offenders are greatly enhanced.

The regular conferencing of local and federal prosecutors provides one example of the enhanced power under the New Criminal Justice (Decker and McDevitt, 2006). The joint review of cases allows prosecutors to select the venue where evidence of guilt in a case is most likely to be admitted and where a conviction will produce the longest sentence. In the aftermath of arrest by local police this may mean either state or federal prosecution. In some cases, double jeopardy can be avoided and prosecution can occur at both levels. One would expect that even the threatening display of these potential powers would result in increased pressure to plead guilty. The suspicion is confirmed in anecdotal reports of offenders in PSN cases who bargain at the state level to avoid being "walked across the street" to federal courts (Scott Decker, 2006, personal communication).

Beyond these joint case reviews, however, there are other examples of note. For instance, in Rochester, New York, both parole and probation agencies conduct "saturation patrols" in which people under supervision in high crime areas are visited at home, where compliance with required conditions is reviewed. The geographic areas to be saturated are determined through the process of crime analysis by the police. The individuals selected for attention are most likely to appear on a list of "most violent offenders," which is shared among local agencies. During the saturation patrols, police are also available, pre-positioned to assist in searches, arrests or other problems. The exceptional powers of search and seizure, which are linked to supervision conditions, thus come to benefit the whole coordinated system.

Crime analysis itself offers another example in which system-wide coordination multiplies the power of agencies (Ekblom, 1998). Although analysts are most likely to reside within a police department and draw a check from that organization, their work serves the collection of participating agencies. Analysts identify the potential targets of collective strategies: the most violent offenders in a community or those regarded as having the greatest negative impact on a community. Investigators pursue these offenders with the goal of arrest or violation based on conditions of pretrial, probation or parole release. At the same time, enforcement action triggers special prosecution initiatives to maximize the likelihood of maximum penalties. Those not immediately eligible for arrest may be brought in through offender notification meetings (see Klofas and Hipple, 2006), at which they are informed that a newly coordinated criminal justice system is prepared to respond to transgressions with maximum potency.

The potential power available in processing criminal cases is thus much greater under the New Criminal Justice than before widespread coordination across agencies. System-wide collaboration and coordination can also go beyond local agencies and their state and federal counterparts in a strategic accumulation and exercise of powers not available to single agencies. In the evolving process of strategic planning, the assemblage of levers to be pulled can also grow to include municipal code violations and other civil processes, as the powers of once more or less self-contained agencies coalesce into a new coercive conglomerate.

This retreat from balkanization in criminal justice is not the result of some grand plan or well-considered design. It was neither spawned nor nourished by blue ribbon commission or influential academic treatise. Instead, it seems to be largely the side effect, or accumulation of side effects, of experiments in problem solving whose results have been regarded as successful. In the apparent absence of deliberate planning the potential consequences of the new concentrations of power seem to have received little systematic attention.

Local Focus

A second characteristic of the New Criminal Justice is that its focus is fundamentally local. Crime control is exercised through the assemblage of partners in criminal justice agencies representing a limited geography—usually a city or county and often only a collection of high crime neighborhoods. Those agencies with broader affiliations, for example local or regional offices of the FBI or DEA, are solicited for their ability to bring with them powers otherwise unavailable locally. Local problems are described and diagnosed and collaborative solutions are devised. In the New Criminal Justice, the local prosecutor and police play the most dominant roles as they lead the effort to use any available resource to address local crime.

Of course, with criminal justice organized and funded primarily at the local level, it is easy to argue that it has always been a fundamentally local enterprise. The President's Commission, however, found little virtue in that argument. In its portrait of the system, local variation is presented as often anomalous or undesirable. These views of the Commission have had two inter-related consequences. First, the roles of the police and the rest of criminal justice were viewed as largely limited to responding to crime and not to a variety of other local needs, and, second, improvement of the system was perceived as coming about largely through standardization.

Under the New Criminal Justice, the subscription to national standards for criminal justice, or to common practice, or perhaps even to the idea of shared principles, is unimportant except to the extent that outside forces, such as appellate courts, can demand it. This is not to suggest that such standards or principles are ignored. They may well be in place, but they are not as relevant to the goals of criminal justice when those goals are locally derived. The President's Commission supported standardization as the key means of reforming the criminal justice system. Under the New Criminal Justice the pathway to reform is through greater effectiveness at crime reduction. Standardization is relegated to the status of a test in which only minimal compliance is demanded in the pursuit of local crime reduction goals.

In their development of theories of community some scholars have described criminal justice as serving a variety of locally relevant functions (Warren, 1972; Duffee, 1990). The New Criminal Justice reflects that view. It recognizes that local jurisdictions may have very different problems. The interests pursued in responding to those problems are defined at the local level and different localities can define them in their own ways. As such, we can expect considerable differences across local criminal justice jurisdictions. The local collaborations may define their community concerns in different ways, may emphasize different solutions, and may utilize their resources differently. The SACSI and PSN sites all selected forms of violence as the targets of their concentrated efforts, but devised distinctively different plans. Incapacitation strategies were common, but some sites also chose offender notification strategies, social interventions, and even strategies to deal with re-entry. In some cases, the work in the frontlines of criminal justice differed dramatically from traditional roles. In Rochester, for example, collaborative strategies led probation officers to work much more closely with police than elsewhere in the state. Probation officers joined police in meeting with newly released probationers; they conducted home visits together and probation officers even used license plate readers to identify probationers who might be driving illegally or violating curfew requirements. Police officers also worked closely with street outreach workers to identify and resolve interpersonal conflicts that were expected to flare into violence. Similarly, in cities such as Milwaukee and Seattle police officers and city attorneys work with code enforcement officers to apply nuisance abatement processes to address persistent problem properties.

The Systems Model of criminal justice argues essentially that there is a common spine to the operation of criminal justice across America. Many of the efforts to reform criminal justice, from improved measurement to better case tracking, have sought to reduce local variation and extend the principles of common functioning based on rationality. The implementation of sentencing guidelines provides one obvious illustration (Ulmer, 1997). Such efforts, it can be argued, often ignore or disregard local interests. In another example, the reform of local jails was often presented as depending heavily on a rational analysis of the jail population (Hall et al., 1985). Short stays or the inability of inmates to post low bail amounts were seen as evidence of inefficiencies that could be overcome. These strategies, however, ignored large differences in the way that localities used their jail space (Klofas, 1990) and disregarded police and neighborhood interests in using jail as a short-term response to street problems (Irwin, 1985; Feeley, 1979).

In its operation, the New Criminal Justice emphasizes local problem analysis and local problem solving. Those goals contrast sharply with the model of standardization promoted as the approach to improvement under the Systems Model of criminal justice. Criminal justice today can take new shapes and forms and adopt processes and roles that are unanticipated and even undesirable under a systems perspective. The New Criminal Justice can legitimize broadly different priorities across communities, including differing levels of tolerance and intolerances across categories of criminal behavior, and it can legitimately lead to different outcomes in terms of adjudication and sentencing (see Nardulli et al., 1988).

Data-Based Problem Solving

There is at least one additional combination of qualities that is important to understanding recent changes in criminal justice. The New Criminal Justice is a data-based problem-solving process. Locally relevant research is at its core. This may be a reflection of improved information technology, including data collection, storage, and retrieval, or progress in crime analysis and particularly crime mapping, or advances in other fields that have been adopted in criminal justice. Regardless of origin, however, the dependence on data as the foundation for problem solving has marked all of the experiments at the foundation of the New Criminal Justice. The Boston Project, SACSI, and Project Safe Neighborhoods all used academics as research partners to assist in the understanding of local crime problems and in the design and assessment of solutions. The most comprehensive of the programs and the most successful at reducing crime engaged their research partners most extensively (McGarrell et al., 2009).

The call for greater research was, of course, a central message of the President's Commission in 1967. Their reports, in fact, laid an important foundation by dealing with such fundamental issues as the measurement of crime. The National Crime Victimization Survey (NCVS) was one innovation that grew out of that interest. The Commission laid out a broad research agenda and also noted the importance of evaluation studies. The report also contained a suggestion that research offices could be useful in some large criminal justice organizations. The clear focus of the Commission, however, was on what today is seen as "basic research" (Tonry, 1997).

In contrast, the research model tied to the New Criminal Justice differs significantly from the approach promulgated by the Commission. The New Criminal Justice places less emphasis on basic research, but draws its strength from what has become known as "action research." Although there are many and sometimes divergent definitions of this approach, all share some common features including a focus on practical problems (see Toch and Grant, 1982). The founder of this approach, Kurt Lewin, spoke mostly clearly on the practice of this type of research with his dictum "no action without research, no research without action" (1948). Action research relies on partnerships between practitioners and researchers in collaboratively defining research problems and solutions through data collection and analysis. Even with these arrangements, though, action researchers strive to maintain high standards of scientific quality.

The action research model is thus a cornerstone of problem solving for the new local collaboratives. In that context, researchers have led detailed analyses of local homicide problems, described patterns of other crimes, analyzed risk among offenders released to local communities, and drawn elaborate portraits of local gun markets using interviews with offenders and other analyses including gun traces. By most reasonable measures, the impact of research associated with the New Criminal Justice has been significant and its practice holds still greater promise (see Dalton, 2003; McGarrell et al., 2009).

The action research associated with the New Criminal Justice has also contributed to our general understanding of crime and criminality. In doing so it has helped to form new bridges between the fields of criminal justice and criminology. The research has reflected the perspective that causes of crime cannot be completely separated from either efforts to prevent it or a community's response to it. Thus action researchers have helped close the gap with studies relating to rational choice, environmental factors and crime, criminal histories, and criminal careers. This applied research has also extended our understanding of the field of deterrence, with contributions both to theory and to research. For example, the concept of "focused deterrence," in which efforts to dissuade offenders are targeted and specific, has been advanced largely through action research studies (Kennedy, 1998). The point is, the New Criminal Justice involves an approach to research that differs from that taken by the President's Commission in 1967, but one that can advance practice as well as basic knowledge in the field.

The paragraphs above describe three characteristics of the New Criminal Justice; other features can easily come to mind. For example, the new model arguably emphasizes substantive over procedural justice, and its approach is largely functional, rather than institutional or agency based. These descriptions, however, seem to overlap with the three more fundamental characteristics noted above: expanded power, local focus, and data-based problem solving. Furthermore, these characteristics appear to be relatively independent of one another. They are also measurable. Finally, they contrast most sharply with key principles underlying the President's Commission's description of criminal justice. These characterizations, therefore, have the virtues of novelty, parsimony, and utility for research.

THE FUTURE OF THE NEW CRIMINAL JUSTICE

The vision of criminal justice presented by the President's Commission in 1967 has certainly had enduring influence. But is there a similar future for what has been described here as the New Criminal Justice? It is easy to find factors that support continued growth and further development of the model, and equally easy to find factors that may relegate it to a brief and perhaps undeservedly scrutinized episode in the history of the Systems Model approach to understanding criminal justice.

There is a strong foundation for the New Criminal Justice. The rich work in community policing has helped return enforcement to its local roots (Greene, 2004). The closely related efforts under the problem-oriented policing umbrella provide support for the broader problem-solving approaches noted here (Goldstein, 1990; see http://www.popcenter.org/). This is also true of the newest permutation, "intelligence-led policing" (Cope, 2004; McGarrell et al., 2007a; Ratcliffe, 2008). Furthermore, the growth of problem-solving courts from drug courts through domestic violence courts, mental health courts, and re-entry courts are all more consistent with the new approach than with the old linear Systems Model (Berman and Feinblatt, 2001).

Many developments in response to terrorism are also consistent with the new directions in criminal justice. Interest in homeland security has emphasized collaboration and cooperation across agencies that are close to or affiliated with criminal justice (National Commission on Terrorist Attacks upon the United States, 2004). The problem area now known as "interoperability" has emerged to address technological problems in communication across agencies including radio frequencies and database compatibility. Perhaps more to the point, U.S. Department of Homeland Security funds have been used to establish "fusion centers" around the country. These high-tech centers bring together federal, state, and local law enforcement agencies for the purpose of sharing information. One recent investigation criticized these centers for gravitating toward a focus on all crimes rather than a more exclusive focus on terrorism (Hall, 2007). Yet the focus on all crimes, all hazards suggests the problem-solving orientation whereby gathering and sharing information across levels of government and across sectors is viewed as capacity building for responding to a variety of problems facing local, state, and federal agencies.

Even with these developments, however, it is also easy to identify potential threats to the New Criminal Justice. One particular area of interest is the system of checks and balances that has become an accepted part of the Systems Model. Today, rather than acting in sequence, agencies can pool their powers in new ways. It seems reasonable to be concerned with the potential for abuse of that power (Wright, 2004; Forst, 1977).

Despite these realignments, however, there has been little sign that either trial or appellate courts have become concerned with the recent coordination of powers within local criminal justice. Yet it is worth noting that, although the increase of power associated with collaboration in criminal justice could raise concerns, an ironic but plausible argument can be made that the broad partnerships will themselves provide protection against the abuse of that power through the range of perspectives represented within the local coalition.

In at least one other area issues have been raised that may affect the continuation and growth of the New Criminal Justice. There is a growing concern in the way that information may be shared across criminal justice agencies. In one example, federal rules, which are designed to protect individuals who are not suspected of involvement in criminal activities, have significantly limited the collection, retention, and sharing of information. Legal requirements for identifying gang membership and procedures for sharing data on gang connections (see 28 Code of Federal Regulations (CFR) 23 et seq.) have had a major impact on developing and using gang databases. The sharing of information is critical to the potency of the new partnerships in criminal justice. Limitations and restrictions on it may have a significant impact.

The degree of regulation from outside may not be the only threat to the growing power within criminal justice collaboratives. It is possible that the level of effort demanded by new organizational roles and arrangements will itself give rise to pressures for transformation. There may be two ways in which this can occur. First, as in Boston and Indianapolis following the initial success of Project Ceasefire, positive results may result in a decline in the intensity of effort. Second, there are indications that the single-minded pursuit of crime reduction that has fueled many of these developments may be difficult to sustain over time (Williams, 2007). This concern is the policy equivalent of regression toward the mean. Regardless of the degree of success, the effort needed may spawn a weariness or fatigue with crime reduction in the minds of criminal justice officials, local politicians, and even the public. That fatigue could reduce the desire for collaboration across organizations.

A consistent theme in research in criminal justice and on the police in particular has been the complexity of the mission (Fyfe, 1997). Police provide a wide range of services for a wide range of their community members. Likewise, crime reduction is only one aspect of the role of local governance. The police, the local politicians that guide them, and the public that elect those officials may each or all grow weary of devoting so much energy and so many public resources into so narrow a mission as crime reduction. They may demand a re-emphasis on a complex role for the police and other criminal justice agencies; one that includes attention to quality of life concerns, and providing a range of services not available elsewhere. More specifically, they may favor tactics such as walking beats or other approaches and programs, which research has suggested are not necessarily associated with crime reduction but may serve other interests (see Braga and Weisburd, 2007). Leaders in other criminal justice organizations may similarly feel the need to re-emphasize traditional roles, and City Hall may measure its success by looking beyond crime control to more comprehensive models of citizen satisfaction or neighborhood order.

A change of focus from crime reduction, the withdrawal of funding supporting cooperation, or a reduction in participation for other reasons could dismantle the New Criminal Justice where it exists and limit is spread across jurisdictions. On the other hand, the model may not be so fragile or restrictive. There would seem to be nothing in local data-based problem-solving coalitions to prevent them from coming together to address a wide range of issues including all of the complexities associated with criminal justice. The New Criminal Justice need not limit itself to enforcement-oriented reductions in crime. The Department of Justice is currently funding collaborative-based programs that will address gang prevention and re-entry in ten cities (U.S. Department of Justice, 2007). There are also other examples of the broad use of this general design to address a range of issues. In Trenton, New Jersey, for example, a revised version of COMPSTAT is being used by a coalition of service providers and police to address delinquency problems through a combination of criminal justice and social services, and in Baltimore COMPSTAT has evolved into GunStat and CityStat.

The brave new world in criminal justice, at least in contrast with that presented by the President's Commission, may be one of community-based problem solving that combines resources and powers from across criminal justice with those of other fields and other services to address a wide range of issues subsumable under a broad concept of community justice (see Clear and Karp, 1999; Karp and Clear, 2002).

A CAUTIONARY NOTE

Although we argue that movement toward a New Criminal Justice represents a fundamental shift in the operations of the criminal justice system and a departure from the Systems Model, we also recognize that there are a number of basic questions regarding this thesis. First, despite the major advance in thinking about criminal justice represented by the rational planning, Systems Model articulated in the President's Crime Commission, it is also clear that in operation the criminal justice system has been loosely coupled and, some have argued, a "non-system" (Freed, 1969; Forst, 1977). If the criminal justice system never truly reflected a rational Systems Model, then to what extent is the New Criminal Justice a departure from existing practice? What does seem clear is that the New Criminal Justice represents a departure from an exclusive predominance of case or people processing by the various components of the criminal justice system.

Second, although throughout the book we provide examples of activities and processes reflecting the New Criminal Justice, serious issues remain about the extent to which these activities and processes reflect common criminal justice system behaviors or whether

we are capturing "aberrations" and experimentation as opposed to system change. This is particularly a threat to our thesis given that our examples draw from our own research experience in several federally funded initiatives, particularly SACSI and PSN. Both of these initiatives focus on violent crime and on gun-, gang-, and drug-related violence in particular. Although these are central problems confronting the criminal justice system, they certainly do not reflect the totality of problems and issues that the police, courts, corrections, and juvenile justice agencies face on a day-to-day basis. Thus, our thesis may be built on atypical innovation in select jurisdictions as opposed to fundamental and widespread innovation across the agencies of the criminal justice system. Research indicating the symbolic nature of much of the supposed innovation in the community policing movement gives caution about overstating the degree of organizational change and innovation occurring in the New Criminal Justice (Mastrofski, 2006).

Having said this, we also believe that there is additional evidence of organizational change which suggests the emergence of a New Criminal Justice. The diffusion of COMPSTAT throughout policing organizations represents a commitment to routine analysis of crime problems as a way of re-orienting focus and resources. COMPSTAT has often involved other arms of local government (e.g., code enforcement, community prosecution), thus reflecting the emphasis on partnerships. Similarly, the community policing movement has fostered new relationships between the police and neighborhood groups, schools, businesses, and other community institutions. The problem-solving movement has emphasized the need to analyze specific crime problems at a local level. Problem-solving courts have emerged that move beyond case processing to attempting to address ongoing drug, disorder, and mental health problems (Feinblatt et al., 1998; Berman and Feinblatt, 2001). The focus on prisoner re-entry represents a similar "problem-focused" approach that may best reflect the movement from systems processing to the New Criminal Justice. Whereas, historically, release from prison would represent the end point of the criminal justice process, particularly with the de-emphasis on parole, re-entry now appears as a feedback loop whereby criminal justice agencies (corrections, probation and parole, police, courts) find themselves needing to establish relationships with social service agencies (housing, drug treatment, transportation, vocational training) and the business community (employment) if they are to effectively address the needs of individual ex-offenders as well as the threat to public safety.

The Systems Model of the President's Commission represented an "ideal type" that brought an important new lens or framework to planning and analyzing the operations of the criminal justice system. The New Criminal Justice also represents an ideal type that we believe captures important trends and developments in contemporary criminal justice. Neither model fully captures the structure and processes of the criminal justice system, nor has anyone effectively measured the extent to which criminal justice systems operate in accordance with the models or the degree of change over time. Yet, to the extent that the New Criminal Justice reflects change in structure and processes, we believe that the model can help criminal justice professionals think about and plan approaches to the problems they confront and can help researchers analyze organizational and inter-organizational change and the impact of such change on both systems and crime, safety, and justice problems.

CONCLUSION

There are, no doubt, a variety of ways in which to consider what is suggested here as significant change in criminal justice. One would be to simply recognize that research has paid insufficient attention to inter-organi-zational links in the field. That condition can be easily remedied. That approach, however, might encourage some to underestimate the significance of recent changes. On the other hand, one may see in this discussion an opportunity to pose the question suggested by Kuhn's analysis of progress in science: Is there enough evidence that is inconsistent with key principles in this field to support a revolutionary rethinking of our most basic theories of how society responds to crime?

In the presidential election of 1964, the Republican candidate Barry Goldwater first put crime on the national political agenda (Cronin et al., 1981). A year later President Lyndon Baines Johnson officially recognized "the urgency of the Nation's crime problem and the depth of ignorance about it" with the creation of the President's Commission on Law Enforcement and the Administration of Justice (Katzenbach, 1967). This history is important because 40 years later it is difficult to fully appreciate the limited knowledge about crime and justice available at the time, and the significance of the contribution made by the Commission's report.

As part of the celebration of the anniversary of the Commission report, Alfred Blumstein addressed the annual research conference sponsored by the National Institute of Justice (2007). In 1967, Dr. Blumstein headed the President's Commission's section on science and technology and he is credited as the chief architect of the systems concept for the Commission (Ritter, 2007). In his remarks he noted that, at the time of its release, the Commission report was the most comprehensive description of criminal justice ever produced. Then he added that it probably still is.

Professor Blumstein is, no doubt, correct on both accounts. A similar point had been made in a 1997 retrospective on the Commission's work (U.S. Department of Justice, 1998). The 1967 report, and especially its description of a criminal justice system, continues to be deeply influential.

But observation today reveals a broad array

of alternative arrangements and practices in criminal justice. Many appear to violate the most basic tenets of the Systems Model. These already seem too numerous and too interconnected to continue to be regarded only as anomalies. There are now sufficient examples to suggest that the Systems Model no longer adequately explains how we address the challenge of crime in the United States.

As important as the contributions of the Systems Model have been, by taking seriously our observations today we may be led to new questions in our research and new designs for our practice. Perhaps those observations will move us further away from questions about how bureaucracies work. Or perhaps they may divert us from the search for the holy grail of "best practice" to be replicated endlessly across undifferentiated settings. Maybe our observations will force us to dig deeper into questions of how communities function or malfunction, how they exercise power, or how the values of those unique communities form, flower, and get translated into the practice of justice. That may be the sort of change of "world view" that Kuhn suggests accompanies a new paradigm in science (1970, p. 111): one he describes by saying "It is . . . as if the professional community had suddenly been transported to another planet where familiar objects are seen in a different light and are joined by unfamiliar ones as well."

CHAPTER 2

Modeling the New Criminal Justice

John M. Klofas

INTRODUCTION

Readers of this chapter are, no doubt, familiar with the 1967 President's Commission's chart of the criminal justice system. That chart made its way into criminal justice iconography shortly after its development by the Commission's Task Force on Science and Technology headed by Professor Alfred Blumstein. Since then it has been reprinted in nearly all criminal justice textbooks produced in the United States. Those few books that do not reprint it in its original form still describe its logic by tracing the route of an offender from the commission of his or her offense through the criminal justice system and to ultimate release at the end of sentence. It seems fair to say that the Commission's chart remains the most recognized image in the field of criminal justice today and the most common description of how cases are handled.

Even the task force members might be surprised by the image's longevity. They described the chart as a "simplified version" of a model of the criminal justice system (1967b). They supported that view by providing numerous more detailed views of the process replete with probabilities and percentages for cases moving through the differing system components. For the task force members the true value of the component charts was in their underlying mathematics. The goal of the task force's "systems analysis" was to use mathematical models to compare ways of designing systems to achieve specific programmatic objectives and to control costs (1967b, p. 53).

When the Commission architects presented their "simplified model" of the system as a whole they cited three virtues:

1 Such models "develop an explicit description of the criminal justice system and its operating modes so that the systems underlying assumptions are revealed."
2 They provide a vehicle for simulating experimentation in those instances for which "live" experimentation is impractical or undesirable.
3 They identify what data must be obtained if essential calculations are to be made of the consequences of proposed changes (1967b, p. 54).

In short, the model of the system can show: (1) how it works, (2) how it might change, and (3) what data are needed to estimate the impact of any changes in one component on other parts of the system.

These goals seem as admirable today as they were compelling for the original task force. That being the case, our task in this chapter seemed unavoidable. As we argue that the original model does not completely describe how cases flow through the criminal justice system today, it seems we are challenged to provide an equivalent diagram of what we see as a more contemporary depiction; but one that can also claim the same virtues as those noted above.

Here, then, we attempt to provide a similar graphic representation of the "New Criminal Justice." There are, however, several important differences between the President's Commission diagram and this one of the New Criminal Justice.

The first, and perhaps the most important, difference between our two depictions relates to how we describe the objectives of the criminal justice system. The task force noted the importance of system goals to the overall design and it went on to describe the criminal justice system as "generally regarded as having the basic objective of reducing crime" (1967b, p. 54). That statement seems quite restrained by today's standards. Now it seems clear that the objective of reducing crime, particularly violent crime, is generally much stronger today than at the time of the Commission (Blumstein, 2008, personal communication). Thus our system diagram places much greater emphasis on the goal of crime reduction than was true of the task force's effort.

In the last chapter we argued that three major factors distinguish the Commission's understanding of the criminal justice system from that underlying the New Criminal Justice. The second difference in these models, then, results from the fact that these factors are prominently featured in the model of the New Criminal Justice. The New Criminal Justice is *fundamentally local in nature*. It is defined by local interests and influenced by local conditions and circumstances. Under the New Criminal Justice, the system also *operates through powerful coalitions of agencies* working together rather than in the linear fashion described by the President's Commission. Agencies combine to prioritize enforcement goals and develop strategies and carry them out together, bringing their combined powers to bear on the problems they identify.

Finally, the third factor defining the New Criminal Justice suggests that the operation of the criminal justice system is now *informed by research in ways not possible in the past*. Today, local analysis, research and intelligence on the crime problem make powerful contributions to anti-crime strategy and operations. Data-based planning and evaluation, often using an action research model, have become increasingly commonplace across criminal justice.

In our model-building venture our course differs from that of the Task Force on Science and Technology in one additional way: we bring a conceptual tool to this exercise that was not readily available to the original task force members. In constructing their mathematical model the task force took a proven and traditional approach to systems analysis (see Whitten and Bentley, 2005). The model is intended to allow calculation of expected levels as cases flow through succeeding stages in the process. The resulting proportions, percentages, and probabilities are the product of classical deductive reasoning. That process begins with and is dependent on certain assumptions about the nature of the issues being studied. A key assumption can be stated in the terms of "set theory" in mathematics. According to that view, something either is or is not a member of a set. For example, behavior is either a crime or not, a case is prosecuted or not, an individual is guilty or not, and he or she receives a sanction or does not. Such absolutes are prerequisites to the calculations that capture the ultimate goal of this approach of systems analysis.

In recent years a rather different approach to system analysis has emerged and found a home in the fields of control systems and computing. In what has taken on the somewhat unfortunate moniker of "fuzzy logic," assumptions about certainty in set membership are unnecessary. Instead, certainty can be replaced with uncertainty and approximation (Kaufman and Gupta, 1991; Klir and Yaun,

1995). Membership in a set is no longer translatable into 0 or 1 but can be characterized as more or less. Variables are thus continuous and range from 0 to 1. Concepts such as slightly, somewhat, quite, and very replace the language of certainty in a system of fuzzy logic. We feel that fuzzy logic provides a useful tool in describing some of the behavior of the criminal justice system.

The differences between the classical logic of the task force and our fuzzy logic can be illustrated by the difference in starting points of the two models. The original Commission diagram begins with a depiction of the amount of crime. That figure is derived from the Uniform Crime Reports (see President's Commission, 1967b) with the assumption that the crime set contains all relevant behavior (anything else would be treated as error) and that whether a behavior is noted as a crime is something that is absolutely true or absolutely false (is or is not in the crime set). The Commission's starting point is thus unambiguous. The model can move forward to try to account for responses to the clearly defined crime set.

The model of the New Criminal Justice begins with the assumption that behavior can be more or less a crime. The diagram thus begins not with a criminal moving through the system but by considering the community context and process that defines the behavior as more or less criminal (see Smith and Vischer, 1981; Eisenstein et al., 1988). This recognizes that different communities may treat similar behaviors differently or that the same community may define behavior differently at different times. The issue seems especially important for understanding lower serious crimes, which, of course, are also the most numerous crimes. For example, police departments often go through periodic waves of enforcement against prostitution (see Morn, 1990). In a model not using fuzzy logic the ebb and flow of prostitution arrests might be reflected as error in the model. In the New Criminal Justice, understanding the local process of definition is central to understanding how cases are processed.

A similar point can be illustrated with regard to findings of guilt. In the Commission diagram a defendant is found guilty or not guilty through a process of trial or plea agreement. Under a fuzzy logic model, however, one might recognize that cases are actually treated as if they differed as to the degree of guilt, not simply as absolute guilt or innocence. For example, an official finding of guilty or not guilty may simply reflect the intensity of investigation (Waegel, 1981), or the value placed on a guilty finding by the prosecutor (Combs, 2007), a defendant's cooperation (Hartley et al., 2007), or the judge's view of the therapeutic consequences of a guilty finding when compared with continuation and eventual dismissal. In drug court, for example, lesser sanctions and treatment referrals may reflect judgments about a defendant's moral identity and lower level of guilt (Mackinem and Higgins, 2007). Likewise, degrees of guilt may be reflected in pleas to lesser charges or the withholding of findings pending completion of treatment. Guilt may also be seen as having degrees in cases in which low charges may be used to get a presumed serious violator off the street when more serious charges cannot be proven. In another example, guilty or not guilty may be the correct legal terminology but that choice cannot reflect the level of culpability one has in cases in which drugs or guns or money are confiscated from suspects but criminal charges are never brought (Ruback and Bergstrom, 2006). These examples illustrate a key difference between the two approaches to diagramming criminal justice being discussed here. Our fuzzy logic model sacrifices the precision of the classical approach to system analysis; in exchange, however, it provides the opportunity to describe and seek to better understand the complexity of the criminal justice system.

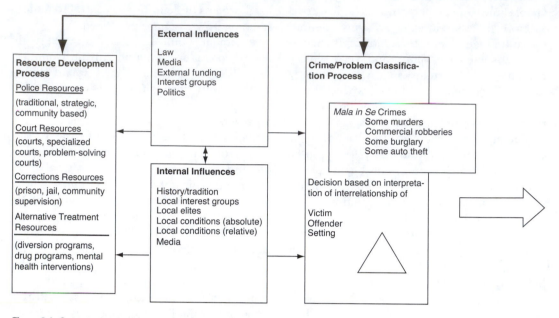

Figure 2.1 Community decision processes.

COMMUNITY PROBLEM ANALYSIS

To understand the way that criminal cases are processed today it is important to consider the way that communities develop and sustain the array of resources used to handle those cases. In this diagram we begin by considering the partnership structures that help define how cases are understood in the community. The influences shaping criminal justice institutions have been examined from a variety of perspectives and include a detailed discussion of the influences of community on courts (Worden, 2007). In this analysis partnerships are an essential ingredient in the New Criminal Justice but can also be understood as varying in their strength and in their make-up (see Murphy and Worrall, 2007). Strong partnerships provide the venue for strategic planning involving a wide array of community interests. When partnerships are weak, planning may be sporadic at best or possibly dominated by a single agency

such as the police. Strong partnerships may give voice to other components of the criminal justice system including prosecution and probation and parole, the courts and federal agencies. They may also extend well beyond the criminal justice system to empower community organizations including treatment and advocacy groups, educational institutions, churches, and community service providers (Ellis et al., 2007). The differences across these partnerships are likely to have important implications for how criminal conduct is understood in communities and how cases are processed. One analysis of community policing has suggested that partnerships that focus on criminal justice agencies and particularly those that form vertically with state or federal agencies are likely to emphasize strong order maintenance practices whereas police partnerships with community organizations will result in a broader range of services and creative problem-solving efforts (Renauer, 2007).

Figure 2.1 illustrates the processes by

which communities develop the resources that they will apply to the problems of crime. These may include a wide range of traditional and non-traditional resources. They may include the number of police and the type of policing they do, the structure of courts including such things as drug court or domestic violence court, the amount of jail space to be used, the development of pretrial release programs, and the number of treatment beds for addicts or other alternatives for suspected or convicted offenders.

The diagram also shows that there are related processes by which communities decide how they will define their crime problem. The definitions will include what communities regard as serious crime, the level of culpability they assign certain offenders, the level of tolerance for some kinds of behavior, and the tendency to view some crimes and criminals as deserving treatment versus punitive interventions.

One major factor influencing how some crimes are regarded is the extent to which victims are regarded as contributing to the offense (see Sobol, 1997). The broadest case of assigning culpability may be related to whether some offenses are regarded as *mala in se*. *Mala in se* crimes are judged "bad in and of themselves" regardless of their legal prohibition and therefore are automatically seen as serious crimes. The concept may be subject to criticism as legally imprecise (Davis, 2006) but observation of case processing suggests its continued utility. In practical application the list of *mala in se* offenses may be small but may vary considerably across communities. It can easily be argued that, with regard to how cases are prosecuted, *mala in se* crimes may include only some murders, commercial robberies, some burglaries, and some auto theft. For example, killing resulting from justifiable homicide or execution is not considered *mala in se*. Likewise death from overdose might not be seen as *mala in se* when a user is seen as partially culpable. Neither may be burglaries of suspected drug houses or other establish-

ments involved in crime. Auto thefts in which cars are "gecked out" for drugs (i.e., loaned to someone) may not be considered *mala in se* whereas thefts by strangers may be. Commercial robberies may be considered *mala in se* as the victim business is generally seen as not sharing culpability. Even these definitions, however, will vary across communities but they all have implications for how cases are processed and for the resources that are dedicated to that processing.

In the second part of the process of defining and understanding crime, communities may assess the particular relationships between individual victims, the offender, and the setting where the crime takes place. This is depicted as the "crime triangle" in Figure 2.1 and relates to questions regarding victims' roles in crime and to the extensive research in what has become known as "beliefs in a just world" (Lerner, 1965). Burglaries in "good" neighborhoods may be treated more seriously than those in high crime neighborhoods, and robbery of known drug sellers may be viewed differently to robbery of someone without a criminal record. In extreme cases, the murder of drug sellers might be seen as different to the killing of people not involved in crime. One may not find a forum at which such matters are decided or a document elaborating the process and outcome of public debate; however, the standards acceptable to a given community will be reflected in the manner in which cases are handled. The handling of those cases and the underlying way in which crime is understood by the criminal justice system and the community are frequently the source of calls for reform.

The ways that cases are handled and the resources available for handling them will reflect a broad range of factors including some whose influence comes from beyond the community's borders as well as those that are unique to that locality (see, e.g., Eisenstein et al., 1988). The two processes described above, the process by which communities develop resources to address crime and the

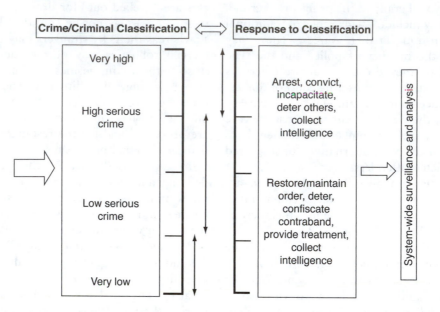

Figure 2.2 Community definition and response to crime and criminals.

process by which they develop definitions and classifications of crime and criminals, are also linked. They affect each other and interact with one another shaping the local criminal justice system and providing direction for how cases will travel through it. Thus communities that come to see some drug offenders as suffering from the disease of addiction may develop drug courts, and communities with drug courts may expand the kinds of people they see as addicted. A similar argument can be made regarding the way that communities may come to regard offenders as mostly criminally culpable and thus opt for expanding jail space as opposed to seeing offenders as needing intervention and expanding alternatives to incarceration.

The complex relationship between how problems are understood and the resources available to address them has long been recognized in studies of decision-making processes. In that field, models of decision making have identified the interdependencies of these two elements and have explored the black box of

influences that shape each of them separately and together. March and Simon (1958) first described how rational decisions are bounded by experience and therefore cannot be seen as fully rational. They go so far as to argue that decision making might best be thought of as using the model of a garbage can that contains both the definitions of problems we see and the resources to address those problems (Cohen et al., 1972). Our conceptualizing of problems, they would argue, is greatly influenced by our understanding of the solutions that lie at hand. That is to say, we can identify problems only to the extent that we already have some understanding of plausible solutions attached to them. The criminal justice system is thus shaped by the interaction of the processes of understanding crime and of developing the resources to address it. Sudnow's (1965) classic examination of the categorization of defendants in a public defender's office and Waegel's (1981) study of how detectives make decisions reflect this type of perspective.

COMMUNITY DEFINITION AND RESPONSE TO CRIME AND CRIMINALS

Before we can consider how individual cases are processed in the New Criminal Justice we must consider one other factor. The specific behavior that is the focus of criminal justice must be matched to the available community resources and the broad categories assigned to the crime problem. Decisions about what specific behavior should be regarded as a crime and how to discriminate between crimes and other behavior are needed. That is to say, some measure related to harm or seriousness is needed. Many measures and submeasures may apply; communities could consider culpability, moral turpitude, extent of injury, breadth or depth of threat, willfulness, and various reasons for mitigation such as age or illness, or costs in pain or inconvenience or economic loss. Whatever the specific categories involved, some indicator of seriousness is reflected. The most obvious place to find such definitions is in the criminal code in which offenses are categorized and matched with presumably appropriate punishments. But even in the face of federal, state or local legislation there generally remains room for local interpretation of laws and local decisions about how laws are applied.

As Figure 2.2 indicates, the community processes of resource development and crime definition produce a ranking of offenses by seriousness as defined in the community (an ordinal scale) and a corresponding set of goals for responses viewed as appropriate based on perceived seriousness. But these definitions and judgments are not stagnant. The classification of crimes and criminals and the related responses may move, at least somewhat, up or down the ordinal scales reflecting redefinition by the community. For example, at times prostitution or gambling may be regarded as quite low in seriousness and at other times they may be regarded as more disruptive and thus more serious. During times and in locations of heightened concern with violence, loitering may trigger police responses unheard of elsewhere or at other times. There may be limits to the extent to which behavior can be reclassified along the seriousness scale but it is clear that crimes may be viewed differently at different times and under different circumstances.

The community process described thus far all feeds into another key component of the New Criminal Justice. Perhaps the most striking development in the field since the President's Commission has been the development and refinement of systems of surveillance and analysis (McGarrell et al., 2007a; Ratcliffe, 2002). The processes discussed above feed a surveillance system that may include 9-1-1, 3-1-1, closed circuit cameras, various information collected in field interviews by the police, and also probation, parole, and prosecution information, gang information, and even information from outreach work and community organizations. A major function of the coalition of agencies formed across the system is to contribute to the pool of available intelligence information. The power to collect data on such a wide range of individuals and behaviors is a significant development within criminal justice.

A related key component of the New Criminal Justice is the analysis of the collected intelligence information and dissemination across the system. Analysts are critical to the problem-solving process as they identify trends in the data, track known offenders, and identify hot spots, temporal distributions, and other patterns (Pattavina, 2005). They also provide evaluation of existing strategies and tactics. Products of analysis serve coalitions from across the local criminal justice agencies and aid in strategy planning, implementation, and evaluation. The system-wide surveillance and analyses processes provide feedback to the community process involving crime and criminal classification and responses to that classification.

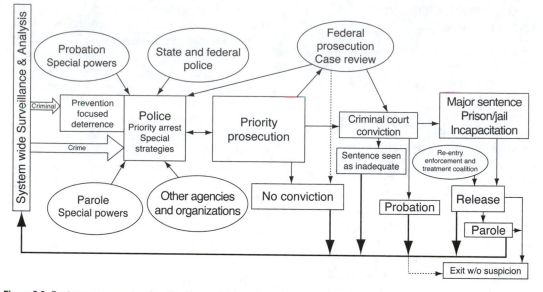

Figure 2.3 System response to classification as high serious crime or criminal.

HIGH SERIOUS CRIME AND CRIMINALS

Figure 2.3 portrays decision making in cases in which the crime or criminal is regarded by the community as high in seriousness. Here, the system-wide surveillance and analysis processes play a critical role in identifying crimes and/or criminals for special attention in the system. That system may be triggered when the surveillance process alerts to either crimes themselves or known or suspected offenders in the community. Once key personnel in criminal justice have identified someone as a serious criminal or an event as a serious crime, the value of fuzzy logic in the analysis can be seen. A presumed perpetrator's legal status may appear ambiguous when considering the way that he or she is treated in the criminal justice system. A person may be subjected to varying degrees of surveillance, restriction, and even sanction with minimal or no court processing.

When a person is recognized or labeled as a serious offender through a process of sur-

veillance he or she may be subjected to a new regimen of prevention efforts. These may include increased surveillance and increased supervision if the individual is on probation or parole. One approach, known as focused deterrence, has become a popular response that focuses on known or suspected offenders even without evidence of specific crimes (see Kennedy, 1997; McGarrell et al., 2006). These programs, based on successes in Boston and elsewhere, involve convincing suspected offenders that the entire criminal justice system has been mustered and is coordinated in its efforts to remove them from the streets through use of conviction and lengthy sentences. A central component of the model, the "call-in," is itself a raw display of coordinated power followed by an offer of services to help avoid the otherwise inevitability of a long sentence (McDevitt et al., 2006).

If the offense or offender is regarded as serious, the course of action is most often designed to lead toward major sentences and incarceration. When analysis shows that a criminal is linked to a crime, or a serious crime or crime pattern is detected, a coalition of criminal justice agencies will focus on producing that outcome. Coalition members can all bring their own special powers and resources to bear on the problem. Their strategies may include worst of worst lists (Bynum and Decker, 2006), gang interventions (McGarrell and Chermak, 2003a), and focused prosecution (Decker and McDevitt, 2006), but together they bring a wide range of powers and resources including:

- different circumstances in which they can search persons and property
- different circumstances in which they can seize and detain persons
- different sanctions that can be threatened or applied
- access to different resources for treatment or referral

- different sources of intelligence information
- different links to other organizations and resources
- different personnel for investigations and enforcement or even simply different hours of availability
- different equipment and methods for investigation and intelligence gathering.

The level of coordination of roles and powers across the criminal justice system as it pursues common goals is new. And that coordination is not likely to end without a satisfactory outcome. An outcome inconsistent with the goal of conviction and incarceration can simply feed back to the system of surveillance and analyses and may support a renewed strategic interest in conviction and incarceration. When release

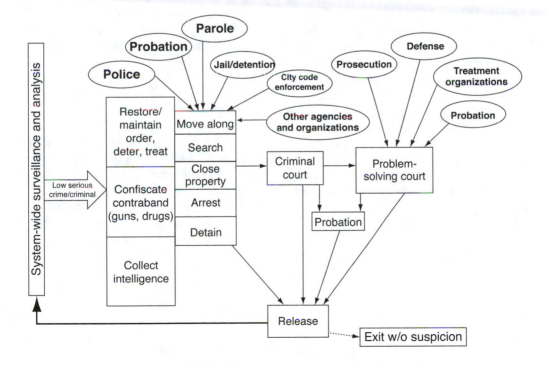

Figure 2.4 System response to classification as low serious crime or criminal.

from incarceration occurs, new system-wide coalitions may come to bear, as enforcement and/or treatment-oriented re-entry programs. Release without prejudice or additional suspicion may occur only after an offender has not come to the attention of the surveillance process for a sufficient period of time.

LOW SERIOUS CRIME AND CRIMINALS

When a crime or criminal is seen as low in seriousness, communities and their criminal justice systems can pursue a range of goals. The purposes of trial and incarceration may be set aside and coalitions of agencies can be concerned with maintenance of order, providing treatment and rehabilitation, or less formal sanctions (Feeley, 1979). They may seek to confiscate guns and/or drugs, they may try to deter individuals with the threat of great penalty, or they may simply try to add to the pool of available intelligence. As conviction and long sentences are not the goal, evidence being disallowed at trial is not the chief concern; the agencies are not pressured to maintain the same high level of standards with regard to evidence and procedures.

Criminal justice agencies may use their power and resources to clear presumed loiterers from street corners, or to proactively seek ways to search cars and persons for guns or drugs or even money. They may seek to close nuisance properties for ordinance violations, or to arrest and briefly (often overnight) detain some offenders. Here again we see the descriptive utility of fuzzy logic. The identified offender may be regarded as more or less guilty despite the lack of adjudication. Restrictions are placed on behavior, and punitive as well as therapeutic interventions can be applied.

In some cases low serious offenders are released at the scene, released with an appearance ticket, or taken to court for arraignment, pleas, and minor sanctions. In some communities an offender may agree to participate in a problem-solving court program such as drug court, mental health court, or domestic violence court. In those cases the coalition of local agencies comes together to provide treatment and surveillance as part of the special court. Even with those goals the agencies involved continue to provide intelligence information through their surveillance efforts. Criminal histories are compiled. Records of affiliation with others or gang involvement are kept. The agencies involved in the local coalitions provide intelligence data through the system of surveillance and analysis before and after release. As noted above, full release without further suspicion or prejudice occurs only when those offenders manage to avoid the surveillance systems for some time.

CONCLUSION

The diagrams above cannot substitute for or replace the President's Commission's original model of the criminal justice system. That skeletal framework continues to provide a useful description of the structure of criminal justice and an ideal type portrait of how cases are processed. We have tried here to reflect what we see as recent and dramatic developments in the field. We have also freed ourselves from some of the key limitations under which the President's Commission labored. Important among those was the recognition that the available data were collected and referenced using the legal taxonomy of crime "which is not necessarily relevant to many important questions regarding crime control" (1967b, p. 66). With the use of fuzzy logic we have described a system in which the concepts of guilt and punishment and even the idea of crime are more flexible and more variable and we think more clearly reflect the operation of criminal justice.

The President's Commission was cautious not to oversell the value of its model at describing how cases are processed. We must provide a similar caution. All models are simplifications and ours, like the Commission's, cannot possibly reflect the complexity of the criminal justice system. The Commission also expected that innovation in the system would continue. Current descriptions of the process must continue to incorporate those innovations in policing, courts, and corrections, and those that cross those boundaries.

In one final note on the potential value of fuzzy logic, it should be noted that there have been two main directions for the development of this approach. In the first, the one important in this analysis, fuzzy logic is used as a conceptual tool for understanding vagueness and building uncertainty into system models. In the second, a more narrow sense, fuzzy logic is a system of logic useful in driving a complicated mathematics that is as capable of explaining numerical outcomes as the more classical systems models. Thus it should be possible to move beyond the conceptual approach taken here to more precise models that more closely parallel the statistically oriented work of the Commission.

CHAPTER 3

Strategic Problem Solving, Project Safe Neighborhoods, and the New Criminal Justice

Edmund F. McGarrell

As noted in the previous chapters, the New Criminal Justice describes justice system processes and interventions that emphasize highly focused local interventions, coalitions formed to reduce crime, and data-driven strategies. When coordinated, these components reflect a strategic problem-solving model that has emerged over the last decade through a series of innovative practices. This problem-solving model also served as a foundation for the U.S. Department of Justice's gun violence reduction program known as Project Safe Neighborhoods (PSN).

PSN was a federal program but with components designed to support locally tailored interventions involving collaborative partnerships and data-driven decision making. PSN was coordinated through the nation's 94 U.S. Attorneys' Offices. This chapter describes some of the innovative criminal justice practices that helped shape the strategic problem-solving model and uses the PSN experience as an example of strategic problem solving. The chapter is informed through the experience of serving as the national research team for PSN, a role that included providing training and technical assistance on strategic problem solving and also conducting research on the implementation of the model across the 94 districts. The argument is not that strategic problem solving was adopted successfully across all PSN task forces—indeed our research shows it was unevenly adopted (McGarrell et al., 2009)—but rather

to describe the model as adopted in a number of jurisdictions.

PSN BUILDING BLOCKS

The PSN initiative built on a number of promising crime reduction programs that emerged during the 1990s. These programs included Richmond's Project Exile, the New York Police Department's COMPSTAT Program, the Boston Ceasefire Program, the Department of Justice's (DOJ) Strategic Approaches to Community Safety Initiative (SACSI), the Bureau of Alcohol, Tobacco, Firearms and Explosives (ATF) illegal firearm market reduction strategies, and Weed and Seed.[1] Certainly the proliferation of problem-solving policing practices, as reflected in the Center for Problem-Oriented Policing (http://www.popcenter.org/default.htm), also served as a foundation for these principles.

Although there were many distinctive characteristics of these various programs, they also share several common dimensions that relate to strategic problem solving. All involved locally driven multi-agency collaborations focusing on locality-specific crime problems. To support this local focus, most involved some type of data-driven process to better understand the dynamics behind the crime patterns that were the target of various law enforcement interventions. For example, COMPSTAT involved the routine review of crime patterns, and ATF's firearm reduction strategies were driven by analysis of patterns from firearms used in crime incidents. Boston's Ceasefire and the SACSI program involved partnerships between law enforcement and researchers who engaged in an action research process (see Chapters 9 and 10 in this volume) that included problem analysis, evaluation of impact, and feedback to the task force. Additionally, the evidence that many of these interventions resulted in significant reductions in crime also challenged prevailing wisdom that police and criminal justice interventions had little impact on levels of crime.

The DOJ architects of PSN appeared to build upon these programs as they created PSN. As suggested by Boston's Ceasefire, Richmond's Exile, and SACSI, the power of the U.S. Attorney's Office would be leveraged to create new multi-agency coalitions focused on local gun crime problems. The U.S. Attorney's Office and the threat of federal prosecution, with corresponding increases in certainty and severity of punishment, for illegal possession and use of firearms was viewed as a mechanism for increasing the deterrence of gun crime. This deterrence-based goal would also be supported by the communication of the deterrence message through direct communication with at-risk individuals (e.g., Ceasefire and SACSI) and community-wide media campaigns (e.g., Exile). Finally, the strategic problem-solving approach of Ceasefire and SACSI would be supported through funding whereby the PSN task forces contracted with a local research partner.

CORE COMPONENTS OF PSN

The basic elements of this strategy to reduce gun crime were operationalized through five core components: partnerships, strategic planning, training, outreach, and accountability.

Partnerships

The PSN program was intended to increase partnerships between federal, state, and local law enforcement agencies through the formation of a local gun crime enforcement task force. The PSN design recognized the limited role of federal prosecutors in many aspects of local crime control and prevention and thus sought to increase partnerships with many elements of the local community. Coordinated by the U.S. Attorney's Office, the PSN task force typically included both federal and local prosecutors, federal law enforcement agencies (particularly ATF and U.S. Marshals), local and state law enforcement agencies, and probation and parole. PSN Coordinators were also encouraged to consider inclusion of local government leaders, social service providers, neighborhood leaders, members of the faith community, business leaders, and health-care providers.

Strategic Planning

Recognizing that crime problems, including gun crime, vary from community to community across the United States, that state laws addressing gun crime vary considerably, and that local and state resources vary across the federal judicial districts covered by U.S. Attorneys' Offices, the PSN program also included a commitment to strategic planning whereby the federal PSN program would be tailored to local context. Specifically, PSN provided resources for the inclusion of a local research partner who would work with the PSN task force to analyze the local gun crime problem and to share the findings with the task force for the development of a proactive plan for gun crime reduction. The inclusion of the research partner was also intended to assist in ongoing assessment in order to provide feedback to the task force.

Training

PSN involved a significant commitment of resources to support training. This included training provided to law enforcement agencies on topics including gun crime investigations, gun crime identification and tracing, and related issues. Training on effective prosecution of gun cases was provided to state and local prosecutors. Additional training focused on strategic problem solving and community outreach and engagement. Initiated in 2001, the DOJ estimated that by July 2005, nearly 17,000 individuals had attended a PSN-related training program.[2]

Outreach

The architects of PSN within the DOJ also recognized that increased sanctions would have the most impact if accompanied with a media campaign to communicate the message of the threat of federal prosecution for illegal possession and use of a gun. Consequently, resources were provided to all PSN task forces to work with a media partner to devise strategies for communicating this message to both potential offenders and the community at large. This outreach effort was also supported at the national level by the creation and distribution of public service announcements and materials (e.g., television and radio advertisements, posters). These materials were direct mailed to media outlets and were also available to local PSN task forces.[3]

> [T]he genius of Project Safe Neighborhoods is the marketing of our product . . . . Our product is fear in the hearts of the criminal. . . . If gun carrying is a big enough liability we can change the minds of would be gun carrying thugs.
>
> (Deputy Attorney General James Comey, PSN National Conference, June 16, 2004)

The outreach component was also intended to support the development of prevention and intervention components. Since fiscal year (FY) 2003 PSN has provided block grant funding to the local PSN partnerships that could be used to support a variety of initiatives including prevention and intervention. Many were built on existing programs such as school-based prevention, Weed and Seed, or juvenile court intervention programs.

Accountability

The leadership of the PSN initiative at the DOJ emphasized that PSN would focus on outcomes—that is, reduced gun crime—as opposed to a mere focus on outputs such as arrests and cases prosecuted. That is, PSN would be measured by the reduction in gun crime. This accountability component was linked to strategic planning whereby PSN task forces, working with their local research partners, were asked to report levels of crime over time within targeted problems and/or targeted areas. In reality, this proved challenging for many of the PSN task forces because of the lack of consistent measures of gun crime in most police departments and the fact that national crime reporting systems do not capture gun crime.

The basic elements and the DOJ's five core components of PSN are illustrated in Table 3.1.

STRATEGIC PROBLEM-SOLVING MODEL

The Project Exile components of PSN, increased federal prosecution and communication strategy, coupled with the Boston Ceasefire focused deterrence approach, were further developed by the strategic problem-solving model developed in the DOJ's SACSI program (Roehl et al., 2008). Specifically, the core components and essential elements of PSN were given structure through a strategic problem-solving process and a set of strategic approaches and interventions developed in Boston, the SACSI sites, and similar crime reduction efforts.

Table 3.1 PSN foundations

Basic elements	DOJ's core components
Increased federal prosecution	*Partnerships*
	Local, state, federal coordinated enforcement
	Community prevention and intervention
	Research partner
	Strategic planning
	Data-driven proactive plan
Focused deterrence strategies	*Training*
	Enforcement training
	Prosecution training
	Strategic problem solving
	Outreach and community engagement
Communication strategy	*Outreach*
	Communicate deterrence message
	Prevention and Intervention
	Accountability
	Meaningful implementation
	Impact on gun crime

The strategic problem-solving model (Figure 3.1), as presented to PSN task forces, was based on systematic analysis of the local gun crime problem.[4] Specifically, crime analysis would be used to identify the geographic patterns of gun crime across a PSN district and within specific jurisdictions of the district. The analysis should also uncover patterns such as linkages to drug sales and distribution, gangs, chronic offenders, domestic violence, illegal gun sales, and related patterns of people, place, and context. On the basis of this analysis, specific strategies would be developed and implemented to address these patterns. As strategies were implemented, the research partner would monitor the level of intervention (dosage) as well as assess evidence of impact. This information could be shared with the task force to allow for revision or modification of strategy. The process was intended to be dynamic and ongoing, allowing for continual revision with the ultimate goal of reducing gun crime.

CORE THEMES

The strategic problem-solving model was also based on a set of core themes. These include focusing resources, using research to help guide action, and expanding the boundaries of involvement.

Focusing Resources

Despite the infusion of significant resources to address gun crime, most jurisdictions across the United States still face too many problem locations, gun offenders, probationers and parolees, outstanding warrants, and former inmates returning to the community to address solely through the PSN program. Thus, a core theme of the strategic problem-solving model was to maximize the impact of interventions (e.g., increased prosecution, media campaign, probation/parole supervision) by focusing on the most serious elements of the local gun crime problem (people, places, and things). Thus, although it may be impossible

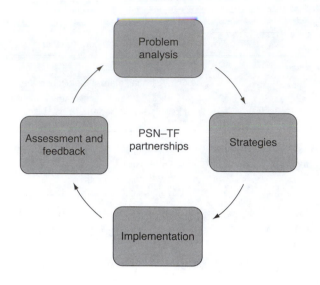

Figure 3.1 PSN strategic problem-solving model.

to increase the supervision of all probationers with a background of firearms possession, it may be possible to identify those suspected to be involved in high-risk activities (gang networks, drug sales) and sunject this subgroup of probationers to police–probation home visits. Although PSN was designed before the publication of the influential National Academies of Science report on the effectiveness and fairness of policing, the model was very consistent with the key finding of this report that the most effective efforts to reduce crime are those that are most focused and tailored to the problem (National Research Council, 2004).

The notion of focusing resources also included attention to recurring problems that may be lost in the routine processing of cases.[5] Thus, in a jurisdiction where gun cases not involving actual violence were found to be routinely dismissed, revised procedures that ensure that every case involving a firearm receives particular attention from police and prosecutors may be an important "system-fix" that can change the message sent to offenders about illegal gun possession.

Using Research to Guide Action

A core ingredient of focusing resources was to use data to identify the people, places, and things driving gun crime at the local level. Experience has indicated that at a certain level there are common elements of much gun violence. Particularly in the nation's urban areas, it tends to involve young men, with offenders and victims often sharing extensive prior histories in the justice system, and to be concentrated in particular neighborhoods (e.g., Braga et al., 2001; McGarrell et al., 2006; Corsaro and McGarrell, 2009; Papachristos et al., 2007; Braga, 2008). These basic patterns, when assessed by the local task force, can help to begin to focus PSN resources. Beyond these patterns, however, there tends to be variation across communities along a number of dimensions such as the link to drug trafficking, the tie to gangs or networks of offenders, the nature of the illegal gun market, and, particularly in rural areas, the tie to domestic violence. Thus, by involving a research partner with the task force, PSN was geared toward identifying these patterns to focus suppression (law enforcement, prosecution), intervention, and prevention resources.

The research partner, as mentioned above, was also intended to monitor implementation of PSN and provide continual feedback to the task force to support ongoing revision of strategies.

Expanding the Boundaries of Involvement

As demonstrated in Figure 3.1, the partnership component of PSN was also a core component of the strategic problem-solving model. At a minimal level, the U.S. Attorney's Office was dependent on local, state, and federal law enforcement agencies to bring gun cases for federal prosecution. The strategic problem-solving model also suggested that the inclusion of other criminal justice system partners could further maximize the impact of interventions. Thus, inclusion of the U.S. Marshal and federal–local fugitive task forces could provide a vehicle for strategic warrant service on offenders thought to be at high risk for gun crime. Building on Ceasefire and SACSI, a number of PSN task forces adopted the "pulling levers" approach of communicating a focused deterrence and social support message to individuals believed to be at high risk of involvement in gun crime (Braga et al., 2001; Kennedy et al., 2001; McGarrell et al., 2006; Corsaro and McGarrell, 2009; Papachristos et al., 2007; Braga, 2008). In both examples, the notion was that increased federal prosecution of gun crime offenders may have greater impact if part of a proactive, comprehensive strategy focused on the people and places driving gun crime at the local level. Specifically, increased prosecution coupled with multiple strategies to communicate to potential offenders the increased certainty and severity for illegal possession and use of guns was central to the focused deterrence strategy.

Similarly, inclusion of community partners, service providers, the faith community, and other local partners was intended to provide additional resources for the development of prevention and intervention programs geared toward reducing gun crime. Community-based prevention programs aimed at the children or younger siblings of gun offenders could potentially yield long-term prevention benefits. Faith-based or victim advocate intervention with shooting victims was hoped to prevent retaliation. Ex-offender mentoring and job placement programs could provide important resources for offenders returning to the community from prison. The value of the strategic model was that limited resources could most effectively be targeted to the critical components of gun violence in the community.

Finally, the inclusion of community members and community leaders was seen as crucial to establishing legitimacy and support for PSN. There was recognition that aggressive prosecution of gun crime offenders was likely to have a differential impact on particular communities. This was particularly true of urban, minority neighborhoods that have been most victimized by gun crime. Focusing resources on the key people and places driving gun crime would disproportionately affect these neighborhoods. Demonstrating that the focus was data driven based on levels of gun crime victimization, that prevention and intervention strategies would accompany aggressive prosecution, and that community leaders would be included in PSN were suggested as critical steps in building community support.

STRATEGIC INTERVENTIONS

Building on the core components of PSN, as well as the strategic problem-solving model, a series of strategic practices and interventions emerged in PSN sites across the country (Table 3.2). These were drawn from the experience in Boston, Richmond, and the SACSI sites. Not all were utilized in all PSN sites, and those that were implemented were adapted to fit local context. Yet these strategic interventions and practices were utilized by a number of PSN task forces with promising results. The strategies are described in more detail in several of the subsequent chapters.

The strategies included incident reviews whereby police officers, investigators, and special unit personnel (e.g., gangs, narcotics), and often prosecutors and probation/parole officers, came together and systematically reviewed homicides and shootings to better understand the dynamics driving gun violence in the local jurisdiction (Klofas and Hipple, 2006). The goal was to generate both strategic intelligence on the people, places, and contexts generating gun violence, as well as tactical intelligence that could lead to enforcement, intervention, and prevention actions.

A second strategy employed in many jurisdictions was the development of a chronic violent offender list identifying individuals believed to be at greatest risk of committing violent gun crime (Bynum and Decker, 2006). These individuals became the focus of investigations and the information was shared with law enforcement and prosecutors with the goals of increasing officer safety and ensuring that these individuals did not "slip through the cracks" of the justice system if arrested.

A strategy derived from Boston Ceasefire and employed in many SACSI sites was the use of offender notification meetings (also referred to as "pulling levers" meetings) at which at-risk probationers and parolees, often with network or gang affiliations, heard directly from justice officials about the renewed focus on gun crime and the commitment to aggressive prosecution for the illegal possession and use of a gun. The deterrence message was coupled with offers of assistance and social support.

Given the threat of federal prosecution communicated in offender notification meetings and in media campaigns, as well as the PSN DOJ commitment to increasing the level of federal prosecution for gun crime, the task forces needed to develop mechanisms to bring gun cases to the U.S. Attorneys' Offices and to decide the appropriate venue for prosecution (federal or local). In many jurisdictions, joint case screening processes were developed whereby Assistant U.S. Attorneys, county or state's attorneys (local prosecutors), ATF agents, and local police officers jointly screened gun crime cases to determine whether the case should be prosecuted federally or locally (Decker and McDevitt, 2006).

In a number of jurisdictions these strategies were intended to be mutually reinforcing. Thus, incident reviews were used to identify groups of chronic offenders believed to be at risk for being involved in violence as perpe-

Table 3.2 Strategic problem solving

Core themes	
Focusing resources	*Strategic practices and interventions*
Maximizing the impact of interventions	Incident reviews
Targeting the most serious gun crime problems (people, places, context)	Chronic violent offender lists
	Gun case screening processes
Addressing recurring problems	Offender notification meetings
Fixing system gaps	Data-driven proactive plan
Using research to help guide action	*Additional strategic interventions*
Unpacking the local gun crime problem	Illegal gun markets/supply-side strategies
Continually adjusting strategies	Re-entry
Expanding boundaries of involvement	Police–probation–parole teams
Criminal justice system partners (local, state, federal)	Directed patrol (gun crime hot spots)
Community partners (expand resources, build legitimacy)	Problem properties/nuisance abatement
	Prevention (street workers, school-based, juvenile gun courts, etc.) and intervention

trators or victims, who could then be called in to an offender notification meeting. Incident review information could be combined with systematic analysis of arrest and conviction data to identify individuals to be included on most violent offender lists. This information could then be used in case-screening decisions in terms of prioritizing the most serious and chronic violent offenders for aggressive federal prosecution. The results of federal prosecution could then be communicated in offender notification meetings to reinforce the focused deterrence message.

A number of jurisdictions also attempted to implement the focused deterrence and incapacitation goals through additional strategies. Building on "promising practices" research evidence,[6] police departments in a number of jurisdictions utilized directed police patrol in gun crime hot spots. ATF implemented supply-side efforts, re-entry programs were developed, police–probation–parole teams conducted home visits, nuisance abatement teams targeted problem properties, and a variety of prevention activities were developed as part of PSN. These efforts were implemented with greatly varying levels of intensity and greater and lesser integration with other PSN strategies. At least at the logic model level, however, the notion of the strategic problem-solving process would suggest that they be focused on those people, places, and contexts that the data analysis suggested as the sources of the gun crime problem.

SUMMARY

As described above, the New Criminal Justice emphasizes locally focused crime reduction interventions, coordinated by powerful coalitions of local, state, and federal law enforcement and criminal justice partners, local government, social services, neighborhood groups, and other community actors. The interventions and coalitions are to be driven by ongoing analysis of crime contexts as well as assessment of the impact of inter-

ventions. When combined, these components reflect the strategic problem-solving model that was included in the design of PSN.

As discussed, these components of the strategic problem-solving model were based upon promising practices that emerged in the Boston Ceasefire Program, SACSI, and Richmond's Project Exile (Braga et al., 2001; Kennedy et al., 2001; Roehl et al., 2008; McGarrell et al., 2006; Corsaro and McGarrell, 2009; Rosenfeld et al., 2005). As will be presented in subsequent chapters, evidence emerged in PSN that, when these principles were implemented, they were associated with reduced levels of gun crime. Additionally, the national assessment found that cities that were the focus of PSN interventions, and where levels of implementation were most intense, had significant reductions in level of crime when compared with non-target cities and low levels of dosage (McGarrell et al., 2009). Given these promising findings, continued development and refinement of the strategic problem-solving model appears warranted as communities attempt to reduce levels of crime and victimization and improve the quality of life, particularly in those neighborhoods suffering from high levels of crime and violence.

NOTES

1 Many of these initiatives are described in more detail in McGarrell et al. (2009). Research on these initiatives is provided in Rosenfeld et al. (2005); Raphael and Ludwig (2003); Silverman (1999); Braga et al. (2001); Kennedy et al. (2001); Coleman et al. (1999). See also Roehl et al. (2008); Dalton (2003); McGarrell et al. (2006); Corsaro and McGarrell (2009).

2 Data compiled by Professor Joe Trotter and colleagues as part of American University's PSN Technical Assistance Program.

3 U.S. Department of Justice, Bureau of Justice Assistance, 2004. See also http://www.psn. gov.

4 By the end of FY 2003, 92 of the 93 PSN task forces had received training on this strategic

problem solving and all task forces were working with a research partner.

5 For example, PSN officials in many jurisdictions report that, for years, illegal possession of a firearm by a felon or concealed carrying offenses, and even crimes committed with a firearm present but no shooting, were routinely treated as non-violent offenses with high rates of dropped charges, dismissed cases, and suspended sentences.

6 Sherman and Rogan (1995); McGarrell et al. (2001); Cohen and Ludwig (2003).

The New Criminal Justice in Practice

This section is meant to put meat on the theoretical and conceptual bones offered up in the first three chapters of the book. This section focuses on important elements in implementing the new collaborative problem-solving models. Material is drawn from evaluations of the major efforts that have helped frame the New Criminal Justice. Chapter 4 draws lessons from the ten-site program known as Strategic Approaches to Community Safety Initiative (SACSI). Dennis Rosenbaum led the evaluation and found that the nature of the working group was among the most significant of the program's developments. Strong leadership, a history of collaboration, and placing a high value on research also helped to distinguish the most successful efforts. Together those factors produced a wide array of intervention programs. Especially important was the ability of researchers and practitioners to work closely together. SACSI provided key momentum for development of the New Criminal Justice.

The remainder of the chapters in this section involve case studies of sites where the New Criminal Justice has been implemented to some degree or another. In the first of these Natalie Kroovand Hipple reports on two Alabama programs that emphasized enhanced federal prosecution of gun cases based on the Project Exile program, which originated out of Richmond, Virginia. The programs each recognized the potential of using federal gun laws in Alabama but they developed differently, found leadership and direction in different places, and faced different obstacles as they each influenced gun crime in their jurisdictions. In Chapter 6, Edmund McGarrell presents a series of case studies that are intended to take the reader "into the weeds" of the problem-solving process. The programs all assembled effective coalitions and drew on the resources of their research partners. While selecting from known interventions, such as enhanced gun prosecution, the sites tailored the programs to meet their needs. In one, an older generation of residents was convinced to exert greater influence over its community in the interests of reducing turmoil that would otherwise lead to police crackdowns. The cases illustrate the complexities of local diagnosis and planning to identify and selectively use leverage to reduce crime.

In Chapter 7 a team of researchers examined the intervention process from the opposite direction. That is to say, they identified cities that had lower than expected rates of serious crime based on their population and city characteristics and they sought to identify the policing strategies that might account for these differences. The investigations found that these cities shared long-term and extensive problem-solving approaches. There was little evidence that any specific program or intervention explained their success. Rather the hard work of focused problem solving and meaningful collaboration appeared to pay off.

The final case study of the Drug Market Initiative in Rockford, Illinois (Chapter 8), extends the ideas of community planning and selective application of leverage. Here long-established drug markets were controlled and crime reduced by identifying key drug sellers, building cases, but ultimately using community interests and the threat of sanctions to reduce open-air drug sales and improve the quality of neighborhood life. Together the case studies, some of which looked from the interventions to their effects on crime and some from the levels of crime back toward possible explanations, provided support for the problem-solving, data-based coalitions so important to the New Criminal Justice.

DISCUSSION QUESTIONS

1   The case studies presented in these chapters show a combination of well-established programs such as enhanced prosecution under Project Exile and a variety of other approaches from pulling levers to community engagement. As you consider these, to what extent do you think they reflect something that might be considered a program available for off-the-shelf application in different communities or a process that involves self-study and planning in different communities? What are the benefits and hazards of approaching intervention from these two perspectives? Which model do you think more accurately reflects the foundations of the New Criminal Justice?

2   Many of the case studies included in these chapters dealt with law enforcement and prosecution powers in criminal justice. What examples are there of other types of interventions in these chapters? What is the range of interventions represented in the Drug Market Initiative? How well does the model of the New Criminal Justice accommodate a range of planning efforts and interventions?

3   These chapters have all focused on strategies for crime reduction. What other kinds of problems does the criminal justice system face? How well would the processes described here fit in approaches to address other problems? How would you adapt the features of the New Criminal Justice to address problems besides crime reduction?

CHAPTER 4

Building Successful Anti-Violence Partnerships: Lessons from the Strategic Approaches to Community Safety Initiative (SACSI) Model

Dennis P. Rosenbaum and Jan Roehl

Among Western countries, inter-agency partnerships have become the coin of the realm for governments seeking more effective strategies to alleviate crime problems (e.g. Crawford, 1997). Rosenbaum's (2002) theory of partnerships delineates the many reasons why inter-agency collaboratives should be more effective than single agencies, including their ability to identify/define multiple sources and components of the problem, their capacity to develop interventions that address different dimensions of the problem, and their ability to coordinate and apply more resources in potentially synergistic ways. In the field of criminal justice/public safety, numerous multi-agency partnerships have been pursued with different levels of success. One of the foundational models of collaborative problem solving, developed in response to urban violence, is the Strategic Approaches to Community Safety Initiative (SACSI). This chapter provides a synthesis of the key findings and lessons learned from the national evaluation of SACSI conducted by the Center for Research in Law and Justice, University of Illinois at Chicago.[1] After describing the SACSI model in practice and discussing some of the factors that contributed to its success, we offer a few cautions and recommendations about partnerships that involve "action research."

BACKGROUND

In the early 1990s, Boston, Massachusetts, experienced an out-of-control level of juvenile homicide and gun-related crime. The police department partnered with Harvard University researchers to analyze the problem in depth and work together with other partners to implement appropriate intervention strategies. This collaboration, called the Boston Gun Project/Operation Ceasefire, was credited with substantial reductions in youth homicides and non-fatal gun violence (see Braga et al., 2001). To see if Boston's approach could be replicated and extended in other cities, the Department of Justice launched the Strategic Approaches to Community Safety Initiative (SACSI)—a multi-agency partnership model designed to effectively address violent crime problems. The success of SACSI eventually led to the nationwide rollout of Project Safe Neighborhoods (PSN), which was based on the SACSI model.

THE SACSI MODEL IN PRACTICE

SACSI was a multipronged anti-violence initiative in ten U.S. cities built upon theory and research regarding problem-oriented policing (Goldstein, 1990), community policing (Rosenbaum, 1994), repeat violent offenders (Kennedy, 1997), and partnerships (Roehl et al., 1996). Adapting the process used in Boston, the SACSI model had several distinguishing characteristics: multi-agency collaboration, integration of research into program planning and implementation, and strategic problem solving, all under the leadership of the U.S. Attorney's Office. In Boston, a multi-agency planning group developed coordinated problem-solving strategies using detailed information about severe juvenile homicide and gun-related crime problems supplied by a research partner and law enforcement officers. Boston's signature strategy—convening offender notification or "lever-pulling" meetings[2] with high-risk offenders that were designed to deter juvenile crime through a combination of warnings of swift and sure enforcement and prosecution for any violence and the provision of social and vocational services—seemed to be a solid success. But it was Boston's collaborative, data-driven, problem-solving *process* that SACSI sought to emulate, not its central intervention strategy. The SACSI approach had much in common with previous collaborative problem-solving efforts, but the integration of a local research partner into the core planning group set it (and Boston) apart from its predecessors.

THE SACSI CITIES

Ten cities were selected as SACSI sites. The five "Phase I" sites were Indianapolis, Memphis, New Haven, Portland (Oregon), and Winston-Salem. The five "Phase II sites"— funded two years later—were Albuquerque, Atlanta, Detroit, Rochester (New York), and St. Louis. The ten SACSI cities are diverse in size, region of the country, and severity of crime (see Table 4.1). As a group, however, they represent America's mid-sized cities, where, by and large, the twin problems of drug trafficking and violent crime came later than they did in the larger coastal cities such as New York and Los Angeles. Nine of the ten SACSI sites targeted homicide, youth vio-

lence, and/or firearms violence. Memphis was the exception, where the SACSI partnership focused on reducing rape and other sexual assaults.

THE NATIONAL EVALUATION

The national evaluation of SACSI, funded by the National Institute of Justice, was a cross-site comparison of the ten sites. The research team documented and assessed partnership formation and dynamics, strategic planning, problem-solving activities, the integration of research into the site strategies and activities, program longevity, and program impact based on local reports and FBI Uniform Crime Reports (UCR) data. The primary methods were: (1) multiple site visits to each program, (2) interviews with SACSI partners regarding processes and activities, (3) a two-wave survey of partnership members regarding interactions, progress, satisfaction, key activities, and effectiveness, (4) observation and recording of meetings and activities by local researchers, (5) attendance at cluster meetings involving all sites, (6) review of project materials and reports, and (7) the acquisition and analysis of UCR data from SACSI and comparison cities.

IMPACT FINDINGS

Using crime data from target neighborhoods reported to local police before and after the SACSI periods and citywide figures for comparison, Phase I researchers in each site reported dramatic decreases in their target crimes, highlighted below (see also Figures 4.1 and 4.2 for illustrations of the drops in homicide rates and in violent crimes in general in the sites during the SACSI periods).[3] In the absence of strong quasi-experimental or experimental designs, we cannot be fully confident that SACSI alone was responsible for the reductions in crime or whether SACSI worked in combination with other factors. But we can say that, although cities of similar

Table 4.1 SACSI cities: population, crime rate, partnership composition and size, and target crimes[a]

| SACSI sites | 2000 Census data | | Violent crime/1000 in the year SACSI started | Composition of core group | Size of core group | Target crime(s) |
	Population	Rank				
Albuquerque	448,607	35	11.45	LE/CJ	15	Homicide, firearms violence
Atlanta	416,474	39	27.81	LE/CJ + ER	15	Homicide, firearms violence
Detroit	951,270	10	23.24	LE/CJ	10	Firearms violence and violations
Indianapolis	781,870	12	11.35	LE/CJ	28	Homicide, firearms violence
Memphis	650,100	18	14.99	Broad based	27	Rape, sexual assault
New Haven	123,626	175	16.84	LE/CJ[b]	27[c]	Firearms violence
Portland	529,121	28	13.72	Broad based	25	Violent crime among 15- to 24-year-olds
Rochester	219,773	79	7.43	Broad based	8	Youth and firearms violence
St. Louis	348,189	49	22.79	Broad based	27	Homicide, firearms violence
Winston-Salem	185,776	107	12.52	Broad based	21	Violent crime among youth under 18 years
Average, cities over 100,000:					Average: 20	
1998			6.91			
2000			6.20			

ER, emergency room; LE/CJ, law enforcement/criminal justice.

Notes

a Data sources: population—U.S. Census Bureau, Summary File 1 (SF 1) and Summary File 3 (SF 3); U.S. rank—*County and City Data Book*, 2000 edition, revised March 16, 2004; violent crime rates—FBI Uniform Crime Reports.

b Became more broad based over time, with addition of full-service offender re-entry organization.

c As it became broad based, it also became smaller, with 10 members by the second wave of the partnership survey.

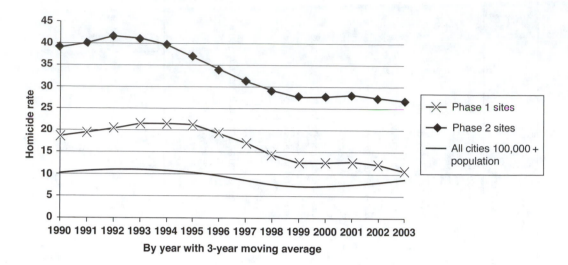

Figure 4.1 Homicide rates, 1990–2003.

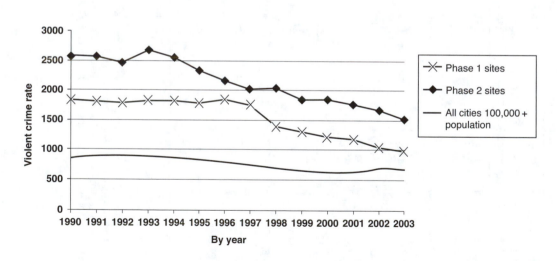

Figure 4.2 Violent crime rates, 1990–2003.

size across the United States experienced decreases in violent crime in the late 1990s, the decreases were significantly greater in the SACSI cities. The drops in SACSI target areas were substantial:

- *Indianapolis* experienced a 53 percent decrease in gun assaults in the target neighborhood versus a 19 percent decrease citywide, and a 32 percent reduction in homicide citywide during the year after interventions in the target neighborhood.
- *Memphis* experienced a 49 percent decrease in forcible rape citywide after the introduction of SACSI.
- *New Haven* experienced a 32 percent decrease in violent gun crimes and a 45 percent decrease in calls for service for "shots fired" citywide after the introduction of SACSI.
- *Portland* experienced a 42 percent decrease in homicides and a 25 percent decrease in other violent crimes citywide after the introduction of SACSI.
- *Winston-Salem* experienced a 58 percent decrease in juvenile robberies and a 19 percent decrease in juvenile incidents in target neighborhoods after the introduction of SACSI.

The impact of the lever-pulling approaches was mixed. Three of four sites found that offenders had indeed "heard the message" about new violence bringing swift and certain law enforcement action. Yet, in those same sites, there was no difference in the recidivism rates of lever-pulling attendees and those of comparison groups of offenders. Researchers in Indianapolis found that a drop in offending was associated with offenders' awareness of increased police stops, probation sweeps, and the like, rather than their awareness of SACSI "offender notification" meetings and messages. Finally, in pre- and post-SACSI community surveys, researchers in New Haven found that residents reported

a decreased fear of crime, increased satisfaction with the quality of life, and a heightened awareness that gun carriers would be targeted.

FACTORS CONTRIBUTING TO SUCCESS

The national evaluation of SACSI included a strong process component that shed light on the program elements needed for the successful execution of partnership strategies. Whether these factors are linked to successful outcomes is more difficult to determine. The SACSI programs faced varying local conditions, were multifaceted, and were led by multidisciplinary core groups. Furthermore, cities with different forms of partnerships and different intervention philosophies also reported achievements in reducing crime. But without a doubt, the field observations, interviews, and surveys helped to document implementation obstacles and uncover broader issues associated with building effective multi-agency partnerships.

The SACSI program featured several central structural components that appeared to be linked to successful execution of strategies. Chief among them were: (1) the leadership provided by the U.S. Attorneys' Offices, (2) the formation of a core multi-agency partnership of decision makers, as well as working groups to carry out program strategies, (3) the integration of research into problem selection, analysis, strategic planning, and assessment, and (4) the implementation of complementary strategies directed at both suppressing and preventing violent crime. Each is discussed briefly.

Leadership of the U.S. Attorneys' Offices

The leadership of the U.S. Attorneys' Offices was a key factor in implementation success. Each U.S. Attorney's Office, through the U.S. Attorney or the First Assistant U.S. Attorney, was able to bring key decision makers to the table and induce them to commit significant resources to SACSI. U.S. Attorneys were generally quite active in partnership building and development, and their involvement was essential for sustaining good working relationships among local, state, and federal law enforcement officials and prosecutors.

In a survey conducted with the agency partners involved in the programs, respondents gave high marks to the involvement of their U.S. Attorneys, second only to the full-time Project Coordinators. The Project Coordinators (usually Assistant U.S. Attorneys) were often cited as leaders of the Phase I core groups, credited with seeing that strategies were carried out and that all partnership members followed through. They were especially helpful in working with non-law enforcement members on prevention and intervention activities.

Core and Working Groups

Each of the SACSI sites successfully formed and maintained a core multi-agency partnership responsible for strategic planning, reviewing research results, and coordinating intervention strategies. Half of the SACSI sites' core groups consisted entirely of law enforcement and criminal justice representatives, whereas the other half were more broad based, encompassing social service agencies, other city agencies, non-profits, schools, the faith community, and others. The majority of the sites also had non-law enforcement partners who worked extensively on SACSI activities (e.g., developing a public education campaign or conducting street outreach) but who were not included in the core group.

The sites with the largest decreases in target crimes—including Portland, Memphis, and Winston-Salem—were more apt to have broad-based core groups (see Table 4.1). In Indianapolis, where target crimes were also dramatically reduced, the core group consisted entirely of law enforcement and criminal representatives, but the working

groups also had strong support from faith-based and social service partners. Core groups appeared to function without substantial difficulty, suggesting that no one model was more effective than others. Throughout the SACSI program, the satisfaction, interest, and motivation of members remained relatively high for all groups.

All sites formed working groups charged with carrying out the daily work needed to implement the intervention strategies. Except for Memphis, all of the sites had a working group composed of law enforcement and criminal justice representatives who concentrated on enforcement, and half of them had a second (or third) working group focused on outreach and prevention.

The combination of core and working groups appeared to be effective for planning and implementation. Working groups shouldered the majority of day-to-day responsibilities. Law enforcement working groups were particularly active and effective. Adult probation agencies, historically marginalized in law enforcement strategies, played central roles in both enforcement and prevention activities.

The Importance of Previous Partnerships

The SACSI projects were built on the foundations of previous collaborative efforts in each city. Previous relationships among partnership members, in both core and working groups, helped SACSI get going quickly. Most of the sites had a history of key law enforcement and criminal justice agencies working together on crime, drug, and gang problems. Some of these previous efforts simply segued into SACSI when that funding became available. Previous working relationships with and among non-law enforcement agencies were less common, but helpful as well. Cities that had developed a culture of conducting business via inter-agency partnerships found the SACSI approach easy to adopt.

Use and Value of Research

Unique to the SACSI projects were the *type of researcher–practitioner relationships* formed and the *nature of the research activities* undertaken. The local researchers were primarily professors from local universities with long-established ties with the criminal justice representatives in the core groups. The researchers became full partners, participating in strategic planning, development, and assessment (i.e., action research). They collected and analyzed traditional and non-traditional data in contextual ways to aid in fleshing out the target problem and in designing and implementing intervention strategies. The local researchers also served as in-house evaluators, providing feedback on strategy implementation and conducting impact analyses to assess effectiveness. Overall, partnership members felt that the integration of research into the planning and implementation of the SACSI initiative was successful and useful.

Local researchers analyzed the target problems through conventional methods, including examining incident, arrest, and probation records; crime mapping; analyses of victim and suspect characteristics and their relationships; and multi-year trend studies. On the creative side, one of the most successful problem analysis tools in half of the SACSI sites was the use of homicide and crime incident reviews, a joint product of researchers and practitioners. Street-level information from diverse agencies and sources (e.g., gang outreach workers and probation officers) was used effectively for strategic planning and prevention.

Several sites developed lists of chronic and high-risk offenders based on arrest and/or probation records, and targeted these offenders with deterrence messages and heightened enforcement, supervision, and intervention. Local researchers in some sites also interviewed target offenders and added specific questions to ongoing Arrestee Drug Abuse Monitoring (ADAM) interviews to gather information on firearms use and attitudes and to assess intervention messages and strategies. Although such interviews were time-consuming and difficult to conduct, they generated some of the most useful research findings for fine-tuning interventions.

INTERVENTION STRATEGIES

The SACSI partnerships developed and implemented an impressive number of intervention strategies. They ranged from prevention to arrest and prosecution, and from the traditional to the innovative. Partnership members reported their perceived effectiveness in solving the target problems as "moderate."

Enforcement Strategies

Each of the SACSI sites implemented both enforcement and prevention strategies, yet all sites, particularly at the start, emphasized enforcement and prosecution. Many of the initial strategies were enforcement oriented—targeting hot spots and repeat offenders, crackdowns, sweeps, saturation patrols, serving warrants, and making unannounced visits to probationers. The SACSI sites were most skilled at implementing enforcement and suppression strategies, and law enforcement, prosecution, and probation agencies committed a high level of resources to these strategies. Key innovative enforcement strategies included:

1 *Offender notification meetings* are modeled on Boston's Operation Ceasefire and based on deterrence theory. The prosecuting attorney's team holds meetings with high-risk individuals, informing them that any violence judged to be within their control will be swiftly and surely sanctioned by law enforcement and prosecution. At the same time, the team offers assistance in obtaining jobs, education, and other services.

2 *Homicide and incident reviews* occur when key agency representatives and street workers meet to review and share information on recent homicides or other incidents of violence. "Grand homicide reviews" typically kick off the process, with representatives from many agencies reviewing cases from recent years and looking for patterns.

3 *"Worst of the worst" offender lists* are compiled from arrest or probation records or by "nominations" from probation and parole officers. The lists of known chronic offenders are used to focus enforcement, prosecution, and supervision efforts.

All of the sites adopted some version of Boston's Ceasefire approach based on deterrence theory. Sites varied in the number of offender notification or lever-pulling meetings held and the emphasis placed on those meetings. Indianapolis, for example, held dozens of meetings, ultimately meeting with several hundred chronic offenders, whereas Portland only held a couple of meetings and worked extensively with about 40 people. There were also variations across and within sites in the extent to which "swift and certain" action was taken following violent incidents (i.e., the extent to which "levers" actually got "pulled"). Geographic enforcement—in which a violent crime would be followed by sweeps and warrants in the area where the crime took place—was more common than targeted crackdowns on associates of the suspects.

Several sites implemented general deterrence strategies using media campaigns and public awareness materials to get out messages of "zero tolerance plus assistance." In most cases, these citywide strategies and high-visibility enforcement were well implemented. St. Louis's core group partnered with a communications agency to develop a public awareness campaign that focused on the five years of federal prison time possible if a felon is caught carrying a gun. Using segmented marketing strategies, more than 10,000 posters were distributed in the target area and radio spots were aired on stations popular with the target group.

Prosecution and Probation Strategies

Prosecution strategies that focused on firearms crimes were central to the SACSI project. Innovative prosecution and probation/parole initiatives pursued within the SACSI model were:

1 *Project Exile:* This initiative was named after Richmond, Virginia's anti-gun project, where an offender with a gun was said to forfeit his right to remain in the community. Although Project Exile is multifaceted, its cornerstones are immediate federal prosecution, stiff mandatory federal prison sentences, and "exile" to federal prison.

2 *Nightlight:* This initiative was named after Boston's Nightlight project. In its generic form, probation and police officers team up to conduct home visits to juveniles on probation and to patrol neighborhood streets to see if these youths are in compliance with curfew and other probation conditions.

3 *Project Re-Entry:* Reaching a national scale, versions of the initiative seek to assist new parolees in re-entering their communities and in adhering to parole conditions. Probation officers (and others) begin working with prisoners in the months before their release to prepare them for their return to the community. Again, warnings about swift and sure response to criminal behavior are given in concert with offers of social and employment services.

A key component of prosecution efforts under SACSI was the unprecedented cooperation between federal and state/local prosecutors. They reviewed cases together to determine in which system the case would be tried, and shared information and resources. New Haven's TimeZup project was typical. Every gun-related crime was reviewed by the U.S. Attorney's Office, local prosecutors, and law enforcement agencies with goals of achieving longer incarcerations, persuading defendants in state courts to plead guilty and to plead guilty earlier in the process, and getting the word out about longer sentences, thus seeking to create a deterrent effect on gun crimes.

Probation officers were recognized as central partners in the SACSI approach, working the continuum from enforcement to prevention. Often paired with police officers, they were key players in lever pulling, Nightlight, and Project Re-Entry strategies; they participated in the development of "most violent offender" lists; and they were primary resources for referrals to jobs, job training, and other assistance.

Portland was one of the earliest cities to launch a Project Re-Entry program, in 1999. Lever-pulling meetings were scheduled with soon-to-be-released gang members while they were still in prison to establish a release plan, and a visit was made to each prisoner's family. A home visit was made immediately after release by a team of probation officers, police officers, and outreach workers, each emphasizing different aspects of the release plan, expectations, and requirements. Over time, most of the work fell to the probation officers. A limited outcome evaluation conducted by the local SACSI research team suggested that this re-entry program reduced the reoccurrence of serious offenses in the paroled group.

Prevention Strategies

Community-based or service-based prevention strategies were given much less attention within SACSI than enforcement approaches, but they were, nevertheless, an important part of the overall model. The "carrot and stick" approach at the core of SACSI—especially the message to at-risk populations that "we will help you if you stop the violence"— required SACSI partners to take seriously their promise of social services. We found that prevention strategies were more prevalent and robust in sites with broad-based representation in the core group and one or more strong non-law enforcement partners. Prevention strategies were provided by probation officers, social service agencies, coalitions of churches, other faith-based organizations, and community organizations. The list of prevention and intervention services provided through SACSI is long, and includes job training, job placement, substance abuse treatment, tutoring, General Equivalency Diploma assistance, mentoring, family-based services, after-school activities, tattoo removal, driver's license replacement, and a school-based rape prevention program in Memphis. Examples of innovative prevention strategies included:

1 *ER trauma intervention:* St. Louis and Atlanta developed emergency room-based programs to gather information (for research and prosecution) and to provide police and social service interventions at a critical moment when the victim, family, and friends are available and attentive.
2 *Faith-based coalitions:* Several sites developed coalitions of churches patterned after Boston's TenPoint Coalition. Church leaders and organizations provided prevention and intervention services, especially mentoring, street outreach, and job assistance.

Winston-Salem's SACSI project was the most heavily involved in prevention and intervention, with several new initiatives launched in addition to more typical prevention activities (e.g., mentoring for youth, family-based services, job skills training and placement, and after-school activities). Teams comprising a police officer, a court counselor or probation officer, a minister, a community representative, and street workers provided coordinated services to high-risk individuals after lever-pulling meetings in a new program dubbed "Operation Reach."

EXPANSION OF SACSI INTO PSN

All ten SACSI projects successfully "morphed" into Project Safe Neighborhoods (PSN)[4] sites, with firearms crimes the main target and rigorous gun prosecution a signature activity among other enforcement, supervision, and prevention strategies. Multi-agency task forces continue to head PSN efforts, and local research partners remain integral to the program as it expands to address local gang problems. The central SACSI concepts of U.S. Attorney leadership, multi-agency partnerships, data-driven strategies, and local research partners continue in these ten SACSI sites under PSN's umbrella. Today, nearly all of the 94 federal districts in the United States employ the SACSI model as part of PSN.

CONCLUSIONS, CHALLENGES, AND LESSONS LEARNED

The impact findings from the national evaluation of SACSI, as well as findings from local evaluations, are consistent with the hypothesis that partnership approaches to public violence can be effective. Looking at crime trends, the Phase II sites enjoyed smaller successes than the Phase I sites. One possible explanation is that the Phase II sites included three of the highest crime cities in the United States (Atlanta, Detroit, and St. Louis) and they often targeted areas of concentrated poverty and high crime. Although these conditions typically hinder the effectiveness of most interventions, St. Louis experienced sizable reductions in target crimes. Phase II sites also differed from Phase I sites in that they

did not have full-time Project Coordinators—a critical factor in successful implementation.

The process data from this national assessment were helpful not only for identifying factors that contributed to successful implementation, as discussed earlier, but also for highlighting areas where difficulties or challenges emerged. Two key issues deserve future discussion and analysis here: the role of non-law enforcement partners in general and the role of researchers in the strategic partnership model.

Partnership Inclusiveness and Focus

In a critical review of the partnership literature, Rosenbaum (2002, p. 171) observes that "the primary substantive issue for public safety partnerships is the failure to be inclusive, thus undermining their greatest strength." The "greatest strength"—diversity of theories, strategies, and tactics—is undermined if non-law enforcement participation is limited. The composition of the partnership will have a heavy influence on the choice of anti-violence strategies. Too often, when law enforcement partners open up their "tool box" of strategies, they only find one tool—arrest or the threat of punishment. Certainly, enforcement was a central feature of SACSI in practice. Most sites, particularly those with heavy law enforcement representation on their core groups, began with and emphasized enforcement and suppression strategies. For many sites, prevention activities were rather limited and implemented late in the SACSI programs. Furthermore, non-law enforcement teams had more difficulties carrying out their responsibilities, due in large part to a lack of adequate resources.

Some SACSI programs shied away from more inclusive partnerships for specific reasons. Inclusive partnerships, not unlike other democratic processes, can be less efficient and, at times, result in more conflict among the partners. In the SACSI partnerships, however, members were generally cooperative and able to reach agreement on goals. Nevertheless, tensions did emerge between subgroups representing different philosophies about how to respond to delinquent youth, such as police and probation officers, law enforcement and community representatives, probation officers and social workers, and researchers and criminal justice representatives. We see this tension as a strength, rather than a weakness, of inclusive partnerships. This dialogue within the partnership, if facilitated by good leadership, is healthy and should, on average, generate more effective anti-crime strategies.

Researcher–Practitioner Relationships

The integration of research and practice was a distinctive and laudable feature of SACSI, but this "action research" process was not without difficulties. Hence, it provided many learning opportunities for both researchers and criminal justice practitioners. Historically, the relationship between researchers and practitioners has been marked by distrust and lack of cooperation. This is not surprising given that each group brings to the table different objectives, organizational cultures, communication mechanisms, methods for validating ideas, and values. SACSI provided unprecedented opportunities for researchers and practitioners to work together in a constructive manner and provide a learning platform for all parties.

One issue that we identified as emergent from this action research model involves the sharing of sensitive records and the need to clarify the roles of researchers and law enforcement practitioners. Researchers must be careful not to overstep their analytic role and become criminal investigators. For example, creating a list of repeat violent offenders—individuals who will then become the target of enforcement and prosecution efforts—is beyond the usual bounds of a researcher's function and raises issues about the protection of human research subjects. As

Braga and Hinkle note (see Chapter 11), "As a basic rule, none of the informational products produced by the academics should be specific enough to result in persons being arrested as a direct result of data being presented." More generally, the federal government has created a rigorous system of regulations and oversight to protect the welfare of all persons who are the subject of human research (Office of Human Subjects Research Protections, 2004). Thus, issues such as voluntary consent, confidentiality, and minimizing harm to the subject can be a challenge for action researchers involved in close collaborative relationships with criminal justice agencies. The gray areas in this partnership require further dialogue and clarification about which activities are "research" and which are not, and who is responsible for each.

Differences in organizational cultures between researchers and practitioners were also noted in several sites, with both parties straining to see each other's point of view at times. Practitioners often want immediate actionable information, whereas researchers need time to collect, clean, analyze, and interpret data. Also, obtaining approval from Institutional Review Boards to interview offenders and others is a time-consuming process. Yet some of the most useful research findings were generated from interviews with attendees at offender notification (lever-pulling) meetings and other high-risk groups. These research findings changed how lever-pulling meetings were implemented in some sites to enhance effectiveness. Finally, as researchers examined the data files kept by law enforcement agencies, they were able to identify areas in which structural enhancements and the collection of new data elements would benefit both future practice and research.

Despite the many obstacles, the SACSI initiative demonstrated that researchers and practitioners can work together to produce effective, evidence-based anti-violence interventions. Perhaps more importantly, they can learn from each other. Law enforcement can learn about new ways to conceptualize and analyze violence problems in the aggregate, design evidence-based interventions, evaluate program effectiveness, and scan the nation for best practices. Researchers, by gaining access to new types of information and confidential decision-making processes, can learn more about how street-level and organizational knowledge is generated and develop a deeper appreciation of the complexities and constraints that exist in organizational and inter-organizational environments.

NOTES

1 This chapter is based on a longer research report, "Strategic Approaches to Community Safety Initiative (SACSI) in 10 U.S. Cities: The Building Blocks for Project Safe Neighborhoods" by Jan Roehl, Dennis P. Rosenbaum, Sandra K. Costello, James R. Coldren, Amie M. Schuck, Laura Kunard, and David R. Forde, June 2005, available online at http://www.ncjrs.org/pdffiles1/nij/grants/212866.pdf.

2 The term "lever-pulling meetings" derived from the assurance given by high-level representatives [such as the Assistant U.S. Attorney, Bureau of Alcohol, Tobacco, Firearms and Explosives (ATF) special agent in charge, homicide commander, FBI, etc.] that, if violence occurred, the representatives would "pull all the levers" available to them (meaning that they would prosecute gun crimes to the full extent of applicable state or federal law, press for re-incarceration for those with probation or parole violations, serve outstanding warrants, etc.).

3 The SACSI evaluation reports are available through the National Criminal Justice Reference Service.

4 For more information on Project Safe Neighborhoods go to http://www.psn.gov.

CHAPTER 5

Project Exile Gun Crime Reduction

Natalie Kroovand Hipple

An initial stage in the research on the implementation and impact of Project Safe Neighborhoods (PSN) consisted of a series of case studies of specific PSN district programs. These site-specific case studies were intended to provide information about how PSN was structured and implemented in different jurisdictions. PSN was developed as a national program tailored to address varying gun crime patterns in local jurisdictions. One of the key roles of the research partner was to analyze these patterns to help inform the local PSN task force. This local nature of PSN also made it important to examine implementation and impact at the local level. Consequently, a series of site-specific cases studies addressed these issues.

In some districts, PSN resulted in a significant increase in federal prosecution of gun crime cases coupled with a communication strategy of a deterrence-based message. This reflected a Project Exile-type strategy. In other districts, research helped isolate particular target areas and dimensions of gun violence (e.g., gangs, drug market locations) and resulted in focused interventions targeted at these dimensions. This reflected a SACSI-type strategy referred to as "strategic problem solving/pulling levers."

As mentioned earlier and given this variation across districts, researchers conducted a series of site-specific case studies as a first step in the national research program. Having decided on this approach, the first challenge

was choosing districts for study. The main criterion for selection was a sense that key components of the PSN strategy had been implemented in a meaningful fashion and had been in operation for a sufficient period to potentially affect levels of gun crime. Researchers reviewed multiple indicators in an effort to identify districts meeting the selection criteria. These included district reports to the Department of Justice (DOJ), interviews with PSN Project Coordinators and PSN research partners, and data and project reports submitted to the DOJ. From these sources, districts were nominated for a possible case study based on:

- evidence of implementation of PSN strategies (e.g., increased federal prosecution, joint prosecution case review processes, incident reviews, offender notification meetings, chronic violent offender programs, targeted patrol, probation/parole strategies, gang strategies, prevention, supply-side strategies, etc.)
- evidence of new and enhanced partnerships (local, state, federal; community, etc.)
- integration of research partners and/or evidence of research-based strategies
- meaningful implementation for a sufficient time period to allow assessment of impact
- sufficient base-rate levels of gun crime to allow assessment of impact.

In effect, these dimensions were employed to ask: Is gun crime being addressed differently in this district based on one or several of the PSN core components?

PROJECT EXILE STRATEGY SITES

The Middle and Southern Districts of Alabama

The state of Alabama is served by three federal judicial districts, with corresponding U.S. Attorneys' Offices (USAOs): the Northern, Middle, and Southern Districts. In terms of PSN, Alabama was unique because the three districts coordinated a common PSN theme, logo, and message. Specifically, Alabama ICE, standing for Isolate the Criminal Element, was the common vehicle used across all three districts to communicate a consistent theme: *Gun Crime = Hard Time*. Two of the three federal districts, the Middle and Southern Districts, were the focus of comprehensive case studies by the MSU research team (McGarrell et al., 2007b; Hipple et al., forthcoming a).

The comprehensive case studies revealed that the two sites largely implemented PSN in a Project Exile fashion. The increased federal prosecution component was coupled with a community-wide strategy of communicating the threat of sanctions. This was a core ingredient of the statewide ICE program and was modeled on Richmond's Project Exile. Simply put, the media campaign was intended to maximize the impact of federal sanctions by communicating the USAO's commitment to federal prosecution of illegal gun possession and use.

The Middle and Southern Districts of Alabama are two of the smaller federal districts in terms of population (ranked seventy-fifth and eighty-second respectively). At the outset of PSN, both districts also suffered from high homicide rates, above the national average per 10,000 population, as evidenced by Uniform Crime Report data from 2001 (Table 5.1). Officials in both districts believed that one of the key causes for the high rate of homicides was extreme prison overcrowding in Alabama that had resulted in illegal gun possession being handled as a minor offense with no risk of incarceration. Indeed, officials shared data demonstrating that a significant number of homicides and gun assaults were receiving either no or minimal prison time in state prisons. The threat of federal prosecution and imprisonment for illegal gun possession and use was considered a potentially powerful tool by these local, state, and federal officials.

Despite having limited resources, both the Middle and the Southern District of Alabama USAOs made it their goal to prosecute as many firearms cases as possible. For both districts, this required excellent relationships with local law enforcement as they would be the ones bringing the cases for federal prosecution. Both districts relied heavily on their Law Enforcement Coordinators to foster new relationships as well as strengthen existing ones. However, each district took a slightly different approach to their task forces and how they would receive possible cases for federal prosecution from local law enforcement.

Table 5.1 Aggravated assault and murder rates, 2001

Site	Aggravated assault rate (per 10,000)	Murder rate (per 10,000)
U.S. average[a]	30.65	0.65
Alabama Middle District	24.31	0.73
Alabama Southern District	24.68	0.85

Note

a 90 federal judicial districts.

Task Force Structure and Gun Case Screening

In response to local law enforcement's concerns about "one more federal task force," the U.S. Attorney (USA) in the Middle District took a different approach to its Alabama ICE task force. Recognizing that law enforcement resources were sparse, the USA still asked agencies to assign an officer to the ICE task force but with the understanding that the officer would remain in his or her own agency and community rather than being assigned full time to the task force. In many respects, the task force member would serve as the point of contact within the local agency. This structure was described by many officials as a key to the success of Alabama ICE in the Middle District.

The task force, known as the Prosecution and Investigative Review Team (PIRT), met weekly at the USA's office in Montgomery. Following the decentralized task force format, members were not required to come every week. However, if they had a case to present or sought updates on previous cases, the PIRT meeting provided a venue for local task force members to communicate directly with a team of Assistant U.S. Attorneys (AUSAs), local prosecutors, Bureau of Alcohol, Tobacco, Firearms and Explosives (ATF) agents, and other local law enforcement officials. Through these meetings, law enforcement officers received immediate feedback on the prospects for federal prosecution as well as continual feedback on existing cases. Interviews consistently revealed that this weekly meeting was a critical component of team building among the local, state, and federal officials involved in the Middle District's Alabama ICE.

In contrast to the Middle District, the Southern District had what they considered a "hybrid" task force model. That is, they decided that a more common "round table" approach in which every contributing agency had someone at the table would not work well for them. What made this task force different

was that the core components were located within the Mobile Police Department, rather than the USAO. The reasoning behind this decision was that the Mobile Police Department is the largest police department in the Southern District and, therefore, had the highest rates of gun crime in the district and would generate the most federal gun cases. The Mobile Police Department chief demonstrated his commitment to PSN by dedicating one sergeant and one patrolman full time to work on ICE cases. Additionally, ATF worked with the Mobile Police Department to develop a case screening system. The screening system was designed to correspond to the elements of a gun crime needed to support federal prosecution. The sergeant became the department's Gun Coordinator, under the Criminal Investigation Division, and was augmented by an officer who was cross-deputized with ATF. This officer worked specifically with an agent dedicated to ICE cases and serve as the liaison between the Gun Coordinator at the Mobile Police Department and ATF.

Both the Middle and Southern Districts believed that training was a key component to their Alabama ICE efforts. Both USAOs realized that local law enforcement officers would need to be educated about federal gun laws, how to investigate cases and write reports, the elements needed for federal prosecution, and case processing. Here, the Law Enforcement Coordinator played a pivotal role in bringing training to law enforcement agencies in the district.

Communication Strategy

In addition to increased federal gun case prosecution, both the Middle and Southern Districts of Alabama focused a considerable amount of their time and energy on their communication strategy. This was a core ingredient in the statewide Alabama ICE program and was modeled on Richmond's Project Exile. Simply put, the media campaign was intended to maximize the impact of federal sanctions by communicating the USAO's commitment to federal prosecution of illegal gun possession and use. According to one criminal justice official in the Southern District, "it was never about locking everyone up but is about getting the message to the criminal population."

Interviews with officials in ATF and the USAO revealed that task force members noticed through the street officer's incident report narratives that the word was out on the street—"don't get caught with a gun." Officers quoted suspects as saying, "I can't get caught with a gun," and "I'm a felon, I can't get ICEd." Officers also reported that suspects increasingly (i.e., since ICE inception) admitted to drugs charges but denied gun possession, suggesting that they were aware of the possible federal consequences. Police and prosecution officials also reported seeing buzzwords in the police report narratives such as "felon" and "ICE" communicated by offenders.

Evidence of Implementation—Outputs

The data clearly indicated that federal prosecution of gun crime offenses increased in the Middle District. Despite the relatively small number of AUSAs (nine in 2000), the number of indictments under U.S. Code Title 922 and 924 violations increased from 15 in fiscal year (FY) 2000 and 20 in FY 2001, to 92 in FY 2003, an increase of over 500 percent. Similarly, the number of defendants prosecuted in federal court increased from 21 in FY 2000 to 103 in FY 2003 and 86 in FY 2004. This increase in indictments and defendants placed the Middle District in the top 7 percent of districts in terms of its percentage-point increase in federal prosecution. The numbers were even more telling when considered in light of the district's population. As one of the least populous U.S. districts (ranked nineteenth least populous out of 94), the Middle District's 2003 rate of defendants per 100,000 population was 9.7. This federal prosecution

rate per 100,000 population was among the top 15 (i.e., fourteenth) of the 94 judicial districts. Thus, evidence suggested that the task force's goal of accepting all gun cases (absent evidentiary problems) was achieved.

Similarly, the Southern District, despite having only 14 lawyers in the criminal division, witnessed the number of indictments under U.S. Code 922 and 924 increase from 46 in FY 2000 to 81 in FY 2002, an increase of just over 76 percentage points. Subsequently, indictments in the same category increased to 109 in FY 2005, a 139 percentage point increase from FY 2000. Likewise, the number of gun crime defendants prosecuted in federal court increased from 65 in FY 2000 to 129 in FY 2005, an increase of over 98 percentage points.

The numbers were even more telling when considered in light of the district's population. As one of the least populous federal judicial districts (ranked eighth least populous out of 90 federal districts[1]), the Southern District of Alabama consistently ranked in the top 7 percent with regard to rate of defendants per 100,000 population. For 2005, the number of defendants prosecuted per 100,000 was just over 16. This rate ranked second among the 90 judicial districts for that year. Clearly, the goal of increased federal prosecution was realized in the Southern District of Alabama.

Evidence of Impact—Outcomes

Ultimately, the goal of PSN was to reduce gun crime. To assess whether the Middle and Southern Districts' PSN strategies had this impact, the outcome analyses focused on gun crime and homicide trends in the city of Montgomery and the city of Mobile respectively. As an initial step in the outcome analysis, annual trends in homicide, armed robbery, and assault with a firearm for each city were reviewed (Table 5.2). In Montgomery, comparing 2002 and 2003 with the previous two years provided evidence of a decline in these crimes, particularly for aggravated

Table 5.2 Gun crime trends—cities of Montgomery and Mobile

	2000		2001		2002		2003		2004		2005	
	M	S	M	S	M	S	M	S	M	S	M	S
Homicide (total)	30	14	27	39	30	34	18	18	25	22	–	32
Aggravated assault with a firearm	319	135	293	121	303	113	244	78	283	92	–	145
Robbery with a firearm	448	497	464	487	543	432	505	374	488	347	–	348

M, Middle District; S, Southern District.

assaults with a firearm. In Mobile, declines were seen in both aggravated assaults with a firearm and robbery with a firearm, though with an upturn in 2005. Homicides increased and decreased from year to year with little discernible pattern over the six-year period, although the base rates were quite small and thus difficult to interpret.

Although trend lines were suggestive of a reduction in gun crime in both cities, to assess the significance of these trends time series analyses were conducted. Time series, considered one of the most powerful evaluation tools, account for crime trends before the intervention point and assess the significance of any change in crime levels following the intervention. Examining Montgomery (the Middle District) first, the time series analyses were based on monthly data from January 2000 through December 2004.[2] Assaults with a firearm had a statistically significant decline ($p < 0.05$) suggesting that there was a maximum likelihood mean reduction of three assaults with a firearm per month immediately after the intervention date of May 2002. This translated into a reduction from approximately 309 gun assaults per year to approximately 270. Homicide also declined, although its significance level was marginal (alpha 0.116). This translated to a reduction from 29.5 homicides per year to 22.8. The analyses did not indicate any effect on armed robbery.

A possible explanation for this decline in violent crimes could be that overall crime

rates were declining at a simultaneous, or similar, rate. If this were the case, the above findings would simply be a result of a general decline in crime. To control for a possible global change in crime independent of firearm offenses, monthly time series analyses of motor vehicle thefts and property offenses were examined. The logic was that, if such a global crime decline occurred, the time series analysis on property crimes would have a similar reduction.

When examining the comparison offenses in Montgomery, there was actually a slight increase in the average number of motor vehicle thefts and overall property offenses, although this change was not statistically significant (Table 5.3). Thus, property offenses remained consistent over the time series period. That is, the comparison variables that account for outside factors (global decline in overall crime) did not change during this same period. This suggests that the reduction in assaults with firearms may be attributable to the PSN intervention.

The research partner working with the Southern District of Alabama took a similar but somewhat different approach to the time series analysis. Data for a large number of crimes committed with a gun were available for analysis. To address the threat that changes in gun crime reflected changes in overall crime trends, the trend in property crime was included as a control variable in the gun crime analyses. Table 5.4 summarizes the results of the ARIMA analysis of the eight

Table 5.3 Montgomery time series analysis—May 2002 intervention date

Crime	Pre-intervention mean	Post-intervention mean	Mean difference (post–pre)	ARIMA model			Intervention coefficient	p-value (s.e.)
				p	d	q		
Target offenses								
Assaults with a firearm	25.78	22.50	−3.28	0	0	0	−3.29 (1.6)	0.038
Armed robbery (ln)	3.64	3.68	0.04	0	0	1	0.049 (0.10)	0.616
Homicide	2.46	1.90	−0.56	0	0	0	−0.558 (0.36)	0.116
Comparison offenses								
MV theft (ln)	4.67	4.86	0.19	0	1	0	−0.017 (0.05)	0.747
Property (ln)	7.09	7.15	0.06	1	1	0	−0.019 (0.021)	0.787

ARIMA, autoregressive integrated moving average; MV, motor vehicle.

models[3] for Mobile. With the exception of sex crimes with a gun, all of the coefficients were negative, suggesting a decline in gun crime. That is, the PSN intervention, after controlling for property crime, had a significant effect in four crime categories (total gun crime, all violent crime with a gun, robberies with a gun, and all assaults with a gun) and in gunshot trauma admissions. There was no reduction in sex crimes and the reductions in homicides and menacing were not statistically significant.

Total gun crime[4] in Mobile after the implementation of PSN decreased on average by about 26 incidents per month, after controlling for property crime. Similarly, violent crime with a gun[5] decreased on average by about 16 incidents per month and robbery with a gun decreased on average by about 11 incidents per month after controlling for property crimes.

In addition to police data, gunshot trauma admissions, representing the number of patients admitted to the local trauma center (i.e., University of South Alabama Hospital), were available for analysis. Trauma center admission for gunshot wounds decreased on average by about two incidents per month after controlling for property crimes. Given the costs of gunshot wounds (Cook and Ludwig, 2000; Miller and Cohen, 1997), this suggests a significant cost saving following the intervention of PSN. Thus, both police and trauma center data suggest that the Southern District of Alabama PSN intervention had an impact on the level of gun crime in Mobile and that this held when contrasted with the trend in property crime.

Challenges Encountered by PSN Task Forces

As with most PSN task forces, ICE officials in both the Middle and Southern Districts of Alabama described a series of ongoing challenges. Foremost for the Middle District were the numbers of federal gun prosecutors and ATF agents. The USAO PSN team was concerned that its ability to effectively prosecute cases referred to the USAO, given the increased desire of local officials throughout the district to refer cases for federal prosecution, would be constrained by the small number of ATF agents and federal prosecutors.

Another challenge related to turnover in key personnel. The Montgomery Police Department witnessed the resignation of the chief of police, who had been one of the key proponents of ICE. Fortunately, the new

Table 5.4 Mobile time series analysis—through August 1, 2006

Crime	Pre-intervention mean	Post-intervention mean	Mean difference (post–pre)	ARIMA model			Intervention coefficient	Property crime	F	R-squared
				p	d	q				
Target offenses										
Total gun crime	130.04	100.49	−29.55	0	1	1	−0.26[a]	0.05[1]		
Violent crime w/gun	52.02	39.94	−12.08	0	1	1	−0.16[a]	0.04[1]		
Homicide w/gun	1.65	1.65	0	0	0	0	−0.27	0.003[1]	1.96	0.04
Sex crime w/gun	0.65	0.79	+0.14	0	0	0	0.139	0	0.240	0.005
Robbery w/gun	39.51	29.81	−9.7	0	1	1	−0.11[a]	0.03[1]		
Assault w/gun	13.44	10.56	−2.88	1	0	0	−2.57[a]	−0.02		
Menacing w/gun	36.04	25.67	−10.37	0	1	1	−6	−0.002		
Gunshot trauma admission	11.10	8.76	−2.34	0	0	0	−2	0.003	3.76[1]	0.09
Comparison offenses										
Property crime	681.42	687.40	+5.98							

Note
a $p < 0.05$.

chief was described as being similarly committed. Similarly, officers assigned to the PSN task force were often reassigned. The district addressed this issue through a commitment to training, and interviews suggested that some turnover was beneficial because the officers assigned to the task force would take their knowledge of ICE and federal gun crime prosecution to their new assignments.

In the Southern District, one of the major challenges for the research partner involved data collection. This was not an uncommon challenge across PSN sites. Despite the desire to collect and use data from across the district, the research partner was forced to concentrate on Mobile for evaluation purposes because of the nature of the data sources. Given the concentration of gun crime in Mobile, however, this was not a major obstacle for the inclusion of research in the PSN initiative.

Similar to the Middle District, the Southern District of Alabama experienced the loss of two major players within PSN: first, the USA and, second, the chief of the Mobile Police Department. However, these changes did not appear to have negatively affected the day-to-day operations of PSN as the program was well established and the new USA and chief of police were supportive. Additionally, the former chief moved to the Sheriff's Department and thereby brought an additional collaborating law enforcement agency to the PSN task force.

Summary

Interviews with officials in both the Middle and Southern Districts of Alabama revealed a consistent emphasis on strong leadership as the key to the successful implementation of PSN. In the Middle District, this leadership came from the USAO and eventually resulted in a high level of participation from local police departments and ATF. In the Southern District, initial leadership stemmed from the Mobile Police Department, supported by the USAO. This leadership element created the environment for other key components such as the PSN task force structure, partnerships, and regular meetings. As the data reviewed indicated, a plausible case can be made that this leadership resulted in changes in how gun crime was addressed within each of these districts and was associated with declines in gun crime in the key PSN target cities.

The next chapter will examine sites that employed a SACSI-type strategy referred to as "strategic problem solving/pulling levers."

NOTES

1 Comparable population data were unavailable for the federal districts of Puerto Rico, the Virgin Islands, Guam, and the Mariana Islands. All comparisons are based on the 90 remaining federal districts.

2 Researchers examined what is known as a distinct zero order, or abrupt permanent change, which is designed to test whether the trend in crime following the May 2002 intervention date was significantly different than the pre-intervention trend. All of the time series conducted adhere to the assumptions of the ARIMA (autoregressive integrated moving average) modeling requirements, specifically bounds of stationarity and invertability (details of the analysis are presented in the technical appendix). Following the argument of Sherman and colleagues (2000) and Hayes and Daly (2003) in the case of evaluation research, researchers employed the less restrictive significance level ($p < 0.15$) to assess significance. This means that researchers considered a change to be significant if it would be unlikely to occur by chance fewer than 15 out of 100 times.

3 Three of the eight models had ARIMA parameters of 0,0,0. The dependent variables in these models were not autocorrelated. The method of analysis in these models, thus, was ordinary least squares linear regression. In those models, the F statistic and R-squared are reported.

4 That is, all categories in the Mobile Police Department database in which a gun was used in commission of the offense and those instances when an offender was in possession of a gun.

5 That is, homicide with a gun, rape with a gun, robbery with a gun, aggravated assault with a gun.

CHAPTER 6

Strategic Problem-Solving Gun Crime Reduction

Edmund F. McGarrell and Timothy S. Bynum

STRATEGIC PROBLEM SOLVING/PULLING LEVERS CASE STUDY SITES

District of Nebraska, Middle District of North Carolina, Eastern District of Missouri, and District of Massachusetts

A series of case studies was also conducted in Project Safe Neighborhoods (PSN) task forces that followed the strategic problem-solving model and that implemented multiple interventions in targeted cities or geographic areas of cities. They included Omaha in the District of Nebraska, five cities in the Middle District of North Carolina, St. Louis in the Eastern District of Missouri, and Lowell in the District of Massachusetts. Full case study reports are available (see Decker et al., 2007; McDevitt et al., 2007, Hipple et al., forthcoming b; Hipple et al., forthcoming c). In the following section, the districts and cities are described, key elements of the PSN intervention are reviewed, and evidence regarding the impact of the intervention is presented.

Context

At the outset of PSN, the four sites had varying levels of homicide and aggravated assault. North Carolina, Nebraska, and Massachusetts tended to have modest levels of violent crime whereas the Eastern District of Missouri had

much higher rates. Table 6.1 indicates these rates (per 10,000) for these four PSN sites. In comparison with other federal judicial districts, the District of Nebraska did not suffer from extremely high violent crime rates, ranked seventy-first overall among federal judicial districts (lowest quartile) for its murder rate and fifty-seventh (third quartile) for its aggravated assault rate. However, Douglas County, which includes Omaha, had a much higher violent crime rate with a homicide rate and aggravated assault rate over twice that of the entire state (Omaha accounted for 80 percent of the district's gun crime) (Table 6.1).

The District of Massachusetts was also below the national average in terms of murder rate but above the national average in terms of aggravated assault rate (Table 6.1). Virtually all of the state's gun crimes occurred in Boston and ten other smaller urban cities within the state (e.g. Brockton, Fall River, Lawrence, Lowell, Springfield, and Worcester). Lowell was one of the first smaller cities to implement a PSN task force and was selected for the case study based on the integration of its research partners and the comprehensive problem analysis that was conducted. Uniform Crime Report (UCR) data revealed that, compared with all U.S. cities with populations greater than 75,000, Lowell placed above average in terms of violent crime and below average in terms of property crime.

The Middle District of North Carolina suffered from more modest violent crime rates

Table 6.1 Aggravated assault and murder rates, 2001

Site	Aggravated assault rate (per 10,000)	Murder rate (per 10,000)
U.S. average[a]	30.65	0.65
North Carolina Middle District	26.57	0.60
District of Nebraska	20.45	0.25
Douglas County	38.29	0.54
District of Massachusetts	36.84	0.24
Missouri Eastern District	35.52	0.73

Note
a 90 federal judicial districts.

(Table 6.1). Specifically, the district ranked thirtieth (third quartile) overall among federal judicial districts when analyzing murder rates, and forty-fourth (third quartile) when analyzing aggravated assaults. Task force officials decided to focus on its five largest jurisdictions: Durham, Greensboro, High Point, Salisbury, and Winston-Salem.

In contrast, the Eastern District of Missouri ranked higher than the U.S. average in terms of both its murder rate and aggravated assault rate (Table 6.1). It also ranked higher when compared with U.S. judicial districts of comparable size. The primary focus area for PSN was the city of St. Louis. The city of St. Louis consistently ranked among the highest three to five cities in the nation in reference to homicide and aggravated assault.

Development and Implementation

Research has shown that one of the characteristics of PSN task forces ranked as high in terms of implementation is previous experience with multiple agency crime reduction collaborations (Zimmermann, 2006). This was true for all of these jurisdictions as they all had a history of multi-agency violence reduction efforts as well as experience of working with a research partner. Specifically, Omaha, St. Louis, and Winston-Salem were all participants in the Strategic Approaches for Community Safety Initiative (SACSI).[1] Officials in Lowell, Massachusetts, were

familiar with the Boston Gun Project, and the police department collaborated with members of the Boston research team in a number of problem-solving initiatives.

Task Force Structure

All of the sites built on this previous experience in developing a PSN task force structure. In Nebraska, two different but related working groups developed: one specific to Omaha and another in Lincoln. The case study focused on Omaha because of its much higher levels of gun crime. The PSN task force in Omaha comprised federal, state, and local law enforcement and prosecutors, the Department of Corrections, the state Crime Commission, Weed and Seed, the local school system, and research partners from the University of Nebraska at Omaha. The working group benefited from the active participation of the U.S. Attorney and the Omaha chief of police. Coordination was provided by a PSN Operations Director with support from the Law Enforcement Coordinator, both housed within the U.S. Attorney's Office. The working group utilized a strategic problem-solving approach that involved regular incident reviews and analysis from the research partners. The working group also relied on routine meetings including gun crime case screening, incident reviews, and a gun, gangs, and drugs enforcement team.

In the District of North Carolina, the U.S.

Attorney's Office coordinated the overall PSN initiative through a Middle District Advisory Team (MDAT) that oversaw task forces in five cities (Durham, Greensboro, High Point, Salisbury, and Winston-Salem). With the announcement of PSN in early 2001, the U.S. Attorney's Office requested that each city send two representatives to be part of the MDAT and this informally formed the skeleton of their task force. As time passed, MDAT moved toward a more formal structure with a Chair and Co-Chair, and each city appointed three representatives to MDAT, one of whom had to be from law enforcement. Non-law enforcement task force members included representatives from social services and local religious groups in addition to others. Additionally, the PSN Project Coordinator served as a MDAT member. The North Carolina Governor's Crime Commission (the fiscal agent), the research partner, probation and parole, and the community engagement partner all attended every MDAT meeting.

Although adapted to the local context, the five task forces included strong partnerships with local and federal law enforcement, local prosecutors, and probation and parole, as well as strong community collaboration with neighborhood groups, the faith community, social services, and the business sector. In addition, the task force worked very closely with a team of researchers from several universities and utilized PSN funds to support the role of service coordinator. Both the research partners and the service providers were integral members of the PSN task forces.

The PSN task force in Lowell built upon the city's experience with community- and problem-oriented policing. The Lowell Police Department was decentralized with officers assigned to one of three geographic districts. The community policing model emphasized partnerships with community groups and other law enforcement agencies. These partnerships facilitated the implementation of PSN. The PSN working group consisted of the PSN Coordinator and federal prosecutors from the U.S. Attorney's Office, local law enforcement including Lowell Police Department detectives, federal law enforcement including the FBI and Bureau of Alcohol, Tobacco, and Firearms (BATF), county prosecutors, probation officers, and research partners from Harvard and Northeastern Universities.

Finally, in the Eastern District of Missouri, the PSN task force was also coordinated in the U.S. Attorney's Office and included representation from federal, state, and local law enforcement, local and federal prosecutors, and probation and parole. It also included the juvenile court, level I trauma center, city neighborhood services, street outreach workers, a media relations partner, and the regional justice information system. The task force collaborated with a research team from the University of Missouri–St. Louis with years of experience working with the local criminal justice system. The overall PSN task force initially met monthly and later moved to a quarterly schedule. Several task force committees met more regularly. For example, the gun case prosecution team met bi-weekly and reviewed all cases involving a gun. There was also a weekly violence review held at the North Patrol station to review the activities of the violent crime task force. Additional task forces were convened at various times to address specific issues and problems.

Community Engagement and Media Campaign

Task forces in all of the sites attempted to build community partnerships and to implement a communication strategy. As noted above, North Carolina used funds to support a community engagement partner and fund service coordinators. Several of the sites collaborated with their Weed and Seed programs as well as with the schools. All included multiple local, state, and federal criminal justice partners. All included media campaigns involving public service announcements (PSAs) and billboards and several utilized strategies such as posters in the jail and on buses and bus benches. The Middle District of North Carolina, Lowell, and Omaha also implemented a series of offender notification meetings to deliver a deterrence and social support message to at-risk populations of probationers and parolees. This followed the "pulling levers" model that originated in Boston and continued through the SACSI program.

Nature of the Gun Crime Problem

The analysis of gun crime problems in Omaha, the Middle District of North Carolina cities, and Lowell indicated that all had significant connections to gangs. In Omaha, gun violence was concentrated in several geographic areas (northeast and southeast) and a significant portion of the gun crime involved gangs and the nexus between gangs, guns, and drugs. Over 28 gangs and 2,600 gang members were identified.

Problem analyses in the five North Carolina sites also suggested that gangs contributed substantially to the gun crime problem. Homicide reviews in several sites confirmed the assumption that gun crime was related to gangs and drugs. Gun crime seemed to be largely driven by chronic offenders and victims, involved drug and gang activity, and included group associations of gangs, groups of chronic offenders, and inter-generational links. Offenders returning from prison were another source of gun crime.

Similarly, gun crime in Lowell involved young males with previous criminal histories, and gang involvement. Analysis of department incident data revealed that young, minority males were disproportionately offenders and victims of serious gun violence. Gang members accounted for a substantial portion of the gun violence problem in Lowell. Based on information from the department's gang intelligence database and a focus group of detectives, 74 percent of gun homicide offenders (14 of 19) and 46 percent of aggravated gun assault offenders (10 of 22) were revealed to be active gang members.

As noted above, St. Louis had very high levels of gun crime and there was a strong spatial concentration of homicide, gun crime, and violent crime. That is, a relatively small part of the city accounted for a large proportion of the violent crime. Indeed, the "top ten" most violent neighborhoods accounted for more than 40 percent of all murders. Gun crime typically involved high-rate offenders at risk for both victimization and perpetration of violence. A substantial number of these offenders and homicide victims were under probation and parole supervision. The analysis did not suggest heavy gang involvement but the distinction between St. Louis and the other cities in terms of gang involvement may have been definitional. St. Louis reported loosely structured neighborhood groups and crews involved in gun crime. Similar groups may have been labeled gangs in the other jurisdictions.

Evidence of Implementation—Outputs

The prosecution data clearly reflected that the goal of increasing federal prosecution of gun crime offenses has occurred in the District of Nebraska. Since the announcement of PSN in 2001 and the full implementation of PSN in the District of Nebraska, the number of indictments under U.S. Code 922 and 924 increased dramatically. For example, in fiscal year (FY) 2001 there were 54 indictments under U.S. Code 922 and 924. This increased to 95 indictments in FY 2002, 166 in FY 2003, and 171 in FY 2005, an increase of 200 percentage points since 2001. Similarly, the number of defendants prosecuted in federal court increased from 63 in FY 2001 to 111 in FY 2002 and 196 in FY 2005. This increase in indictments and defendants placed the District of Nebraska in the top 9 percent in terms of its percentage point increase in federal prosecution. The numbers were even more telling when considered in light of the district's population. The federal prosecution rate of 11.0 per 100,000 population was ranked eighth among the 90 federal judicial districts in 2003.

Similarly, the Middle District of North Carolina also made a commitment to increase the threat of federal prosecution for gun crimes. The number of cases filed under U.S. Code 922 and 924 increased steadily since the inception of PSN. From FY 2000 to FY 2004, the number of cases increased from 104 to 187, an increase of almost 80 percentage points. Similarly, the number of defendants increased from 5.8 defendants per 100,000 population in FY 2000 to 8.1 defendants per 100,000 population in FY 2004. This placed the Middle District of North Carolina at the top of the second quartile when comparing defendants per 100,000 population for the 90 federal districts.

In the Eastern District of Missouri, a total of 1,381 individuals were indicted for gun crimes by the U.S. Attorney's Office or the St. Louis Circuit Attorney's Office between January 2002 and October 2005. The majority of indictments (82 percent) were reported by the U.S. Attorney's Office. In total, the U.S. Attorney's Office averaged 17.4 indictments per quarter. The number of federal indictments peaked in the second and third quarters of 2003 and then again in the second quarter of 2004. Thus, similar to Omaha and the Middle District of North Carolina, the results suggested that the U.S. Attorney's Office and the St. Louis Circuit Attorney's Office made a large number of indictments during the intervention period. In addition, the majority of individuals indicted were sentenced to a lengthy term of incarceration.

In Lowell, federal prosecution was used more strategically and as a focused deterrence threat. Partly this reflected the belief, in contrast to many other jurisdictions, that Massachusetts state law provided substantial penalties for illegal gun possession and use. The threat of federal sanctions was used in a series of offender notification meetings

with gang members who were warned that continued involvement in gun crime would result in federal prosecution. A particularly innovative strategy with several Asian gangs was to use a pulling levers strategy with adults in the community that urged them to exercise control over the youths who were believed to be involved in gang violence.

All of these jurisdictions coupled the increase in federal prosecution (or the threat thereof in Lowell) with a variety of other interventions and strategies. All included the integration of research partners. All of the sites with the exception of St. Louis conducted systematic incident reviews. St. Louis relied on homicide file reviews and other sources of crime information conducted by a team of researchers experienced with the St. Louis Police Department. All of the sites except Lowell developed chronic violent offender programs and Lowell used detailed network analyses of gang structures. All but St. Louis utilized offender notification meetings that combined the deterrence message with social support. St. Louis utilized a complementary set of strategies, including stories in a local neighborhood-based newspaper highlighting homicide and gun crime prosecutions as well as victimization. Additionally, all of the sites included law enforcement strategies such as directed police patrol in gun crime hot spots and police–probation–parole home visits. All developed mechanisms for federal and local prosecutors to screen gun crime cases. Finally, all included various prevention and intervention strategies in collaboration with schools, social service providers, and neighborhood leaders and organizations.

Evidence of Impact—Outcomes

Each case study included an assessment of the impact on gun crime. This was often conducted in collaboration with the local PSN research partner. Thus, the specific measures and target areas were driven by the local program. This makes comparability across sites problematic. Readers interested in the details of each evaluation are directed to the original case studies (Decker et al., 2007; McDevitt et al., 2007; Hipple et al., forthcoming b; Hipple et al., forthcoming c).

For Omaha, the research team initially reviewed the annual trends in three firearm-related crimes: homicide, armed robbery, and aggravated assault. Given the relatively small number of homicides with a firearm (ranging from 24 in 2000 to 15 in 2004), the analysis focused on total violent gun crimes, which was a composite of homicide with a firearm, aggravated assault with a firearm, and armed robbery with a firearm.

Following discussions with the local research team, February 2003 was designated as the intervention date. This was the point of PSN implementation when law enforcement training had occurred and there was a significant increase in federal prosecution for gun crimes. Overall, in Omaha the average number of firearm offenses per month reduced from 77.35 per month before intervention to 61.62 per month after February 2003. These preliminary findings were suggestive of a reduction in gun crime. However, to assess the significance of these trends, the research team conducted a time series analysis.

The time series analysis was based on data in monthly format from January 2000 through June 2005. When the total number of firearm offenses was examined at the aggregate level, the ARIMA (autoregressive integrated moving average) models showed a statistically significant reduction ($p < 0.01$) from pre-intervention to post-intervention. The analysis indicated that there was a statistically significant reduction in the overall number of firearm offenses of 20 percent per month between pre- and post-PSN intervention.[2] Table 6.2 displays the statistically significant decline in overall firearm crimes from the raw number of offenses.

The trend in gun crime was compared with the trend in property crime. There was no statistically significant change in property crime during this period. Thus, there was no evidence that the decline in gun crime was due to some factor influencing all crime in Omaha. That is, the comparison with property crime was consistent with an interpretation that PSN led to a reduction in gun crime in the District of Nebraska.

As noted, the Middle District of North Carolina focused resources on five cities in their efforts to reduce gun crime: Durham, Greensboro, High Point, Salisbury, and Winston-Salem. Given the small population of Salisbury, and corresponding low rates of gun crime, and the fact that High Point was subject to an independent National Institute of Justice evaluation, the focus was on the cities of Durham, Greensboro, and Winston-Salem.

Table 6.2 Time series analysis—February 2003 intervention date

Crime	Pre-intervention mean	Post-intervention mean	Mean difference (post–pre)	ARIMA model			Intervention coefficient (s.e.)	p-value
				p	d	q		
Targeted offenses								
Total firearm offenses (ln)	4.32	4.08	−0.24	0	0	2	−0.23 (0.08)	0.003
Comparison offenses								
MV theft (ln)	5.78	5.60	−0.18	0	2	2	−0.01 (0.02)	0.544
Burglaries	269.5	285.4	15.9	1	0	0	11.9 (15.9)	0.453

ARIMA, autoregressive integrated moving average; MV, motor vehicle.

Consultation with the local research partners suggested that the appropriate intervention date was May 2002.

Given the small to medium population base for these cities, the base rate of gun crime was relatively low. Consequently, consistent with Omaha, the focus was on total firearm offenses (a composite measure of homicides, assaults, and robberies committed with a firearm). Table 6.3 shows the average number of monthly firearm offenses for each site pre-intervention and post-intervention. As indicated, the total number of firearm offenses declined in all three of the sites between pre-PSN intervention and post-PSN intervention.

In the next step of the analysis, time series analyses were conducted for each of the three sites. The results suggested a statistically significant decline in firearm offenses in two of the three sites. Winston-Salem showed a statistically significant decline between pre- and post-PSN intervention with total firearm crimes declining by just over nine per month. Greensboro had a statistically significant decline in total firearm offenses of approximately 13 per month between pre- and post-PSN intervention. Durham also experienced declines in total firearm offenses although they did not attain statistical significance and thus could reflect chance variation.[3]

In Lowell, Massachusetts, the gun violence intervention strategy was targeted toward Asian youth gangs who the analysis had shown were disproportionately involved in gun crime. The intervention began in October 2002. This date represented the start of police raids on gambling houses and, as a result, an increase in arrests for related crimes. The goal of the raids and arrests was to send a message to Asian youth gangs to stop all violence.

The specific focus of the PSN-Lowell intervention was on gun assaults involving gang-related youths. Aggravated assaults with a gun declined from 4.94 per month in the pre-intervention period to 3.56 per month for the post-intervention period.[4] This represented a 28.02 percent decline in aggravated assaults with a gun—or one fewer gun assault per month. To test whether this result was the likely result of the PSN intervention, the change in prevalence of gun assaults within Lowell was compared with the change in prevalence of gun assaults in several Massachusetts cities: Brockton, Boston, Fall River, Lawrence, Springfield, and Worcester.

Table 6.4 shows the monthly average number of gun assaults before and after the introduction of the targeted deterrence intervention in Lowell compared with the difference and percent change across all cities. As the table shows, Lowell experienced the greatest decrease in aggravated gun assaults after the introduction of the intervention.[5] Overall the findings of this comparison analysis were consistent with the finding that PSN-Lowell may have resulted in a reduction in aggravated assaults with a gun, consistent with the simple pre–post test analysis.

In St. Louis, PSN was implemented in two target neighborhoods. The evaluation contrasted the trend in the two target or intervention neighborhoods with the trends in contiguous neighborhoods as well as control

Table 6.3 Total monthly firearm offenses, pre-PSN and post-PSN intervention for three target cities

City	Pre-intervention average	Post-intervention average
Durham	76.75	68.90
Greensboro	70.42	57.43[a]
Winston-Salem	50.46	41.23[a]

Note
a Independent samples *t*-test $p < 0.001$.

Table 6.4 Comparison of pre- to post-intervention change in aggravated assaults with a firearm in select Massachusetts cities

| City | Aggravated assaults with a firearm | | | |
	Pre-intervention monthly average	Post-intervention monthly average	Difference	Percent change
Lowell	4.94	3.56	−1.38	−28.02
Boston[a]	37.61	36.50	−1.11	−2.94
Brockton[b]	8.76	8.04	−0.72	−8.27
Fall River[a]	2.52	4.75	2.23	88.86
Lawrence[b]	1.62	3.18	1.56	96.52
Springfield[c]	27.55	46.57	19.03	69.07
Worcester	7.48	6.59	−0.89	−11.92

Notes

a Boston and Fall River data are missing last three months from series. Post-intervention monthly average computed by dividing total by 24 months.
b Brockton and Lawrence data are missing first year 2000 from series. Pre-intervention monthly average computed by dividing total by 21 months.
c Springfield data are missing last six months from series. Post-intervention monthly average computed by dividing total by 21 months.

neighborhoods in other parts of the city that also had high levels of gun crime. The data were limited to broad analyses of aggravated assault involving a firearm, robbery, and homicide before and after the intervention in the first quarter of 2003. Table 6.5 details the percent change in violent crime incidents from pre- to post-intervention.

As displayed in Table 6.5 there were substantial declines in incident rates for aggravated assault involving a firearm over the analysis period and across neighborhood groups. The overall magnitude of change was greatest for the control group (39 percent decline). In contrast, the intervention neighborhoods experienced a 7 percent decline in aggravated assault offenses.

The decline in armed robberies was also substantial, although again it was apparent across intervention, control, and contiguous neighborhoods. For the intervention group, the rate of robbery declined 16 percent between the pre- and post-intervention periods. The contiguous neighborhoods experienced a similar decline (13 percent)

whereas robbery rates in the control neighborhoods declined 41 percent.

Similar to robbery and assault incidents, homicides declined in all of the neighborhoods. Homicide rates declined 21 percent in the intervention neighborhood, 51 percent in the contiguous neighborhoods, and 41 percent in the control neighborhoods.

The final comparison of incidents across the neighborhoods involved weapons offenses. Consistent declines above 34 percent were observed in the intervention, contiguous, and control neighborhoods following the PSN intervention.

From the standpoint of violent crime in St. Louis, the review of gun assaults, robberies involving a firearm, homicides, and weapons incidents revealed positive news. From an evaluation standpoint, however, the results raised questions about the cause of the decline. The fact that the decline was generally smaller in the intervention neighborhoods than was the case in the control and contiguous neighborhoods suggested that some factor other than the PSN intervention

Table 6.5 Comparison of pre- to post-intervention change in violent crime incidents

Neighborhood group	Pre-intervention quarterly average	Post-intervention quarterly average	Difference	Percent change
Aggravated assaults with firearm				
Intervention	14.65	13.72	−0.93	−6.57
Contiguous	4.96	4.12	−0.85	−18.61
Control	3.32	2.24	−1.08	−38.97
Robbery with firearm				
Intervention	9.30	7.93	−1.38	−15.96
Contiguous	4.89	4.30	−0.59	−12.80
Control	3.42	2.26	−1.16	−40.84
Homicides				
Intervention	1.24	1.00	−0.24	−21.28
Contiguous	0.43	0.25	−0.18	−51.81
Control	0.23	0.15	−0.08	−40.00
Weapons offenses				
Intervention	4.92	3.48	−1.45	−34.44
Contiguous	1.72	1.12	−0.60	−42.01
Control	1.23	0.87	−0.36	−34.54

caused these declines. The most generous interpretation from a PSN standpoint is that PSN had a citywide impact. However, a highly plausible rival hypothesis is that some factor other than PSN was producing the declines in gun crime across the city.

Thus, in looking at the impact analyses across these jurisdictions, promising results emerge. Every city included witnessed a decline in gun crime. Lowell, Omaha, Greensboro, and Winston-Salem experienced statistically significant declines and they appeared to be significant when contrasted with the comparison crime trend. St. Louis also witnessed a decline in its two treatment neighborhoods but this was true in contiguous and control neighborhoods as well. Durham witnessed a decline but it was not significant.

The next chapter seeks to examine the variation across the nation's cities in terms of patterns and trends in violent crime. Why is it that some cities have avoided the increase in violent crime experienced in many communi-ties in 2005–6? The thought was that there may be policing strategies in such communi-ties that have played a role in stemming the increase in violent crime which could serve as promising practices for other police depart-ments and local governments.

NOTES

1 A task force team coordinated by the U.S. Attorney's Office participated in SACSI as an "unfunded" site.

2 As the natural logarithm of offenses was used in the analysis, we report a factor reduction of −0.23 between pre- and post-intervention. To convert from the log form to a percentage change in the actual number of offenses, we use the standard formula [exponential (beta coefficient)−1], or in this case [exponential (−0.23)−1], which equals −0.205. This equates to a 20 percent reduction in gun offenses.

3 Salisbury was included in the original analysis. It experienced a decline but it did not attain statistical significance. The base rates were too low to allow for meaningful assessment.

4 This difference in mean was significant using a two-tailed test ($p < 0.05$).

5 As the series reported here do not reflect identical time periods, we tested whether using only common periods across the sites changed the results. For example, we restricted the analysis to a comparison between the changes one year (12 months) pre-intervention to one year (12 months) post-intervention. In this analysis and others, Lowell still demonstrated the greatest decline in aggravated assaults with a gun.

CHAPTER 7

Identifying Effective Policing Strategies for Reducing Crime

Natalie Kroovand Hipple, Edmund F. McGarrell, John M. Klofas,
Nicholas A. Corsaro, and Heather Perez

In 2006, the Police Executive Research Forum (PERF), working with police chiefs and mayors, raised the concern that, following a steady decline in violent crime which began in the early 1990s, the nation's cities were experiencing an increasingly violent crime trend. A number of potential factors were identified as the possible sources behind an increase but the primary intent of PERF reports and forums had been to draw attention to this possible upward trend in violent crime so that the nation could act in such a way as to prevent this from escalating to a violent crime epidemic such as that experienced in the mid- to late 1980s. In response to these types of concerns, the Bureau of Justice Statistics (BJS) requested that the Sagamore Institute conduct a study that could point to promising policing strategies that might inform local, state, and federal policy with the goal of violent crime prevention and control.

As the PERF project indicated, there is variation across the nation's cities in terms of patterns and trends in violent crime. We sought to study this variation as a way of identifying cities that have avoided the increase in violent crime experienced in many communities in 2005–6. The thought was that there may be policing strategies in such communities that have played a role in stemming the increase in violent crime which could serve as promising practices for other police departments and local governments.

Among the cities that appeared to have a lower trend in homicide and robbery than predicted were Chicago (IL), El Monte (CA), Tampa (FL), and Topeka (KS). Background information was gathered about each city and site visits were conducted. It should be noted that this represents an exploratory study intended to identify promising strategies and interventions. The research did not include a formal test of the effectiveness of these strategies on violent crime.

Two teams of researchers conducted site visits in May and June 2008. The researchers had previous contacts in two of the sites (Chicago and Tampa), and two sites were considered "cold calls" (El Monte and Topeka) as the research team had no existing contacts in those cities and spent considerable time setting up these visits. The site visits were based out of the police department. That is, the police department in each city served as the central focus of the visit. Once contact was made, background information was provided about the study and the reasons why the city was chosen, and the police department was asked to set the agenda. The researchers provided some suggestions as to which other outside agencies might be included in the site visit but for the most part this was left up to organizers on site. On site, interviews were semi-structured and varied in length.

DESCRIPTIONS OF THE SITES

Chicago

Located on the western shore of Lake Michigan, Chicago has a population of over 2.7 million people. Caucasians comprise almost 42 percent of the population and African Americans comprise over 36 percent of the population. Chicago also has the third largest South Asian American population in the country. The largest law enforcement agency in the Midwest and the second largest in the country, Chicago Police Department has six police areas, 25 police districts, 280 police beats, and roughly 15,700 sworn police officers.

Tampa

Tampa is one of three incorporated cities located in Hillsborough County, Florida. Hillsborough County covers over 1,000 square miles of which 84 percent is unincorporated. Sixty-four percent of residents in Tampa are Caucasian. Tampa is part of the Tampa Bay Area, which covers a five-county region including Hillsborough, Pinellas, Polk, Pasco, and Manatee Counties. The Tampa Bay Area is served by the U.S. Attorney's Office of the Middle District of Florida. Violence reduction efforts in Tampa are largely driven by a multi-agency coalition serving the greater Tampa Bay Area, of which the Tampa Police Department is a key partner. The data used in the analysis, however, were specific to the city of Tampa.

Topeka

The City of Topeka is 55 square miles and is located in Shawnee County, which is 600+ square miles. According to the chief of police, Topeka is a city in a rural area that has big city problems. Local officials reported wide income inequality among the residents of Topeka.

The Topeka Police Department staffing level is set at 294 sworn officers. As of May 2008, they had 266 sworn officers with 14 in the academy, meaning that the department was short by 25–30 officers from previous years (approximately 10 percent), making it difficult to keep up with attrition. The city is divided into 12 patrol areas, which fall into six zones. The current chief has been in place just over 18 months. He is a veteran police officer and former police chief of the Kansas City, Kansas Police Department.

El Monte

The City of El Monte is located 12 miles east of Los Angeles in Los Angeles County. The city is just over 10 square miles and it is quite ethnically diverse. Hispanics constitute the majority of the residents, followed by Asians and then Caucasians.

The El Monte Police Department staffing level is set at 161 sworn officers. As of June 2008, the department employed 145 sworn officers, a deficit of 16, again approximately 10 percent under staffing levels. The current chief of police is a 37-year veteran of the police department.

SITE VISITS

One of the challenges in this study was the need to be open to novel approaches to crime prevention and control while at the same time having sufficient structure to make the site visits efficient and productive. Our approach was to employ semi-structured and open-ended interviews with a variety of police, prosecution, local government, and community representatives based on broad categories suggested in previous research as representing promising components of policing practices (e.g., Weisburd and Braga, 2006; National Research Council, 2004). We also drew upon the research team's experience with Project Safe Neighborhoods and a series of case studies that suggested promising strategies for addressing gun crime consistent with those suggested by Weisburd and Braga and the National Research Council. This research has suggested that very focused interventions, including focused deterrence strategies, driven by research and crime analysis, developed and implemented through strategic partnerships, and employing problem-solving processes, hold promise for reducing violent crime. These principles undergird what Klofas, Hipple, and McGarrell (see Chapter 1) have referred to as the "New Criminal Justice." Klofas et al. argue that contemporary criminal justice practice has been significantly influenced by three key concepts: (1) working coalitions, (2) local problem and resource focus, and (3) data-based problem solving. Consequently, our site visits attempted to assess whether these sites had formed working coalitions and partnerships, were employing data-driven problem-solving processes, and were utilizing locally focused interventions targeting individuals, groups/gangs, contexts, and hot spots believed to be driving violent crime.

The second main limitation of this research is that we cannot isolate the specific causal mechanisms nor can we test whether it is these identified promising practices that may account for the lower than anticipated level of violent crime in these four cities in contrast to the other cities included in the sample of cities with populations over 100,000. We suspect that at some level virtually every police and sheriff's department can point to some external partnerships, some degree of problem solving, and some degree of data-driven crime analysis. The extent to which these processes do, or do not, drive highly focused crime control interventions is likely to relate to the level of integration and coordination of these principles, the level of organizational commitment, and the resulting intensity of implementation. We are not in a position to measure these qualities across a large sample of jurisdictions but rather will attempt to point to promising practices that are common across these four cities.

Chicago

One of the challenges in discussing crime prevention and control efforts in Chicago is that so much is occurring at any given time.[1] Chicago has been a leader in community policing with resulting widespread partnerships. The Chicago Police Department has adapted and modified COMPSTAT into a comprehensive system for reviewing crime patterns and providing crime intelligence information throughout the police department, has decentralized policing structure and accountability, and has developed highly focused interventions aimed at gun crime and the nexus of guns, gangs, and drugs. The police department has made significant commitments to technology related to information sharing as well as an extensive camera system. Chicago has a vibrant and very focused Project Safe Neighborhoods initiative aimed at gun crime as well as a significant public health initiative utilizing street-level outreach workers seeking to prevent violence (Skogan et al., 2003). Many of these initiatives overlap, thus making it very difficult to isolate the crime reduction impact of any given strategy. With these qualifications in mind, Chicago does exemplify the key principles described above as promising: working coalitions, locally focused problem solving, data-driven problem solving, and violent crime–focused interventions.

For nearly two decades the Chicago Police Department has made an enormous effort to transform the department to a community-oriented policing mission and style. Known as the Chicago's Alternative Policing Strategy (CAPS), this has involved reorganization of the department into a neighborhood-based structure, extensive training of police in principles of community policing, and support for the development of neighborhood-based leaders and associations. Over the years, this has been reinforced through the reorientation of city services to a congruent neighborhood-based focus. The result has been neighborhood-focused coalitions of police, community members, business owners, schools, and city services engaged in problem solving related to crime and disorder.

An additional somewhat unique characteristic of CAPS is that it has been supported by a long research partnership with a team of researchers including Wesley Skogan, Dennis Rosenbaum, Susan Hartnett, and colleagues. This allowed ongoing assessment and feedback to support revision and refinement of CAPS and benchmarking of both internal organizational change as well as external partnerships. Skogan's (2006) recent book summarizing two decades of this research suggests that, although challenges remain, for example in building relationships with non-English speaking Hispanic communities, considerable progress has been accomplished in terms of both organizational transformation and meaningful police–community relationships.

Perhaps aware of research suggesting that community policing alone appears to have a limited impact on reducing crime (e.g., Weisburd and Braga, 2006), the Chicago Police Department implemented a number of crime-focused strategies. Several of these reflect the concept of developing data-driven capacity to analyze local crime problems and to drive interventions. Building and expanding on the New York Police Department's COMPSTAT program (Silverman, 1999), the Chicago Police Department developed two crime pattern review programs supported by a major technological innovation. The weekly crime pattern review meetings include the Violent Incident Strategy Evaluation (VISE) and the Deployment Operations Center (DOC) meetings. The meetings are coordinated and supported by the Bureau of Crime Strategy and Accountability.[2]

The VISE meetings focus on homicides, aggravated batteries with a firearm, and public violence with a firearm within a particular area of the city and then more specifically in police districts within the area. Violent crime trends are reviewed, incidents are mapped, and local commanders are expected to be able to both discuss trends and patterns and present plans for responding to emerging violent crime problems. The DOC meetings complement the VISE meetings with a more intensive focus on violent crime hot spots known as level one and level two deployment areas, which typically consist of a small number of police beats within police districts. The information shared is very detailed in terms of the individuals and groups involved in violent crime incidents, sharing of intelligence (e.g., gang conflicts), and targeting of known, chronic offenders. This is also an opportunity for local commanders to request the assistance of other units (e.g., gangs, narcotics, additional patrol) to address the problem. The weekly meetings are complemented by daily bulletins focused on homicides and firearms crimes. In addition to sharing information, these meetings and related communication vehicles all reinforce the department's focus on and commitment to reducing homicide and violent gun crime.[3]

The data-driven meetings and intelligence-sharing processes are supported by the Citizen Law Enforcement Analysis and Reporting (CLEAR) program. Winner of the Innovations in Government and the IACP iXP Leadership in Technology Awards, CLEAR is described as the largest transaction police database in the nation. The CLEAR database integrates extensive information sources including crimes, arrests, field contact information, gang intelligence, warrants and corrections, and much more. Indeed, reflective of the partnership theme, the database includes information from the Illinois Department of Corrections and federal law enforcement including the Drug Enforcement Administration, and Bureau of Alcohol, Tobacco, Firearms and Explosives. It includes both confidential and secure information available to police managers and officers utilizing mobile computer terminals to access information, as well as public information to support the CAPS community partnerships.

The amalgamation of these initiatives combines resource sharing, technological advances, and centralized accountability with decentralization that facilitates very focused interventions at a local level targeted at the individuals, groups, and contexts driving crime within neighborhoods and street blocks.

Tampa

Law enforcement officials in the Tampa Bay Area like to think of their community as one small town even though its five-county metropolitan area is the third largest in the United States, houses over 4 million residents, and continues to grow at a fast pace. In discussing their ideas on local relations officials attributed their small-town feeling to the gentle influences of a southern culture of hospitality. Such feeling seems consistent with the area's history of successful annexations with the City of Tampa, including its most recent in 1988. Whatever its ultimate source, cooperation and collaboration seem deeply engrained in the attitudes, values, and working relationships within the local criminal justice system.

Strong and positive working relationships are reported across all law enforcement agencies and across all levels from local to state and federal. The foundation of these is based in strong partnerships that function at the organizational and individual level. Local officials speak of friendships that sometimes go back multiple generations and that permeate organizational boundaries today. These partnerships result in working relationships that go well beyond mutual aid. The agencies in this area work closely together in everything from assuring success on prosecution of cases to formulating anti-crime strategies and carrying them out. As law enforcement and prosecution leaders described them, the links between their agencies are strong and continue to be held together by personal as well as professional ties. At one juncture officials described the many bridges in the area as helping to connect the parts of their community. In other cities officials might have focused instead on the islands that separate their community into distinctly different parts.

It was also clear in Tampa that the existing positive relationships help give shape and direction to the local Project Safe Neighborhoods initiative, which, in turn, provides the forum for exercising these healthy partnerships. Thus, years into the effort, regular meetings are still well attended and still function as a venue for strategy development. The local U.S. Attorney and particularly the Law Enforcement Coordination Manager have been instrumental in maintaining this process.

It is interesting to note that alongside the enforcement partnerships in the Tampa Bay Area there exists a parallel but largely separate partnership among relevant social agencies and treatment programs. At present, services are coordinated through the offices of the largest county in the area. The idea behind this organizational arrangement is that the county facilitates greater stability in service delivery than individual private organizations, which may be more strained by the ebb and flow of grant funding and local budgets.

The service providers have formed their own close-knit organizations both as a function of being together and to some extent as a function of being separated from the enforcement side. The plan of service work is clearly multidimensional and focuses on providing alternatives to crime and gang membership, preventing gang recruitment, and providing a range of theoretically and geographically widespread interventions.

The relationship between enforcement efforts and treatment efforts is perhaps best illustrated in the agenda for the monthly Project Safe Neighborhoods meetings. Both groups are brought together in the discussion of planning and strategies. They also report to each other on their separate efforts. The treatment providers, however, are dismissed from the meeting when the details of enforcement operations are discussed. This pragmatic but limited notion of partnerships is sometimes later ignored as treatment and enforcement staff will join together in planned community programs and activities.

The combination of collaboration and respect for different areas of operation across enforcement and treatment professionals is matched by another area of agreement. There is a shared understanding across these groups on how best to understand the overall problem of crime in Tampa. Both groups look at crime in the Tampa area as somewhat transient, often changing but never out of control and otherwise largely lacking in drama. That is not to say that they do not regard it as serious. They certainly do. But they do not see it as intractable or as a permanent feature of the Tampa social structure. It is not highly organized. Local gangs are most often fragmented and young people often shift allegiances in them. Serious and significant crimes occur with regularity. It is a problem but not a sign of social failure or societal degeneracy. There is a shared belief that many crimes can be prevented and all of them can be cleared by arrest. In short, those who work in and with the criminal justice system are optimistic about what they can accomplish. That optimism is built on a shared understanding of the nature of crime in Tampa.

The level of agreement and optimism about crime in Tampa is accompanied by a growing body of shared information about the problem across the region. Although the engagement of university researchers is sporadic, there is extensive sharing of data on trends and patterns in local crime. This is accomplished through the broad engagement of crime analysts from the Hillsborough County Sheriff's Department and other Tampa area police departments in the regional planning sessions associated with Project Safe Neighborhoods. The U.S. Attorney's Office distributes the products of crime analysis, including written reports and crime maps, at the monthly meetings. Crime analysts also attend those meetings and provide briefings on crime patterns across the region. Participating enforcement leaders have built the analysis of these data into the collaborative planning process and also use the data products in their own agencies.

In conclusion, Tampa area enforcement agencies have incorporated all of the three critical elements of modern policing that were identified earlier in this report. In the Tampa area data have been increasingly integrated into a process of strategic planning. There is a widely shared perspective on local crime, which supports and encourages police efforts to control the problem. Finally strong partnerships are found across agencies addressing crime in the Tampa area.

Working relationships among law enforcement seem particularly strong in the Tampa area. Local, county, and federal police agencies work well together. These relationships seem to reflect cultural and historical patterns in the region. They also seem to benefit from the energetic efforts of organizers who have managed to formalize relationships and implement specific anti-crime initiatives. Treatment-oriented partnerships also seem strong although they do not have the history or focus of the enforcement partnerships. Enforcement and treatment agency leaders in the Tampa area are not surprised to find that the community has lower than expected crime in some categories, considering its size and population make-up. Those leaders tend to see this as a reflection of strong working connections especially in the areas of enforcement and prosecution.

Topeka

Officials in Topeka expressed the view that their citizens have a poor "self-image" of their city. There exists a sense of hopelessness, that is, that nothing can be done to change what is happening in the city, such as crime and the quality of life. In an effort to change the citizens' perceptions of the city, the Topeka Police Department committed very formally and very publicly to partnerships. The Topeka Police Department has taken a stance that crime control is not just the responsibility of the police department and that partnerships would be the only way to engage the community and combat the problems. Additionally, high ranking officials in Topeka expressed the need and desire to remove the "secrecy" of what goes on in their organization. The chief of police stated that he wanted "transparency." Although this did not mean inviting the public into ongoing crime investigations it did mean trying to involve the community, especially the citizens, in public safety.

The Topeka Police Department is a member of a group called Safe Streets of Topeka/Shawnee County. Safe Streets was started by a local reverend in response to a homicide. The group has grown substantially over the past 12 years and has gained not-for-profit status (501(c) (3)). Within Safe Streets is the Safe Streets Coalition, which specifically addresses crime and safety concerns. A brochure on their website (http://www.safestreets.org) states that their action plan is to "[e]ngage every man, woman, and child to help combat crime at home, at work, at school and at play". Although the Coalition has been around for over a decade, typical meeting attendance was around 15–30 people. The police department has always had a designated representative at these meetings. But over the last two years, and as a testament to the importance of partnerships, attendance has soared to over 150 people at every monthly meeting.

The focus of the Safe Streets Coalition right now, as well as the police department, is to make Topeka the "Safest Capital City" with a population of over 100,000 in the country. The mission is: "To build a comprehensive, multifaceted coalition of community members called the "Safest Capital Team' in an effort to reduce crime and substance abuse in Topeka/Shawnee County." Using a sports metaphor, they have written a playbook on how they plan to do this. Ten "teams" make up the Coalition, each with a captain. The teams are:

- Business
- Education
- Faith Community
- Government
- Health Care
- Law Enforcement
- Media
- Neighborhoods
- Non-Profit
- Parent/Youth.

The police chief is the captain for the Law Enforcement team. Right now there are 17 plays. Each play includes the description of the play, the reason for the play, the target group, the target area demographics, the time frame to run the play, the resources needed to run the play, the desired or projected outcomes, and the play coordinator and his or her contact information. What is quite evident from talking with Coalition team members is how very committed the police department is to this coalition and how the police department recognizes the importance of the community. As someone within the police department put it: "Crime is just not a police issue, it's a community issue. The partnerships have gotten us over the hump."

A smaller city such as Topeka, for obvious reasons, does not have the volume of violent crime found in Tampa and Chicago. Therefore, problem solving and resource focus are directed more toward property crimes than violent crimes. This is not to say that the police department ignored violent crime or does not consider it important. The focus on analyzing and proactively responding to property crime is seen as building the capacity to address violent crime as well. When patterns of violent crime emerge, the department is well positioned to rapidly respond with the ultimate goal of preventing further violence. Thus, whereas violent crime is not the dominant focus it remains a top priority and is included in ongoing analysis and strategic planning.

As an example, Topeka has focused recently on gasoline pump drive-offs, which mainly include situations in which patrons pump gas and then drive away without paying for it. This crime is a larceny as defined by the Uniform Crime Reports and offers a very simple solution: require patrons to pre-pay for their gasoline. After trying twice unsuccessfully to pass a city ordinance to oblige all gas stations to require pre-payment for gasoline, the police department searched for another avenue. The police department entered into a partnership with the Petroleum Marketers Association. The Petroleum Marketers Association, in cooperation with the police department, mailed out letters to all of the gas stations in the area asking them to voluntarily become "pre-pay." The response to the letter was described as "incredible." The police department estimates that 90–95 percent of all gas stations in the Topeka area are now voluntarily "pre-pay" stations and that the reduction in the number of larcenies reflects the compliance. According to the Topeka Police Department, those stations that did not voluntarily comply continue to show high levels of gasoline theft.

Another issue facing Topeka was larcenies from vehicles. The police believe that these are truly more preventable crimes. Research into the crime showed that items were being stolen from *unlocked* cars, from *open* garages, or when they were left in plain sight, on a car seat for example, presenting too many opportunities for would-be thieves. The Topeka Police Department undertook a multifaceted approach. First, they created flyers/door knocker hangers to put on windshields and houses. These notices explained what the police were seeing—a cell phone left on a passenger seat, a garage left open at night, a GPS device left suctioned to a windshield—and how simple steps taken by citizens could empower them to reduce crime in Topeka. This "Lock It, Remove It, or Lose It" is campaign one of the plays (#1) in the Safest Capital City Campaign through the Safe Streets Coalition. The police department was able to partner with area stores such as Walmart. Walmart would play the short public service announcement clip on their flat screen televisions located at their entry doors to help remind patrons of their role in preventing crime.

Topeka utilizes a combination of formal and informal partnerships. The police department has dedicated 12 community officers who work side by side with the 12 code compliance (i.e., non-sworn) officers. The code compliance officers will soon be moved to fall under the supervision of the police department, enhancing their response. Additionally, the Topeka Police Department has school resource officers in every middle school and finds that these officers are a good source of intelligence. The community has taken on some basic patrol duties, supported by Safe Streets and the police department. Many of these relationships are fostered through the Safe Streets Coalition. Community members are trained and given special identifying clothing and then patrol their neighborhoods. These patrols are in close contact with police and can communicate things that are happening when the police are not there.

Finally, as can be seen from the above description, data-driven problem solving is the backbone to the police department's efforts. The Topeka Police Department engages in a COMPSTAT-style meeting, which occurs weekly. These meetings include all officers holding the rank of lieutenant and above. The Topeka Police Department is also in the process of hiring two more crime analysts to bring the total to three full-time crime analysts.

El Monte

Officials in El Monte report that, in 2002, a focus of the new police administration was to connect with their residents who had a poor self-image of their city and a sense of hopelessness about changing their quality of life. At the same time, they also sought to identify and empower those residents who wished to take a more active role in their neighborhood and deter crime. Here again, formal partnerships emerged as a key component of the police department's efforts to change the community's way of thinking.

The El Monte Police Department has taken a somewhat different, yet still very successful, approach to formal partnerships. The El Monte Police Department created a Community Relations Office, a major referral resource for those with problems who come into contact with police officers in the community. This is a "one-stop shopping center" where community members can go for a variety of services, beyond that of just formal law enforcement. For example, El Monte residents are eligible for *free* counseling services with a certified counselor or one of several counselor interns from a local university. The Community Relations Office is also a place where the police department offers assistance with jobs, clothing, and shelter as well as houses specialized officers dedicated to tackling specific community issues such as graffiti, gangs, or panhandling. Another example is that former gang members can visit with the gang resource officer and receive help with job placement or arrange for *free* gang tattoo removal through a partnership with a local medical facility. Police officials believe that community relations maintains so many positive relationships with families over time and that community relations officers are often able to prevent serious criminal activity before it comes to fruition.

Faced with limited resources, the El Monte Police Department felt that decentralizing some of their resources would help focus them. El Monte took a more formal approach by dividing their jurisdiction into 65 areas that they call "reporting districts" or RDs. Each RD has one officer assigned to it and a police captain oversees the entire RD program. The role of an RD officer is an extra responsibility to the officer's assigned patrol or investigative duties. Patrol officers still respond to calls for service and investigators still maintain a case load. Officers are trained in approaches to working with the community. An RD officer is responsible for knowing the people in his or her area and developing responses to any problems that may arise in the area. The relationships that an RD officer develops within his or her reporting district help to create a sense of trust that reciprocates between the RD officers and the community. This sense of trust is intended to improve the community's self-image about the city as well as work to eliminate the sense of hopelessness about improving quality of life. RD officers are asked to develop two short-term projects and one long-term project over a 12-month period. The projects are included in minimum standards that each RD officer must meet each year, and officers are evaluated on their progress toward meeting those yearly goals.

One requirement of RD officers is that they hold what is called a Park, Meet, and Greet (PMG) on each street in their district each year. The police department found that, when they tried to hold community meetings, set a place and time and printed and distributed thousands of flyers, only a handful of community members would attend. Therefore, they decided to try another approach—the PMG. A PMG involves the RD officer enlisting the help of another officer to close off a street. Officers park their cars and turn on their lights and sirens to get the attention of the local residents. They also go house to house and knock on doors, announcing that a meeting is being held and asking the residents to participate. As people come out of their houses to see what is going on, the officers convene an informal neighborhood meeting.

They introduce themselves, talk about what crime they see occurring in the area, and then ask the residents what they are seeing and what their concerns are. One PMG meeting will draw more people than a planned and advertised community meeting.

For the El Monte Police Department, one of their key partners is the El Monte City Schools, the public school system. They have a dedicated school resource officer on each high school campus and other officers assigned to the middle and elementary schools. The El Monte Police Department sees this as a very important and vital partnership. The schools see it that way as well. When funding for school resource officers was in jeopardy, the school district matched funding provided by the police department in order to keep the officers on campus. Both the schools and the police department have described this resource as invaluable. The schools view the police department as a resource, both personally and professionally. The schools see how the school resource officers are able to bridge the relationship between schools and families. Communication becomes a key element as many families with at-risk youth do not know about the resources available to them until told by the school resource officer.

The El Monte Police Department has one dedicated crime analyst who works very closely with officers from all facets of the police department. Additionally, each officer has the capability to request e-mail alerts based on information in the CAD (i.e., computer-aided dispatch). The crime analyst has the ability to query any information that the dispatcher includes in the call for service. For example, an officer may request to be notified every time a certain address appears in a run. The department analyst can also set up e-mail alerts for any of the community partners.

Similar to Topeka, El Monte has focused considerable resources on property crime. A local example would be the focus on graffiti. Graffiti has long been a problem in El Monte and has long been high on the priority list for the department. In 2002, the police department decided that the problem was big enough to assign one full-time detective to focus on the issue. This focus on graffiti is meant to have a positive effect not only on the physical appearance of the city but also on the juvenile taggers and their families. Housed in the Community Resource Center, the goal is to help both the city and these families.

Officials decided to focus on graffiti because of its very conspicuous effect on the quality of life in the community and the "broken windows" (Wilson and Kelling, 1982) effect it would have if it was left visible in the community, not to mention the endless recidivism if the suspects are not pursued and dealt with through the court system with an attitude modification program, monetary fine, probation, or incarceration. One official likened it to the three E's of traffic enforcement (i.e., education, enforcement, and engineering) but instead called them the three E's of graffiti abatement (enforcement, education, and erasure). All three legs of this tripod are needed to be sufficiently adequate to balance the total weight of the problem. Otherwise, it is not a successful program. There is a 24-hour graffiti hotline that anyone can call when they see graffiti and the goal is to have it removed or covered up within 24 hours of the phone call. School resource officers are trained in how to spot potential taggers and the graffiti detective teaches an in-service program to all officers on an as-needed basis about graffiti trends, patterns, and laws.

The graffiti detective has worked very closely with the District Attorney's Office and the local courts to develop a detailed response to those caught tagging. First-time offenders are treated with some leniency as the approach is often informal. Taggers, often along with their parents, meet with the graffiti detective and are given the opportunity to go straight. If the graffiti detective decides that the offender needs a more formal approach, he will issue a citation to juvenile informal traffic court with a recommendation to the judge for restitution (which the offender can "work off" through community service), counseling, and/or the TORCH (Teaching Obedience Respect Courage and Honor) Program, which is delivered by the police department. There is also the option for parenting classes if the graffiti detective sees the need. However, if an offender is convicted, California law mandates that there automatically be a one-year delay for that offender receiving his or her driver's license. However, an offender can agree to clean graffiti in a specific area of town for one year in lieu of the one-year delay.

The graffiti detective has also worked closely with the Prosecutor's Office to develop a formula for restitution based on the cost of all the materials needed to remove the graffiti such as special chemicals, paint, vehicles, ladders, ropes, etc. A very conservative estimate is that it costs the City $10.00 per square foot to remove graffiti. This does not include the salaries of those working to remove the graffiti or the cost of any damage (e.g., a broken window). Additionally, the cost to replace a reflective street sign is $400.00. These signs often lose their reflective coating when graffiti is removed. It is important to note that the graffiti detective's biggest source of intelligence comes from the school resource officers, reflecting the importance of the partnership with the schools. More often than not, a tagger will also tag textbook covers, backpacks, and the like. Their particular moniker or "art" is passed on to the graffiti detective who then may compare it with graffiti sites.

SUMMARY

A set of common themes emerged across the four varying sites (Table 7.1). First, each community has placed significant attention on building strong partnerships with other components of the criminal justice system, local government, the business community, and neighborhood groups and residents. These could be formal partnerships such as CAPS in Chicago and Safe Streets in Topeka or more informal partnerships such as that between the El Monte Police Department and the City School District or the active group in Tampa organized through the U.S. Attorney's Office. These partnerships multiplied the resources available for crime reduction efforts as well as set the stage for legitimizing the ongoing efforts of the partners. Additionally, these partnerships fostered information sharing among their members.

Second, each community has established regular processes for analyzing crime patterns, feeding this information to officers and managers, and building accountability for crime prevention and control into the mission of the department. This ranged from formal COMPSTAT-style meetings in Chicago and Topeka to regular sharing of crime patterns through other means such as task force-type meetings and e-mail. By understanding the people, places, and contexts driving local crime problems and coupling these with ongoing assessments of interventions, each site is able to uniquely tailor anti-crime responses as well as hold managers, the police department, and multi-agency collaboratives accountable for current trends in crime. Additionally, such knowledge of crime problems and anti-crime resources allows these communities to borrow promising anti-crime initiatives from other communities and implement them in the best way that serves the local context.

Third, each department has decentralized policing services to focus on specific neighborhoods and reporting districts. This, too, enhances information sharing and accountability. Similarly, schools emerged as important locations to focus resources. The result of these partnerships, local focus, and data-driven processes is highly focused, deterrence-based interventions. This is consistent with one of the key findings of the National Academies of Science review of effective policing strategies that called for very focused

Table 7.1 Summary of core components by site

City	Working coalitions	Local problem and resource focus	Data-driven problem solving	Focused interventions/ focused deterrence	Leadership and commitment
Chicago	CAPS (neighborhood groups, businesses, schools, city government); CPD, U.S. Attorney's Office, Cook County Prosecutor, Department of Corrections	Level One and Level Two deployment areas; focus on homicide and gun crime	CLEAR information system coupled with VISE and DOC meetings	PSN collaboration with Cook County Attorney and U.S. Attorney's Office to increase penalties for illegal gun possession and use	Chicago Police Department; U.S. Attorney's Office, ND IL
Tampa	Active group comprising regional enforcement and prosecution working with PSN and U.S. Attorney's Office. Separate treatment coalitions	Widely shared view that crime problem is manageable and controllable. Treatment services coordinated through a single county	Crime patterns and trend data shared regionally by crime analysts. Verbal and written presentation including maps common	Focus on violent crimes and gangs—prevention, alternatives; enforcement and prosecution working closely on tactical operations	History of good working relationships strengthened by active leadership through U.S. Attorney's Office, MD FL, and Exec LECC
Topeka	Safe Streets task force	Safest Capital City Campaign	COMPSTAT-style meetings; increasing crime analyst staff; utilize crime mapping	Gasoline pump drive-offs; larcenies from vehicles	Commitment from the chief of police as well as other LE heads
El Monte	Community Relations Office; partnership with El Monte City Schools	Reporting Districts; Park, Meet, and Greets; school resource officers	Dedicated crime analysis personnel; utilize crime mapping; CAD-based e-mail alerts	Graffiti abatement	Commitment from the chief of police. El Monte City School District

CAD, computer-aided dispatch; CAPS, Chicago's Alternative Policing Strategy; CLEAR, Citizen Law Enforcement Analysis and Reporting; CPD, Chicago Police Department; DOC, Deployment Operations Center; Exec LECC, Executive Law Enforcement Community Coordinator; LE, law enforcement; MD FL, Middle District of Florida; ND IL, Northern District of Illinois; PSN, Project Safe Neighborhoods; VISE, Violent Incident Strategy Evaluation.

interventions geared toward specific contexts and crime problems (National Research Council, 2004).

Finally, one additional ingredient that was evident in these four cities was leadership. The specific people and roles varied across the sites but in every jurisdiction clear leaders were evident who continually placed emphasis on the expectation that the police, working in concert with other community partners, were responsible for preventing and controlling violent crime. This emphasis, in turn, translated into an expectation that ongoing problem analysis would be occurring and that leaders throughout the organization would know what was currently happening in terms of violent crime trends; that department personnel would work in collaboration with multiple formal and informal partners; that problems would be examined at the local level; and that participating partners would bring resources to bear on these local problems resulting in very focused interventions specific to the area and the type of crime. In short, leadership leads to accountability, which is the final ingredient evident in the four site visit cities.

Although each of these core components has its promise, there are also inherent limitations (Table 7.2). We would not be surprised to find that, in places where, in contrast to the four study sites, the homicide and robbery rates have continued to rise, there may indeed be one or more of these core components in place. However, we would venture to guess that these core components, if present, are not integrated into a community's way of doing business, making those limitations even more apparent.

One of the limitations of this exploratory investigation is that it was not possible to systematically assess and test the specific dimensions of these common themes. On one level it is likely true that every police department in the nation can point to partnerships, routine crime analysis, local focus, and focused interventions. Thus, the question remains of whether these dimensions discriminate practices and processes that more or less effectively prevent and control violent crime. Likely this is an issue of "the devil is in the details." The details, in turn, likely include the quality and quantity (i.e., "dosage") of the resulting interventions. In all

Table 7.2 Summary of promising practices

Strategic component	Promise	Limitations
Working coalitions	Coalitions with other criminal justice agencies, government, research partners, and businesses can bring additional resources; partnering with community can increase legitimacy and sharing of information	Research suggests that community policing and associated relationships alone do not reduce crime
Local problem and resource focus	The criminal justice system operates under a uniquely local understanding of its crime problems and its anti-crime resources	Local issues may limit
Data-driven problem solving	Understanding the people, places, contexts driving local crime problems coupled with ongoing assessment of interventions	Timeliness of data
Focused interventions/focused deterrence	Increasing efficiency and effectiveness of crime control strategies	Absent meaningful community partnerships may be perceived as unjust targeting and harassment by police

four cities, evidence pointed to the effective integration of all of these components resulting in intensive and focused interventions (Figure 7.1). The next step should be to take each of these dimensions and create measurable components for each, that is, create performance metrics. First, this would allow a police department to measure its success over time, further increasing the accountability component that this research has shown to be so important. Second, this would also allow for comparisons to be made across police departments and permit benchmarking of best practices and the routine assessment of the link between these managerial and strategic processes and the level of violent crime.

NOTES

1 An additional factor is that, in late 2007, the Mayor of Chicago appointed a new superintendent of the Chicago Police Department who was sworn in on February 1, 2008. As is common in any organization with new leadership, there are changes occurring within the police department. This has included modifications in some of the Chicago Police Department programs noted below. The programmatic information described in this report is accurate as of 2007.

2 This role now falls under the Bureau of Professional Standards.

3 Under the new Superintendent, VISE and DOC meetings have been combined into one meeting known as the Crime Analysis Review Meeting (CAR).

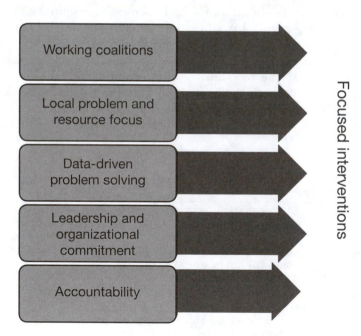

Figure 7.1 Suggested core components of effective policing strategies.

CHAPTER 8

The Rockford Drug Market Intervention: Design, Process and Impact Assessment of a Pulling Levers Strategy in Illinois

Nicholas A. Corsaro and Edmund F. McGarrell

In 2007, police officials in Rockford, Illinois, decided to take a very different approach to addressing its open-air drug markets and the neighborhoods negatively affected by the drug markets. The approach was data driven. Specifically, it built on a promising practice developed in High Point, North Carolina, it included a problem analysis of the drug market in Rockford, and it included an assessment of the impact of the intervention. It involved partnerships between the police, federal and local prosecutors, social services, key community leaders, local residents, and the business community. Finally, it was a highly focused intervention. Rather than addressing all drug sale activity in the city, the decision was to focus initially on one specific market in a particular neighborhood. If this intervention proved successful then the plan was to move to a second drug market. Given this, the Rockford drug market intervention represented the central characteristics of the New Criminal Justice.

BACKGROUND—ROCKFORD

The city of Rockford is home to just over 150,000 residents and is the third largest city in the state of Illinois after Chicago and Aurora. The city covers roughly 56.7 square miles. Over 72 percent of the city's population is white and 17 percent of the population is African American. The per capita income for the city was just over US$19,000, with a median household income of US$55,600 according to the 2000 U.S. Census.

Rockford, like most American cities, experienced peak violent and property offenses in the early to mid-1990s. Specifically, when comparing violent and property crime rates in Rockford at the turn of the century with those peak years of the 1990s, violent offenses declined by roughly 32.8 percent while property offenses declined by 25.8 percent according to the FBI's Uniform Crime Reports. Of course, these fluctuations in crime patterns are most relevant and important to the Rockford Police Department (RPD), which relies on the trends to ultimately craft strategies and responses to these problems.

RPD is home to over 300 officers and operates on an annual budget of just over US$40 million. RPD went through a major change in administration when a new police chief was appointed in the spring of 2006. RPD also underwent the switch in 2006 from collecting data consistent with the Uniform Crime Reporting (UCR) system to collecting data consistent with the National Incident-Based Reporting System (NIBRS).

To better place the crime situation in context and to understand the challenges faced by RPD's new leadership, it is instructive to compare reported crime in Rockford to the national crime context. Rockford placed in the second highest quartile (i.e., the top 50 percent) of all large U.S. cities for property crime offenses according to the 2005 UCR.

However, Rockford was in the bottom 3 percent of all large U.S. cities for violent crime index offenses including homicides, rapes, and assaults. Thus, the new law enforcement administration was charged with the task to create and implement strategies to address the fact that, although Rockford was a relatively non-violent city compared with other large U.S. cities, it placed in the top half of all cities for property offenses.

THE LINK BETWEEN DRUG MARKETS AND HIGH CRIME AREAS

According to several high-standing officials in RPD, drug markets are the driving force behind the high property crime in the city, which is consistent with previous criminological research that suggests a strong relationship between drug markets and property offenses (see Pettiway, 1995; Rengert and Wasilchick, 1989). As is often the case, thefts and burglaries often concentrate around drug markets because users are often attempting to establish funds to finance their drug use (Rengert, 1996). Drug market-driven crime is particularly challenging for RPD because Rockford is triangularly located within an easy driving distance to Chicago (IL), Madison (WI), and Cedar Rapids (IA). Thus, there are a number of avenues available for narcotics trafficking into the city of Rockford.

To get a more detailed picture of the extent to which drug markets and crime in certain areas were related, research analysts in RPD were charged with the task of identifying the extremely high crime locations. In early 2007, RPD analysts used spatial data analysis and crime-mapping techniques to diagnose those crime hot spots that had the most index offenses, including property and violent crime as well as drug-related offenses, such as drug arrests and drug complaints. Results from these analyses indicated that two neighborhoods in particular experienced unusually high index and drug offenses in the

city. One high crime area was located on the east side of the city, whereas the other area was located on the west side, referred to as the Coronado Haskell neighborhood. Combined, the two target areas consisted of six police beats (i.e., two beats in the Coronado Haskell neighborhood and four beats in the eastern side of the city) and comprised less than 4 percent of the total city population.[1] Not surprisingly, both of these areas shared boundaries with established Weed and Seed prevention programs because of the persistent history of high crime and focused police efforts in these neighborhoods. Thus, law enforcement and community resource officers were intimately familiar with both high crime hot spot locations.

Of the two chronic crime hot spots, RPD decided to first concentrate heavily on the Coronado Haskell high crime neighborhood because it was slightly smaller than the high crime neighborhood on the eastern side of the city, it was more of a residential-based area, and specific citizens within the neighborhood were very involved in the local Weed and Seed programs and had already established open communication with community resource officers from RPD.[2] Figure 8.1 displays the geographic boundary of the Coronado Haskell target neighborhood.

Figure 8.2 compares the monthly rates (per 10,000 residents) of violent,[3] property,[4] drug,[5] and nuisance offenses[6] between June 2006 and April 2007 in the Coronado Haskell neighborhood with those in the remainder of the city of Rockford over this same period.[7] It is apparent that violent, drug, property, and nuisance crimes were much higher in the target neighborhood than in the remainder of Rockford before the intervention strategy that was to be adopted to address these issues was implemented. On the basis of this analysis, RPD officials decided to attempt to implement a drug market reduction initiative in the Coronado Haskell neighborhood that was originally used in High Point, North Carolina.

Figure 8.1 Street map of the Coronado Haskell community.

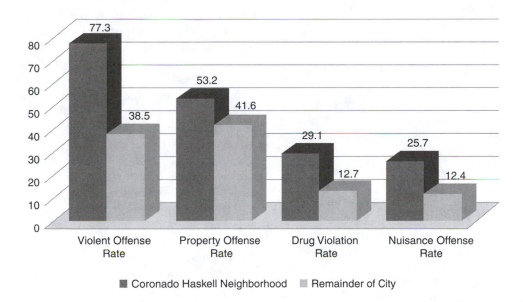

Figure 8.2 Monthly offense rates comparing the Coronado Haskell neighborhood with the remainder of Rockford between June 2006 and April 2007.

HIGH POINT DRUG MARKET INTERVENTION

Beginning in 2004, the High Point Police Department (HPPD) in North Carolina decided to try a relatively new and different approach when dealing with open-air drug markets and the crime and disorder associated with the illegal drug trade in high crime neighborhoods. Rather than reactive enforcement that focused on incarcerating individual dealers and individual sellers, HPPD set out to use a more systematic, data-driven, and proactive project that was inspired by Boston's Operation Ceasefire (Braga et al., 2001; Kennedy, 1997) and similar strategic policing approaches (Braga et al., 2008; Corsaro and McGarrell, 2009; Kennedy and Braga, 1998; McGarrell et al., 2006). At the heart of these strategies was a multi-stage approach that concentrated on increasing sanctions for repeat offenders for youth-, gun-, and gang-related violence. In addition, task force members in these various strategies focused their efforts on deterrence-based messages designed to inform previous offenders that future violence would not be tolerated, and that conforming in a more positive and pro-social way would actually yield benefits. These strategies were also adopted by many sites in the national Project Safe Neighborhoods (PSN) initiative (McGarrell et al., 2009).

The HPPD also had experience implementing a PSN strategy targeting local gun and gang crime, and thus had already established a strong multi-organizational working relationship with key institutional partners (i.e., District Attorney's Office and U.S. Attorney's Office) and community partners (i.e., West End Ministries, High Point Community Against Violence, and community residents) in their violence reduction programs (Frabutt et al., 2006). Specific to open-air drug markets, HPPD implemented the West End Initiative in a community that experienced persistent drug problems in the neighborhood.

Law enforcement officials in High Point conducted several months of investigations in the West End Initiative, and were able to compile very thorough cases against a number of individuals who sold drugs in the neighborhood over the period of the investigation (Frabutt et al., 2006). In May 2004, officials from multiple law enforcement agencies, federal and local prosecution, and corrections officials as well as community members in the West End neighborhood conducted a call-in of 12 verified drug sellers from this area. Unlike several of their fellow dealers who were prosecuted and incarcerated because of their violent criminal histories, these offenders would be given a second chance with charges held over their heads. At the meeting they heard about the lack of tolerance for drug dealing from community members as well as a strong deterrent message from the various criminal justice officials who were present.

Importantly, the task force presented a locally produced 10-minute film that showed the previous High Point PSN initiative, which added credibility to the seriousness of the deterrence-based message. Offenders at the notification were able to see first-hand the potential positive support they were being offered as well as the heavy sanctions they faced if they continued to sell drugs. The drug sellers at the call-in were also offered a variety of social services (e.g., treatment, housing, employment) to assist their transition out of drug dealing. The West End Initiative produced an average crime decrease of 57 percent over four years in that neighborhood. Also, according to surveys taken from local residents as well as police, the open-air drug market literally disappeared overnight in the target neighborhood (Frabutt et al., 2006). In sum, the High Point initiative was heavily based in a strategic framework in the use of strategies that were consistent with previous drug market research (Mazerolle et al., 2007).

Rockford law enforcement officials were made aware of the strategies and success of the High Point initiative at a Community Oriented Policing Services (COPS) meeting and were interested in replicating a similar approach in their community. Officers in Rockford contacted officials in High Point and made a site visit to better follow the blueprint of the West End Initiative.

ACTION PLAN

The chief of RPD invited David Kennedy of John Jay College of Criminal Justice to help develop a strategic plan of action and to demonstrate to officers in the department the purpose of, and procedures on how to successfully implement, a "pulling levers" intervention. Kennedy helped develop the pulling levers initiative in Boston (Kennedy, 1997) and had worked closely with HPPD officials to adapt the model to address open-air drug markets. After RPD officers and officials were made aware of the multiple stages and procedures of the drug market pulling levers strategy, they decided to implement the initiative in the Coronado Haskell target neighborhood.

One of the obvious problems in the Coronado Haskell neighborhood was the fact that a high amount of illegal drug distribution occurred on the property of an abandoned school. The vast parking areas and large open ground of the school offered a number of discreet ways into and out of the property, which was conducive for both drug dealers and drug buyers. Also, a number of drug-related crimes such as vagrancy, prostitution, and property thefts were concentrated around the abandoned property. Thus, even within a high crime hot spot, illegal drug distribution, property, and nuisance offenses were not simply randomly distributed but rather were concentrated in an area with a history of illegal narcotics distribution.

As a first step toward focusing on abating high crime in the target area, RPD boarded up the property and locked the gates, mounted a camera on the building, and helped clear out

trees and other materials that helped facilitate discreet drug dealing at this location. RPD also met with residents in a local community meeting to get a better understanding of the concerns about the crime that was obviously being driven by the presence of the open-air drug market. It is important to note that law enforcement officers believed that the proactive response in tightening security around the school helped facilitate increased community participation in local meetings because of the fact that residents were able to observe an immediate commitment on the part of the officers in dealing with drug selling in the neighborhood.

RPD officials also contacted several key criminal justice agencies, social service agencies, and community groups to ensure that members from various agencies and groups were willing to work together toward achieving the goals of the intervention program. The drug market task force in Rockford was composed of the following key members:

- Rockford Police Department (local law enforcement)
- Rockford Prosecuting Attorney (local prosecution)
- U.S. Attorney (federal prosecution)
- Rockford Human Services (social service provisions)
- local parishioners (community outreach)
- community development leaders (community outreach).

Following the High Point model, the next stage was for RPD officers to conduct an intensive and thorough investigation of drug dealing in the target area by relying on multiple sources including cooperating witnesses as well as extensive police surveillance, including still photography and video recording of the drug buys. The investigation lasted approximately eight weeks. Narcotics detectives conducted a modified incident review (see Klofas and Hipple, 2006) to facilitate this process. Through the detailed investigation and incident reviews, RPD was able to identify and build strong cases on 12 individuals who persistently sold drugs in the neighborhood. Although these 12 individuals were identified as chronic drug distributors, many did not actually reside in the Coronado Haskell neighborhood. RPD was focused on building cases against dealers who sold drugs within the neighborhood, regardless of the location of their home inhabitance.

After the investigation was complete, a committee that consisted of both law enforcement (i.e., the lead narcotics officer and deputy chief) and prosecution (i.e., Assistant U.S. Attorney and Assistant State's Attorney) reviewed the cases made against the 12 individuals who had become the specific targets of the focused investigation. More specifically, the committee reviewed the criminal histories of the offenders and determined that only non-violent offenders who did not have extensive criminal histories of violence and gun offending would be eligible for the notification call-in. Ultimately, five individuals did not have an extensive and violent criminal history and were selected as eligible participants for the notification, while the other seven offenders were the target of focused prosecutions to serve as a crackdown that would communicate a deterrent message.

PUBLIC NOTIFICATION

The culmination of the investigation, inter-agency cooperation, and community mobilization came together in early May 2007, which was roughly three months after the initiation of the program. Table 8.1 outlines the stages that RPD and the inter-agency working group took in the target neighborhood which made the initiative known to the public. Although the investigation and implementation phases had been under way for several months, most of this work was "behind the scenes," at least from the perspective of community residents as well as the drug offenders in the target neighborhood. The actions and stages outlined below made the offenders, the residents in the target neighborhood, and the rest of the public in the city of Rockford aware of the initiative.

Public Notification, Stage 1: On Monday May 7, 2007, the RPD hosted a community meeting in the gymnasium of a local parochial school in the Coronado Haskell neighborhood. During the meeting, law enforcement officials informed the citizens that they had been conducting a thorough investigation and that immediate action was about to ensue. RPD believed it was necessary to inform the citizens and community groups that a series of wholesale changes were coming to the neighborhood. This was consistent with research

Table 8.1 Public notification of the Rockford Pulling Levers drug program

Procedure	Date(s)	Key methods
Stage 1	May 7, 2007	Met with community members to inform them that something was about to happen in their neighborhood
Stage 2	May 7–8, 2007	Arrested chronic and violent drug offenders in the target neighborhood
Stage 3	May 7–8, 2007	Contacted non-violent and low-risk drug offenders to ensure their appearance at the notification meeting
Stage 4	May 9, 2007	Held the notification meeting at a parochial school gymnasium in the target neighborhood
Stage 5	May 10, 2007	Initiated a neighborhood sweep for nuisance violations and seized apartments in target area

suggesting that informing residents that a crackdown is going to occur is vital when trying to foster and enhance police–community relations (Webb and Katz, 2003, pp. 36–7).

Public Notification, Stage 2: On both Monday May 7 and Tuesday May 8, 2007, RPD officers arrested the seven drug dealers they had built cases against who had violent and chronic criminal histories. During these two days, six of the seven individuals were arrested and charged with multiple counts of illegal narcotics distribution and were given very large bonds, in excess of $500,000. The seventh offender was arrested a few days later. Although RPD had determined weeks before this focused crackdown that these seven offenders were ineligible for the notification call-in, they decided to wait and perform a concentrated arrest effort at the same time as the call-in to amplify the magnitude, severity, and certainty of arrest.

Public Notification, Stage 3: During the same two days of the focused crackdown on violent offenders (i.e., May 7 and May 8, 2007) RPD officers contacted the five individuals who were eligible for the pulling levers call-in, as well as their families, and, when needed, the pastor of a local church in the target neighborhood to assist with the notification. This was a somewhat delicate matter because, during these same two days, RPD officers were focusing on the arrest of the seven violent drug dealers in the neighborhood. It was certainly expected that word on the street that RPD was engaged in a crackdown on drug offenders in the area would have filtered to the sellers who were being invited to the call-in.

Thus, there was some skepticism from the notified offenders that RPD was simply trying to lure them to a meeting and arrest them as well. The pastor of a local ministry was very helpful in generating assurance that the notification was indeed legitimate and not simply a ploy used as a sting operation to generate an arrest. In addition, the chief of RPD wrote a letter to each of the five individuals notified that police were aware of their previous illegal activities and that no arrest would be made during the meeting, which was set for Wednesday May 9, 2007. RPD also encouraged family members of the five notified offenders to accompany them to the meeting to provide social and moral support.

During this same period, RPD reached out to residents in the Coronado Haskell neighborhood to make them aware of the upcoming notification meeting. They used a variety of contact strategies, which included an automated land-based telephone line, locally referred to as "reverse-9-1-1," as well as hand-delivered fliers to residents by police officers who patrolled the neighborhood. Almost 400 calls were placed on the automated voice system, and several hundred flyers were passed out in the neighborhood.

Public Notification, Stage 4: On May 9, 2007, the pulling levers call-in took place at the same local parochial school gymnasium that had been used a few days earlier to inform residents that a change was going to occur. Those present at the notification included many of the residents of the Coronado Haskell community, the multi-agency working group, which included law enforcement, prosecution, social service providers, local ministry, and outreach members, and the five notified offenders and their family members. The meeting began with residents in the community speaking out in public concerning the toll that the drug market and drug dealing were having in the neighborhood. A prevailing theme of this component was residents stating that "our children deserve better" and that change had to occur to eliminate the drug dealing, prostitution, and nuisance-related offenses that accompanied the open-air drug markets in the neighborhood.

After the community-driven message, all of the residents from the neighborhood were thanked for coming and were dismissed from the remainder of the session. The five notified offenders and their families accompanied the multi-agency working group into a small classroom where they each received an individualized bound notebook. In the notebook were photographs of each person selling drugs, a copy of the letter by the police chief stating that they would not be arrested at the notification hearing, and a list of complaints against each offender that remained unsigned. The chief informed the group that they could easily go down and get the complaints signed by a judge to issue a warrant for arrest, and that each person would be subjected to the same focused prosecution that the seven violent offenders would receive. The multi-agency task force gave each offender 72 hours to determine if they wanted to enroll in the social service provision component of the program, although all five decided to enroll that night.

Successful enrollment entailed several stages. First, each person met with the director of Rockford Human Services the night of the call-in for an immediate needs assessment, which lasted approximately 20 minutes for each person. For example, if an offender was a drug user, and most were, they were placed in immediate treatment care. A more thorough needs assessment was made within the week. The purpose of the assessment was to identify and help reduce and remove some of the immediate threats to successful completion.

Each offender would be subjected to drug testing and would be expected to meet with social service providers for regularly scheduled meetings. In addition, when possible, social services assisted with legitimate employment opportunities when needed. Most important, each offender was warned that any violation of this probationary period would be met with extreme consequences, which meant that all previous drug offense complaints would be pursued whether the violation was drug related or not. Thus, they sent the message: when we say last chance, we mean just that. Indeed, several months later one of the five offenders from the call-in was arrested for shoplifting in a local convenient store. The multi-agency task force pursued all previous drug offenses in court and the individual was convicted on all counts several months later. This was considered important for maintaining credibility both on the street and among the agents who helped build cases against these individuals. After the notification call-in, officials focused on an intensive follow-up in the Coronado Haskell neighborhood.

Public Notification, Stage 5: On May 10, 2007 (the day after the call-in), RPD crafted a response to help "clean up" the target neighborhood. From dawn until dusk, a mobile command unit was parked in the middle of the Coronado Haskell neighborhood. Along with community development leaders, RPD focused an intensive sweep throughout the neighborhood issuing citations for maintenance code violations (e.g., weed and lawn care, parking, trash, and litter violations). Interestingly, a public official who resided in the neighborhood was issued a citation, affirming the "no tolerance" message of the sweep. At the end of the day, a street sweeper went through the neighborhood as a symbolic message that the streets were now "clean."

RPD and building code officials seized five apartments in the neighborhood with nuisance and code violations. These were locations where landlords and owners of the properties had been made aware that they were renting to known dealers, but did not cooperate with law enforcement and code officials to remedy the nuisance-related problems. Human service officials also participated in this process by providing immediate shelter for residents within the units and homes who were not involved in illegal drug distribution from information based on the investigation several months earlier. Specifically, human services provided assistance with the move out and had already found similar housing in another location, and even provided financing of one month's rent for each family at their new residence. In sum, the task force took great care to ensure that residents in the seized apartments did not experience any unnecessary strain.

FOLLOW-UP

Following the action taken in early May 2007, RPD maintained intensive patrols in the Coronado Haskell neighborhood for several weeks, in addition to the regular beat patrols performed by law enforcement. It became apparent during community meetings that residents in the neighborhood were concerned about outside drug buyers and drug dealers who either may have been unaware of the intervention strategy or would simply try to take advantage of the void through a "replacement" capacity. The presence of these actors would have the real potential to contaminate the efforts that had been made in the neighborhood. The task force believed that it was important for citizens in the target community to observe a continued police presence following the intervention to affirm the commitment to reduce crime in the community, even when many of the drug dealers were no longer living in the neighborhood.

In addition to the immediate and intense patrol efforts in the target community following the stages that were carried out in May 2007, RPD continued to make violent, drug, and nuisance offenses in the Coronado Haskell neighborhood a high response priority. Residents noted after the intervention that they felt a sense of "empowerment" in their community because they had helped stimulate the change that had occurred. RPD wanted to ensure that residents would continue to feel empowered to address crime problems, and thereby committed to responding swiftly and assuredly to potential crime problems. Finally, RPD presented outcome and impact findings of the intervention to the citizens in the neighborhood at a one-year follow-up at the local school where the original meeting was held.

ASSESSING IMPACT

Although the multiple strategies of the Rockford pulling levers drug market intervention came to the public's attention in May 2007, assessing the impact of the strategy is a somewhat challenging proposition. There are a number of factors that make an intervention analysis a challenging task.

First, we have to choose a "pre/post" intervention date in order to conduct the analysis. The majority of the tasks were performed in May 2007, at least from a public notice and outcome analysis. Law enforcement in Rockford continued intensive saturation patrols in the Coronado Haskell neighborhood for many weeks after the intervention. We decided to use May 2007 as the discrete intervention period understanding that police saturation in the area following the intervention would likely have yielded more reported offenses in the neighborhood simply by the process of enhanced police presence. Sufficient post-intervention data should minimize this concern.

Second, Rockford underwent a change from the UCR system to the NIBRS in the early spring of 2006. A detailed trend analysis is virtually impossible because of the change in the reporting structure, which limited the analysis to only a single year of pre- and post-intervention data. Although we were able to run time series models with the available data, these results, although promising, were methodologically limited.[8]

Third, the lone neighborhood that could be used as a control or comparison site was the other high crime neighborhood in the eastern part of Rockford (discussed earlier). Unfortunately, from an evaluation design perspective, a few months after the intervention in the Coronado Haskell neighborhood, RPD implemented a similar strategy in the other part of the city. Thus, there are no data available for a control site comparison analysis. As an alternative, the trend in crime in the target neighborhood was compared with the trend in crime in the remainder of the city.

Finally, at the present time we do not have data from residents in the Coronado Haskell neighborhood that would provide more detail about the knowledge of, perceptions of, and beliefs concerning the intervention. Although we plan to assess resident perceptions, the current impact assessment is limited to official police offense data with roughly one year of pre- and one year of post-intervention data in the target area, using the remainder of the city of Rockford as a baseline comparison.[9] Specifically, to assess whether the May 2007 pulling levers drug market intervention had both a pronounced and a sustained impact, we rely on the use of official RPD offense data using the remainder of the city of Rockford (i.e., Rockford overall city minus Coronado Haskell community) as a surrogate for trend comparison purposes. Offense data from RPD is subjected to a more rigorous reliability check than standard calls for service data because of the fact that law enforcement officers in RPD enter information on a given

offense into a computerized system after an investigation, which details the circumstances of the event. Thus, the categorization of offenses is subjected to an internal reliability check as all officers who took part in a given investigation are expected to report and ultimately cross-validate the data.

Figure 8.3 compares the monthly rates (per 10,000 residents) of violent, property, drug violation, and nuisance offenses from May 2007 to May 2008 in the Coronado Haskell neighborhood with those in the remainder of the city of Rockford over this same period. Whereas Figure 8.2 showed that the target area was subjected to higher rates of each offense type before the intervention, this was not the case when examining one year's worth of post-intervention data. Figure 8.3 shows that violent, drug, property, and nuisance assaults were much lower than in the remainder of the city for almost all offenses here except for drug violation rates, which became very similar to the remainder of Rockford.

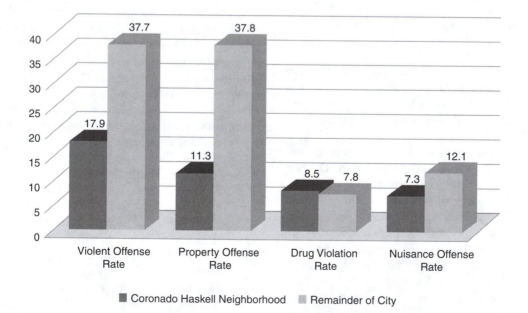

Figure 8.3 Monthly offense rates comparing the target neighborhood with the remainder of Rockford between May 2007 and May 2008.

Specifically, monthly offense percentage declines in the Coronado Haskell community were observed for violent crime (–76.8 percent), property crime (–78.7 percent), drug crime (–70.7 percent), and nuisance crime (–71.2 percent). Comparatively, the remainder of Rockford also experienced percentage declines in violent (–2.1 percent), property (–9.1 percent), drug (–38.5 percent), and nuisance (–2.4 percent) offenses, although not to the same level or extent as was observed in the target community. A more detailed evaluation of impact that relies on the use of growth curve modeling shows that the Coronado Haskell neighborhood experienced a statistically significant decline in non-violent offenses and a substantial although non-statistically significant decline in violent offenses, whereas no such significant declines were seen in the remainder of Rockford during this period (see Corsaro et al., 2009). Thus, the analysis of offense data certainly suggests a strong and sustained impact that has made the target community "on par" with the remainder of Rockford in terms of violent and non-violent crime.

CONCLUSION

The Rockford Drug Market Initiative was a strategic, multi-agency, and community approach designed to combat drug markets in a high crime neighborhood in an effort to eliminate drug and related offending and to make a once high crime community a better place to live. The strategy has shown great promise in achieving those goals, as evidenced by the reduction in offenses seen one year post implementation.

The purpose of this chapter was to document the various steps that the RPD undertook to actually implement the pulling levers strategy. Specifically, RPD was very true to the pulling levers framework by observing the approach used in High Point, North Carolina, garnering multi-agency and outreach support prior to implementation,

conducting a detailed investigation to better understand the dynamics of the drug markets in the target community, implementing the crackdown and pulling levers program, and following up their actions in the target neighborhood in both the short and long term. Our purpose was to document the specific detail concerning these multiple stages to provide both process and context that were so vital to apparent program success.

As part of the ongoing research it will be important to examine whether the Coronado Haskell community is able to maintain low drug-related and violent crime for a sustained period of time. The issue of whether the drug market crackdown, the pulling levers program, and the attempt to strengthen community participation can generate long-term reductions in crime is an important question to address, particularly when dealing with the pulling levers approach to combat open-air drug markets. Further research concerning citizen participation and resident reaction is necessary to better understand the community dynamic throughout this process.

In terms of community participation and resident reaction, an important aspect for which greater understanding is needed is the extent to which the drug market intervention can result in community building and racial reconciliation between community members, the police, and the criminal justice system. Traditional drug enforcement has had a differential effect on the African American community in particular. John Jay College's David Kennedy, noted above as an architect of the drug market intervention program, has argued that the process of the police and community working together in the drug market intervention program, whereby there is a joint effort to eliminate the drug market but also to provide new opportunities to non-violent drug dealers and thereby avoid incarceration, has generated such police–community reconciliation.[10] Further, this reconciliation may be a key ingredient of enhanced collective efficacy within the neighborhood (Sampson et al., 1997)

The pulling levers strategies developed in Boston and implemented in Indianapolis, Minneapolis, Chicago, and other cities have shown potential long-term impact; however, these programs dealt with more violent and gang-driven violent crime and homicide. The utility of the pulling levers approach in more unstructured and somewhat haphazard open-air drug markets, such as those in Rockford, will remain the focus of future research for quite some time. The Rockford strategy discussed here shows promising immediate and medium-term (i.e., one year of post-intervention data) offense reduction in the target community, which adds support to the idea that drug markets can be altered with a strategic and dynamic intervention approach. Whether these results are generalizable and valid in the long term should continue to be the focus of research and law enforcement, through implementation, replication, and assessment.

Finally, the Rockford drug market intervention reflects the core elements of the New Criminal Justice. The approach was data driven and problem based. It was highly focused on those neighborhoods within Rockford that suffered from open-air drug markets and the crime and disorder associated with such markets. Additionally, it reflected a powerful set of partnerships among local and federal law enforcement, city government, social services, neighborhood groups, businesses, and local residents. The intervention was not focused on case processing across the agencies of the criminal justice system but rather on strategic focusing and communication with at-risk individuals and local residents alike.

NOTES

1 The Coronado Haskell neighborhood houses approximately 2,700 residents, whereas the east neighborhood houses nearly 3,200 residents.
2 This program was locally referred to as "ADP (Alternative Drug Program) West" and is seen in Figure 8.1.
3 Violent offenses are an aggregate measure of homicides, robberies, and assaults (both aggravated and simple).
4 Property offenses are an aggregate measure of stolen, vandalized, damaged, and destroyed property offenses.
5 Drug offenses are an aggregate of drug/narcotic and drug equipment offenses.
6 Nuisance offenses are an aggregate of prostitution, curfew, loitering, vagrancy, and disorderly conduct offenses.
7 We would ideally display one year of pre-intervention data to address the concern of seasonality. However, although data for the entire year of 2006 are available for the entire city of Rockford, specific data in the Coronado Haskell neighborhood only date back to June 2006 because of a change in the reporting system. Thus, we display ten months' worth of pre-intervention data in both the target community and the overall remainder of the city (overall city minus target community) for the sake of consistency.
8 We were able to estimate a series of autoregressive integrated moving average (ARIMA) time series models with the data available here, using May 2007 as the pre/post abrupt, permanent transfer function date. The models converged and showed a statistically significant decline in non-violent offenses ($p < 0.05$) and a marginally significant decline in violent offenses ($p < 0.10$) in the target area, while the remainder of the city did not experience a significant change. However, the use of only 24 periods of monthly data is roughly half the number of observations needed for a robust and reliable analysis. Thus, we present alternative bivariate trend analyses in this section.
9 A more detailed analysis of impact is available in Corsaro et al. (2009).
10 Kennedy has made this a core element of the Drug Market Intervention Training Program sponsored by the Bureau of Justice Assistance (http://www1.cj.msu.edu/~outreach/psn/DMI/default.htm; see Kennedy, 2009).

SECTION 3

New Knowledge for New Practice in Criminal Justice

One of the key findings from Project Safe Neighborhoods (PSN) was that the integration of research was associated with overall implementation effectiveness (Zimmermann, 2006; McGarrell et al., 2009). Yet the integration of research was uneven across the 93 PSN task forces. The findings suggest that research partnerships are important but not automatic. This section provides insight into the promise and challenge of research partnerships in criminal justice by examining the new roles that research and researchers are playing in criminal justice. In Chapter 9 Lois Felson Mock describes the history of involvement in action research at the National Institute of Justice (NIJ). Mock is a good source on this as she not only oversaw many action research projects while a key staff member at NIJ but also was the chief proponent of preserving a strong action research role as a fundamental part of PSN. Here she also outlines the lessons learned over her career in supporting action research.

Other chapters in this section were written by researchers with considerable experience of working closely with criminal justice agencies. In Chapter 10, James Frabutt and his colleagues describe the complex roles of researchers in PSN in North Carolina. There, researchers were successfully integrated into the local criminal justice system planning process and utilized gun crime surveillance systems that drew on researcher and practitioner expertise. The authors describe what they regard as key elements of their successful research partnership.

In Chapter 11 Braga and Hinkle provide their perspective on practitioner–researcher partnerships based on their own partnership in Boston. Both note that these types of partnerships have often been mutually unsatisfactory and they offer complementary lessons on bringing these two diverse cultures together. Key to true partnership in their view is recognition of the limitations of their own roles and recognition of the expertise of their partners. Developing trust, they argue, is the most critical factor for mutually productive relationships. Even with that, Braga points out, academics must take care to maintain high standards that will serve their interests in the university as well as in the community.

Cultural contrasts between the academic and practical worlds of criminal justice are the focus of Chapter 12, Jack Greene's essay. He notes the politics of policing and the record of external criticism that has often made these organizations defensive. Furthermore, the craft aspects of policing may be seen as clashing with the measurement focus of researchers. Academics have often had their own vulnerabilities as policy studies and values have often seemed to meld together. Trust is a tricky issue in these usually disconnected worlds. As Greene points out, however, working through these partnerships is producing a new generation of both police leaders and researchers.

In the final essay in this section (Chapter 13) Wesley Skogan draws on his long years of experience as a researcher working with the police in Chicago. Such partnerships, he argues, must deal with widely different perspectives on such issues as time lines and the timeliness of research and on perceptions about its usefulness. Practitioners may push for tactically useful findings but researchers will need to focus on longer horizons and larger pictures. His work proves that solid partnerships are possible but not without conscious and deliberate effort.

DISCUSSION QUESTIONS

1 These essays have described key differences between academic and practitioner orientations in criminal justice. Of course, key similarities also exist including an interest in high-quality information and research that is useful. How does action research address issues of validity and reliability in research? Do partnerships require compromises on such fundamental issues? Can you develop the argument which would conclude that action research has the capability of assuring high degrees of these important data characteristics?

2 Much of what is needed in criminal justice can be captured under the concept of evaluation research. Practitioners and their funders often need information on whether something works or under what circumstances it works. How can the insider role in a research partnership address questions of potential bias that may result from long-term, planning-focused relationships? What is the role of research partners when it comes to the question of evaluation?

3 Greene argues that research partnerships can influence the future of research as well as practice. What sort of skills and sensibilities are these partnerships likely to engender for researchers and for practitioners? How will partnerships change expectations in the future? What skills and sensibilities do you think the best researchers and the best practitioners are likely to need in the future?

CHAPTER 9

Action Research for Crime Control and Prevention

Lois Felson Mock

INTRODUCTION

Traditionally, the criminal justice system has had a linear structure, starting with police or law enforcement activities and leading to prosecutor/court actions and finally to correctional and probation/parole processes in its efforts to control crime and process offenders. Each of these three criminal justice components acted as an independent entity and offenders were processed from police to courts to corrections, without overlap in responsibilities. Crime prevention was not a primary criminal justice function, but was left to social service and community organizations and neighborhood groups.

Beginning in the mid-1990s, however, this linear structure began to change, as the system began to incorporate a *problem-solving model* in its efforts to prevent and control crime, beginning with its adoption by law enforcement departments. The ineffectiveness of previous crime control programs had led to a new focus on Herman Goldstein's "problem-oriented policing" model, which viewed and responded to crime incidents as more than individual events, but more broadly as symptoms of larger problems associated with particular persons and/or situations, requiring a more comprehensive response. Pioneering police departments began to incorporate preventive strategies and to target problematic

locations and offenders. This led to increased success in their law enforcement programs and they began to be adopted more broadly in the policing community nationwide. In addition, as successes became more widely recognized, this problem-solving perspective began to spread from police to prosecutor/courts and corrections agencies.

As this problem-solving model became more widely adopted by criminal justice system components, it began to be utilized not only as a tactical response to a particular local crime problem, but also as a strategic process for addressing broader, more complex urban crime and disorder problems. Furthermore, this new strategic perspective required that the three components of the criminal justice system work together rather than as isolated entities, to combine their resources in their efforts to solve crime and disorder problems at the local and city levels.

This problem-solving model was evidence based and required sound and systematic research to identify and understand problems, to design interventions, and to assess and evaluate their effects. And this new, non-linear, more holistic approach to crime and disorder required a new, more comprehensive model for criminal justice research and evaluation as well—an approach that has come to be called *action research*.

DEFINITION OF "ACTION RESEARCH"

"Action research" refers to a particular approach to the research process in which researchers engage in an active partnership with one or more practitioner/operational agencies to solve problems. More specifically, in the National Institute of Justice (NIJ)-related context, this approach involves the collaboration between criminal justice researchers and criminal justice/law enforcement agencies in a data-driven, strategic problem-solving process to solve crime and disorder problems in local communities.

This problem-solving collaboration operates as follows. The research partner takes a key role in *problem identification*, collecting and analyzing detailed data on the sources, characteristics, patterns, and contexts of the problem in question and presenting this analysis to the agency partners. Together they discuss these findings and jointly *develop intervention strategies* designed to target the specific problem identified. These are likely to be precisely focused interventions aimed at particular neighborhoods, particular offenders, and particular criminal activities identified as causing the problem being addressed. The operational partners then utilize their resources and expertise to *implement these strategies*, involving additional agencies (including social service and community agencies) if called for by the strategic plan. The research partner remains involved in the implementation process, carefully *monitoring* the conduct of the interventions and providing *feedback* to the practitioners so that flaws are immediately detected and strategies can be refined to better target the problem elements. Finally, the research partner provides an *assessment* of the program implementation and impacts on both the service delivery system and the target crime and offenders.

This action research approach represents a departure from the traditional criminal justice research model, in which scholars maintained their independence from the problem-solving/program development process and were involved only as evaluators of its ultimate impact on crime. They may have been present throughout the process, but only as observers (or process evaluators) and had no active role in the process itself. In fact, in many cases, evaluators were selected for a program "after the fact" and had no direct observation data on program development and implementation.

HISTORY AND EVOLUTION OF NIJ INVOLVEMENT IN ACTION RESEARCH

The NIJ (the research and evaluation arm of the U.S. Department of Justice) has been at the forefront of the development and support of this new type of criminal justice research, and it has had a pioneering role in the advancement of the strategic problem-solving approach within the criminal justice system.

In 1994, NIJ funded three multi-agency/researcher partnerships aimed at solving local youth firearms and violence problems. Two of these—programs in Atlanta and St. Louis—resulted from a joint NIJ/Centers for Disease Control and Prevention solicitation and, although they succeeded in creating working partnerships and integrating research into their planning process, both faltered at the program implementation stage and were not able to effectively conduct the interventions they had developed. In *Atlanta*, the program was too broadly based to be a realistic response, given local resources, but laid the groundwork for later success in action research efforts. In *St. Louis*, the program placed too much reliance on a single mentoring strategy, which the local task force was never able to implement fully and which appeared to have little impact to the extent that it was conducted.

The third problem-solving effort occurred in Boston and in this site the entire action research process was successfully completed.

The Boston Gun Project, or "Operation Ceasefire," assembled an inter-agency working group of criminal justice agencies, schools, youth services, faith-based groups, and researchers. In this program, researchers from the Harvard Kennedy School played a central role in the partnership throughout the problem identification and strategy design, implementation, and assessment phases of the program. A set of innovative strategies was developed to target violent youth gangs in two high crime target areas, including "offender notification" deterrence meetings (at which gang members were warned of consequences if they engaged in gun violence and were offered services if they abstained), "operation nightlight" police/probation home visits to serious offenders, and supply-side law enforcement interventions against illegal gun trafficking to youth in the city. These strategies were successfully implemented by the task force agencies and refined based on researcher monitoring and feedback. The results were astounding: Boston had no gun youth homicides for 2½ years; there was a 25 percent decrease in gun assaults per month and a 32 percent decrease per month in shots fired calls citywide; and there was a 44 percent decrease per month in youth gun assaults in the Roxbury target area.

Based on the unprecedented success of the Boston program, NIJ became involved in two major initiatives formed to capitalize on its elements. The first of these was based on the beneficial partnership between the Boston Police Department and Harvard researchers and led the Institute to create a program of *Locally Initiated Research Partnerships* in which 39 local police/researcher partnership grants were funded nationwide between 1995 and 1998. Although these grants did not replicate the entire range of the action research elements, they promoted a wide variety of police/researcher collaborations, benefiting both communities. Police departments were able to use research data to understand local problems more thoroughly

and to develop more strategic interventions. In turn, researchers were able to consolidate relationships with local departments and get access to police data for their studies. NIJ conducted an overall assessment of this initiative and learned much about the formation and maintenance of successful partnerships, advancing the concept of information-led policing.

The second initiative resulting from the Boston success was a major Department of Justice program launched in 1998, entitled *Strategic Approaches to Community Safety Initiative (SACSI)*. Five initial cities (Indianapolis, Memphis, New Haven, Portland, and Winston-Salem) were funded to replicate the action research process outlined above, with separate grants given to the practitioner agencies and the research partners. Their task was to create a multi-agency/research partner task force, select a serious local violence problem and conduct a strategic problem-solving process to understand its sources, design and implement targeted interventions, monitor and refine these interventions, and assess the impacts on the system and the target crime. The following year, five additional cities were funded: Albuquerque, Atlanta, Detroit, Rochester, and St. Louis. Most of the cities selected gun violence as their target crime, but Memphis selected sexual assault and Winston-Salem chose youth violence in general. An independent cross-site assessment was funded by the Institute to document the action research process and its effects (see Chapter 3). This study found that the multi-agency partnerships, although often taking time to become established, functioned well. In addition, results showed that research was effectively integrated into problem identification, strategy design, and intervention refinement, with local research partners then conducting impact evaluations for their task forces. This process resulted in a wide variety of interventions designed to fit specific local problems and resources, ranging from enforcement to deterrence to prevention.

Finally, the assessment team found that violent crime decreased in SACSI cities more than in other cities of similar size, although a direct causal link could not be established because of the comprehensive nature of the program and the lack of experimental control of extraneous conditions.

When the G. W. Bush administration took office, Attorney General Ashcroft named gun violence as the highest priority of the Justice Department. Therefore, in 2001, the Department of Justice announced the initiation of *Project Safe Neighborhoods (PSN)*, a firearms violence reduction program run through the nation's 93 U.S. Attorneys' Offices.[1] Building on the promising outcomes of the Boston and SACSI programs, as well as Richmond's Project Exile firearms prosecution program, PSN utilizes the action research/strategic problem-solving model. In each of the 93 districts, separate PSN programs have been initiated. Local collaborative partnerships have been formed between criminal justice agencies (local, state, and federal prosecutors and law enforcement, probation/parole, juvenile justice agencies, corrections), relevant social service and community organizations, and local research partners. Gun violence problems have been fleshed out through research data collection and analysis; strategies have been developed targeting the problem elements identified. The research partners have monitored the implementation of interventions by practitioner agencies and have provided feedback for strategy refinement. And, in most districts, researchers are now engaged in process and impact evaluations of the program's effects, not only on the justice system, but on the gun violence problem addressed.

NIJ is one of the core PSN agency partners, represented on the central Firearms Enforcement Assistance Team (FEAT), and is responsible for overseeing all strategic problem solving and research elements of the initiative. The Institute's role in PSN is implemented through a consortium of expert researchers operating under a grant to Michigan State University (MSU). Through this grant, research-based training and technical assistance have been provided to the individual task forces on issues related to strategic problem solving and research activities. In addition, MSU is performing the functions of a research partner for the overall initiative, conducting a series of cross-site studies of promising strategies emerging from the initiative and a series of comprehensive case study assessments of the program process and outcomes in districts that have implemented the PSN action research/problem-solving model as designed. Although definitive findings are not yet available in all sites, some of the more advanced districts are already producing promising data showing a positive program impact on local criminal justice processes and on reducing the gun violence problem addressed.

In addition to these major initiatives, NIJ has engaged in other activities to advance the field of action research. In 2003, the Institute conducted a *workshop* to discuss a number of special problems that researchers may confront when engaged in this type of problem-solving partnership, such as human subjects and privacy concerns and reconciling the different goals and cultures of the practitioner and academic communities (see, for example, Chapters 11–13). Also in 2003, NIJ and IACP conducted a *roundtable* to discuss means for enhancing and promoting partnerships between law enforcement departments and university-based researchers. Furthermore, the Institute has conducted *action research program evaluations* in a number of cities (Los Angeles, Indianapolis, Detroit, and Milwaukee) to assess the effectiveness of the overall problem-solving process or to evaluate specific intervention strategies developed through the action research model. And, finally, NIJ is currently funding a large-scale evaluation of a *multi-site anti-gang initiative* that is being conducted by the Department of Justice, based on the PSN strategic problem-solving model.

LESSONS LEARNED FROM NIJ ACTION RESEARCH

As a result of this extensive NIJ program of action research conducted as part of the growing body of strategic problem-solving initiatives targeting crime prevention and control, some important lessons have been learned about the process and its effects.

First, and most important, in the traditional model of criminal justice research, when the role of the researcher was as an independent evaluator brought in to measure effectiveness after program implementation, too often study findings were inconclusive or showed that the program "didn't work." This led to the cynical view that practitioners could do little to reduce crime and disorder. The action research model, however, has shown that, when researchers and their evidence-based studies are involved in the development and implementation of programs as well as their assessment, agency programs can be effective in reducing crime and increasing public safety and security. What criminal justice agencies do does matter.

More specifically, lessons have been learned about the creation of successful *partnerships* for strategic problem-solving programs. For example, both line- and policy-level collaborations should be formed to establish and approve new practices and implement them effectively. Initial collaborations may have to be restricted to criminal justice agencies and researchers, especially in those activities that examine crimes and criminal histories of individual offenders. But other agencies must be added during program implementation stages so that social and other services may be offered as part of the program strategies. Experience also shows that regularly scheduled meetings of the partnership groups are needed to maintain commitment of all parties. Finally, program resources, responsibilities, and credit must be shared by all agencies involved in the partnership so that all members feel equally involved in the decisions, activities, and outcomes of the initiative.

Lessons have also been learned regarding the *role and integration of research* in the strategic problem-solving process. The *research partner role* should include the following activities: data collection for problem identification; problem analysis to suggest interventions; the monitoring of agency implementation of program activities; feedback of the findings of the monitoring to agency partners so that they can refine and improve their policies and practices; and the evaluation of program impact on the service delivery system and the target problem. And, to ensure the necessary acceptance and *integration of the research* into program activities, the researcher and agency partners must share program goals and must understand each other's capabilities and limitations as they implement the initiative, compromising so that each agency's requirements can be met.

Regarding the nature of the *strategic interventions* themselves, lessons learned from this history of action research initiatives have shown that interventions may include the entire range of suppression, deterrence, and/or prevention activities, with comprehensive programs combining all types of strategies often being most effective. In all cases, however, interventions should be targeted to particular problem elements (offenders, victims, settings, and contexts) as these are identified through research. And finally, interventions should utilize the combined capabilities and resources of all partner agencies, resulting in a more comprehensive response to the problem.

LIMITATIONS OF ACTION RESEARCH

There are several limitations to action research that must be considered when deciding on its suitability. First, it is appropriate for use only in researching and evaluating strategic problem-solving programs addressing crime and disorder (or other social problems).

There are other issues that require other types of research, including survey research and other data collection methods to answer specific criminal justice questions, independent assessments of existing policies or practices, and randomized experiments among others. In addition, because the research partner in action research is a participant in the design and implementation of the program, his or her role as evaluator loses credibility through an appearance of a loss of objectivity and independence. This limitation must be addressed and may be minimized through the adoption of such scientific practices as the setting of standards for the impact evaluation before the implementation of the program, so that findings must meet certain criteria established ahead of time; the establishment of an independent certification for research partners requiring evaluation objectivity; and the involvement of an independent research monitor during the evaluation phase who will provide a second evaluation analysis to corroborate that of the main research partner.

SUMMARY AND CONCLUSION

In conclusion, through its involvement in the "New Criminal Justice" and its strategic problem-solving approach, action research offers a number of key benefits for success-ful crime prevention and control. These include: *increased understanding of the target problem* through data collection and analysis; *improved problem-solving strategies* designed to focus on specifically identified problem elements; *pooled agency resources* to conserve costs and expand the range of practitioner capabilities and expertise; *program refinement and system improvement* based on research partner monitoring and feedback during implementation; and *more knowledgeable evaluation* conducted by a researcher with complete knowledge and understanding of all aspects and phases of the program.

Because of the effectiveness of this new type of partnership research, criminal justice agencies have been increasingly successful in their strategic problem-solving initiatives and this process has been gaining wider and wider use as an important approach to crime prevention and control. It has been instrumental, as well, in changing the traditional linear, "independent agency" criminal justice model to a more interactive, "multi-agency" form, more suitable to addressing local crime and disorder problems.

NOTE

1 Mariana Islands and Guam were treated as task force.

CHAPTER 10

Added Value through a Partnership Model of Action Research: A Case Example from a Project Safe Neighborhoods Research Partner

James M. Frabutt, M. J. Gathings, Lynn K. Harvey, and Kristen L. Di Luca

ACKNOWLEDGEMENTS

The Center for Youth, Family, and Community Partnerships at the University of North Carolina at Greensboro is the Project Safe Neighborhood Research Partner for the U.S. Attorney's Office, Middle District of North Carolina. These efforts are currently supported by Project Safe Neighborhoods funding (180-1-07-001-BB-245) awarded by the U.S. Department of Justice through the North Carolina Department of Crime Control and Public Safety, Governor's Crime Commission. Research efforts from 2002 through 2005 were supported by Project Safe Neighborhoods funding (Award #2002-GP-CX-0220 and 180-1-03-001-BB-094) through the U.S. Department of Justice, Office of Justice Programs. Any opinions, findings, and conclusions or recommendations expressed in this material are those of the authors and do not necessarily reflect the views of the Department of Justice.

RESEARCH, PARTNERSHIP, AND ACTION

Most frequently used to examine public health and environmental issues, community-based action research is becoming an increasingly popular methodology intended to develop relationships with communities through the facilitation of a collaborative atmosphere in which complex issues of public interest are addressed (Israel et al., 2003; Minkler and Wallerstein, 2003; Viswanathan et al., 2004). Although numerous terms are used throughout the literature (i.e., participatory research, action research, participatory action research, constituency-oriented research, emancipatory research, empowerment research, and discovery research), a recent evidence report/technology assessment commissioned by the U.S. Department of Health and Human Services drew on several experts and published writings to define community-based participatory research as an approach that "combines research methods and community capacity-building strategies to bridge the gap between knowledge produced through research and translation of this research into interventions and policies" (Viswanathan et al., 2004, p. 2).

In action-oriented research, the researcher not only provides data analysis expertise but also acts as an agent of social change (Balcazar et al., 2004). Moreover, by supporting community efforts to identify problems and their associated violence reduction strategies, the researcher is able to provide the necessary knowledge to effect lasting, efficacious changes to programs and policies, and, in doing so, improves the functioning of public institutions. Authors underscore that participatory action research is an evolving process that involves collaboration between researchers and stakeholders in the design and conduct of each research phase (Cornwall and Jewkes, 1995; Israel et al.,

2001; Turnbull et al., 1998). Mutual, active engagement in the research process includes activities such as formulation of research questions, data collection, interpretation of findings, and dissemination of products and research findings (Small, 1995, 1996). Participatory action research features egalitarian partnerships between community members and researchers. As a result, the reflexivity of the researcher–stakeholder relationship sets a foundation for knowledge acquisition and mutual education.

ACTION RESEARCH TO SUPPORT COMMUNITY SAFETY

In May 2001, President G. W. Bush introduced Project Safe Neighborhoods (PSN), a comprehensive and strategic approach to gun violence reduction. The PSN gun violence reduction plan comprised five essential elements: (1) partnerships, (2) strategic planning, (3) training, (4) community outreach and public awareness, and (5) accountability. PSN called upon each U.S. Attorney "to implement this national initiative, working in partnership with communities and state and local law enforcement agencies" (Bureau of Justice Assistance, 2002, pp. 2–5). Building on the foundation of multi-level partnerships, PSN featured an explicit focus on strategic problem solving around communities' gun violence issues. In fact, federal support was included (up to $150,000 over three years) as part of the PSN initiative for "research partners/crime analysts" to assist with both the strategic planning and accountability elements of the initiative. By design, the research partners were meant to be included as an integral member of the violence reduction partnership, focusing on increasing:

> the capacity of PSN Task Forces to design data-driven strategies that produce measurable decreases in firearm-related violent crime and to improve the long-term ability of federal, state, and local

partners to work together to understand, prosecute, and prevent firearm-related violent crime within their jurisdictions.

> (Bureau of Justice Assistance, 2002)

ACTION RESEARCH IN THE MIDDLE DISTRICT OF NORTH CAROLINA

When the research partner grants became available and PSN was in the launching phase across the Middle District of North Carolina, the Center for Youth, Family, and Community Partnerships (CYFCP; formerly the Center for the Study of Social Issues) at the University of North Carolina at Greensboro submitted an application. The application was a natural fit on two important levels. First, the opportunity to engage in research that moved beyond outreach and service and into the realm of university–community engagement (Boyer, 1990; Kellogg Commission, 1999; Lerner and Simon, 1998) was in line with the philosophical orientation of CYFCP (MacKinnon-Lewis and Frabutt, 2001). Importantly, there was a direct synergy between the purpose and goals of the PSN research solicitation (i.e., featuring a partnership approach to applied inquiry) and the mission and vision of CYFCP.[1] Second, the PSN research partner solicitation offered a formal mechanism to solidify and deepen an already existing track record of research and partnership with local criminal justice partners (Frabutt et al., 2001; Quijas et al., 2001).

CYFCP began to serve as the PSN research partner for the Middle District of North Carolina on October 1, 2002. The interdisciplinary research partner team consisted of a principal investigator (Frabutt), two co-investigators (Harvey and Cureton) and a graduate research assistant. CYFCP partnered with and drew on the expertise of the Center for Community Safety (CCS) at Winston-Salem State University, a community-based center which helps shape the way that local communities respond to violence impacting residents. As a hub for decision making on violence prevention, the Center spearheads the use of new approaches, and draws upon new partners, in addressing significant local public safety issues in Winston-Salem and Forsyth County. CCS was created in 2001 as an outgrowth of a Department of Justice initiative (Strategic Approaches to Community Safety Initiative, 1998), whose purpose was to foster academic–community partnerships that developed research-based interventions to address serious crime and safety problems in communities.

The U.S. Attorney's Office of the Middle District of North Carolina, in consultation with the Middle District PSN task force, selected five initial target localities as the focus of PSN efforts: Durham, Greensboro, High Point, Salisbury, and Winston-Salem. Currently, eight PSN sites are engaged in these violence reduction efforts in the Middle District. Uniquely, the three additional sites are countywide initiatives in Alamance, Cabarrus, and Orange Counties in which multiple law enforcement agencies and city partnerships are engaged in collaboration. Research partner efforts are therefore dedicated to fourteen cities across seven counties. The cities range in population from approximately 1,991 to 241,752 and the counties range in population from approximately 123,776 to 449,078 (Table 10.1).

Table 10.1 Population of the Middle District of North Carolina PSN target localities

Locality	Population estimates[1]
Cities	
Burlington	47,692
Carrboro	18,611
Chapel Hill	53,416
Concord	66,107
Durham	214,492
Graham	14,277
Greensboro	241,753
Haw River	1,991
High Point	95,630
Hillsborough	6,240
Kannapolis	41,273
Mebane	8,283
Salisbury	29,461
Winston-Salem	201,955
Counties	
Alamance	139,786
Cabarrus	157,179
Durham	246,824
Forsyth	331,859
Guilford	449,078
Orange	123,776
Rowan	134,540

Note

1 City and county population estimates are for July 2006. This information may be retrieved from http://www.osbm.state.nc.us.

Research activities centered on these target localities can be classified into four general domains that emerged based on local need, federal reporting requirements, and ongoing input from the Middle District PSN task force. The major research foci are: (1) overall, cross-city data collection, (2) initiating crime incident review processes, (3) evaluation and consultation on existing and new crime reduction strategies, and (4) city-specific or event-specific research questions. These efforts are briefly summarized in Table 10.2 and are articulated more fully in the paragraphs that follow.

Overall, Cross-City Data Collection

To review data on firearms enforcement and firearms crime from the 93 PSN task forces across the country, the Bureau of Justice Assistance requested that research partners complete a standardized reporting form on a semi-annual basis. Contacts were established within each police department, District Attorney's Office, and the U.S. Attorney's Office to collect these data according to a set timeline. Although submitting this semi-annual report to Michigan State University (Research Technical Assistance Partner for PSN) was a requirement of the federal grant, the more important use of these data was in creating a local feedback loop whereby data and trends remained at the forefront of PSN planning and evaluation.

It was critical to local community and law enforcement partners that extant research and state-level crime analyses were regularly infused into local discussion, planning, and strategic problem solving. Therefore, the research team often distilled crime trend data and disseminated the most important observations back to PSN task forces, community groups, and other interested parties in the form of fact sheets or research briefs. For example, the research team worked in collaboration with the Middle District Outreach Partner (responsible for heightening community awareness of PSN) to provide one-page violent crime summaries for each target city. The summaries were then included in customized presentation packets that the Outreach Partner provided to local speakers' bureaus and PSN task forces. As representatives went out to make community presentations and requested volunteers, they were citing the most currently available crime data for their local community.

Table 10.2 Middle District research partner efforts and description

Research effort	Description
Overall, cross-city data collection	Data were collected and compiled onto the Semi-Annual Researcher Reporting Form, which includes major categories such as crime measures, arrests and seizures, and local and federal prosecution outputs
Initiating crime incident review processes	To derive timely and operationally meaningful descriptions of gun violence in target cities, crime incident review processes were initiated in the cities of Salisbury, Durham, Greensboro, and Winston-Salem and the counties of Alamance, Cabarrus, and Orange
Evaluation/consultation on existing and new crime reduction strategies	Once localities have defined their gun violence problem, the research team provided assistance in selecting and evaluating strategic interventions
City-specific or event-specific research questions	To be responsive to the need of local communities for tailored data or responses to specific questions, the research team engaged in "mini-projects" to address local questions

Crime Incident Review Process

From the outset of the research team's involvement in Middle District PSN efforts, there has been a clear need to use crime incident reviews as a tool to develop operationally meaningful definitions of gun violence in each of the target communities. Crime incident reviews bring all participants in a local criminal justice system together, from local agencies such as police, prosecutors, probation, and parole, to federal agencies such as the DEA, FBI, ATF, and U.S. Attorneys' Offices, in a review of recent cases for the dual purposes of (1) gaining new information and insight into crime trends within a community and (2) facilitating communication between criminal justice agencies (Klofas and Delaney, 2002). The crime incident review process compels each agency to share known information about incidents of crime including, but not limited to: information concerning the suspect and victim; previous arrest and conviction histories; gang affiliation; friends and acquaintances; and current probationary status. For a typical review, the research team would assist with and/or coordinate (1) a survey of police and probation/parole officers of the most violent offenders and most violent locations, (2) a review of trend data on focus offenses, (3) a review of victim and offender demographic profiles for focus offenses, and (4) an actual review of crime incidents. A final deliverable was a summary report of the major themes, observations, and conclusions from the crime incident review process (Cureton et al., 2004; Harvey and Frabutt, 2004; Di Luca, 2007; Di Luca and Sellers, 2008).

The research team's involvement in the crime incident review process can be viewed as both an applied research endeavor and a capacity-building activity. Providing conceptual, research, and organizational support for crime incident review efforts allowed each jurisdiction to conduct locally specific analyses of their gun problems, and also embrace a systematic and problem-focused approach to violent crime prevention. As a result of bringing multiple law enforcement and judicial agencies together in a collaborative atmosphere, the range of intra-system information shared was broadened. A format and structure for collaborative problem solving was modeled. As the research partner role was time-limited in nature, one objective throughout crime incident reviews was to provide the framework for a successful review, assist as needed, and provide analysis and feedback. The ultimate goal, and true test of the sustainability of problem-solving methods, was to empower and enable criminal justice partners to work strategically and systematically well beyond the direct involvement of the research partner through PSN.

Evaluation/Consultation on Existing and New Crime Reduction Strategies

The third domain to which the research team directed its efforts centers on assessing and modifying strategic interventions based on empirical data. The research team provided assistance in selecting and evaluating strategic interventions once target cities have defined their gun violence problem. In Greensboro, as in other cities across the Middle District, notification sessions with violent offenders have been a critical component of the overall crime reduction strategy. The notification strategy itself is a widely used problem-oriented policing strategy adopted from the Boston Ceasefire project (Braga et al., 2001; Kennedy et al., 2001) and is specifically designed to prevent recidivism among violent offenders. Featuring a bilateral technique that depends upon both law enforcement and community members for its success, repeat violent offenders are invited to a meeting to receive a unified message that violence will no longer be tolerated in their community. Law enforcement "notifies" offenders of the consequences they will incur should they choose to continue their involvement in gun crime and violence in the community, and that they will be prosecuted to the fullest extent of state or federal law, depending upon which statute carries the more stringent penalty for violation. Community members deliver a warmer version of the message and offer assistance to offenders who choose to desist from further criminal involvement. A third component of the strategy involves resource delivery: needs assessments are conducted with each willing offender, with a strong emphasis on educational background, employment skills, and substance abuse treatment. Interested offenders are directed to job skills workshops and GED testing as a means to make lasting, positive lifestyle changes.

Although notification sessions in Greensboro had been occurring for over five years, the Greensboro Community Violent Crime Task Group (GCVCTG) was committed to raising the profile of this program and decided to increase local elected officials' awareness of the program's intent, components, and overall effectiveness. The research partner team collaborated with the co-chairs of the GCVCTG to produce for City Council a brief presentation on the comprehensive strategy and a summary handout of the efficacy of the notification sessions across the District.

Most recently, the research partner team has worked with the Durham Police Department to evaluate its offender re-entry notification program, STARS (Strategies To Abate and Reduce Senseless Violence). This process incorporates the notification strategy, calling upon law enforcement officials and community members to develop a lasting partnership devoted to violence reduction in their community. Data for the STARS analyses were provided by the Durham Police Department, consisting of offender demographics, call-in session attended, and an offense history for each offender who had attended a session within the past two years. Overall program effectiveness was examined, yielding positive results. Specifically, the rate of weapon offenses per month was reduced by 57 per-

cent in addition to a 75 percent reduction in the rate of violent offenses per month, a 33 percent decrease in the rate of drug offenses per month, and a reduction of 40 percent in the rate of crimes against persons (Gathings and Frabutt, 2005). In another analysis of the STARS program, a sub-sample of data for notification participants was selected to explore the program's impact on offenders over time. Data indicated that most recidivism occurs within the two years following program participation, with a sharp decline in re-offending three years after notification attendance (Gathings and Frabutt, 2006). Based on these results, the research team provided expertise on sustaining program efficacy over time.

Another example of impacting practice through strategic use of data occurred through a roundtable format hosted by the research team. Via roundtables, the research team has a platform for infusing research into local practice across the District through information dissemination, best practice sharing, and strategy development. Through both formal (e.g., Middle District advisory team meetings) and informal networks, PSN partners identify topics that are of interest or concern in their communities and forward these as potential roundtable topics. To date, the research team has convened for roundtables discussing the issues of youth and violence, re-entry, and crime analysis. In this role, the research team brings national- and state-level research to the fore to paint a broad picture of what is known about the topic, as well as local-level research to better inform partners in their strategy building processes. The roundtable forum brings researchers and front-line practitioners together to engage in dialogue that promotes strategy development and the sharing of information and best practices across the District. Independent of the training and research partners, Project Safe Cabarrus successfully convened a law enforcement roundtable focused on gang-related issues; this is an example of the sustainable impact of research and training efforts being incorporated into PSN efforts at the site level.

Of particular interest, the crime analysis roundtables have provided a unique and valuable forum for building strong foundations to strategic violence reduction. Working with more than 20 police and sheriff's departments, it is clear that the data sets of one agency differ from those of another. This is largely owing to variations in incident reporting processes, coding, database and record management systems, sophistication of software, personnel dedication, and a multitude of other factors. Understanding that sound data provide the baseline for fairness in PSN strategy building, the Middle District partners committed to identifying crime analysis roundtables as a priority. These roundtables are convened to promote information sharing and best practices and also to shepherd new PSN site crime analysts into understanding the value of their work and of leveraging peer support and mentoring.

City-Specific or Event-Specific Research Questions

As PSN was implemented and brought to scale across the target cities of the Middle District, there were occasions in which a city had a particular need that research and problem-solving methodologies could address. Law enforcement and/or community groups had begun to define the problem of interest, or the research questions themselves, and the research team worked collaboratively to refine (and sometimes narrow) the scope of the inquiry and provide appropriate support, data collection, and analyses. The research team has been committed to maintaining flexibility and providing support to address these issues as they arose. The West End and Daniel Brooks Initiatives in High Point and the New Hope Initiative in Winston-Salem provide such examples.

The research team collaborated with David Kennedy of the John Jay College of Criminal Justice, High Point Police Department, and the Winston-Salem Police Department to conduct preliminary inquiries into the development, implementation, and impact of the strategy in three neighborhood sites (Frabutt et al., 2004; Harvey, 2005a; Sumner et al., 2005). A derivative of the notification program, the West End Initiative in High Point is a novel police- and community-driven strategy to address illicit drug dealing in street-level, open-air markets. The strategy uses crime-mapping information to target drug dealers, drug suppliers, and street-level drug sales that impact community safety in a clearly defined neighborhood. Building on a statistical and mapping foundation, extensive intelligence is gathered on both networks of individuals involved in the local drug market and individual patterns of criminal behavior. Evidence is compiled against the identified offenders, including surveillance information and undercover buys. A community-driven component of the strategy includes contacting those individuals identified as "significant others" within the offenders' lives. The offenders are invited to attend a notification session, where they are offered assistance and resources to make a change in their lifestyles. If offenders choose to participate in the program, which places heavy emphasis on attaining employment and substance abuse counseling, arrests and charges that could have otherwise been made are not acted upon.

Pre- and post-intervention crime data were collected and semi-structured interviews were conducted with law enforcement officers and community members to assess the initiative's impact. Drug and violent crimes declined immediately after the notification. Burglary, drug sales, assault, and robbery (by knife or strong-arm) all declined after the notification. Before the notification, these four crimes accounted for two-thirds of the total number of crimes; after the notification they accounted for less than one-fifth of the crimes. Based on the success of the West

End Initiative, the project was expanded to include an additional intervention site within the city of High Point, the Daniel Brooks neighborhood.

As before, the research partner team logged the processes, activities, and outcomes associated with the initiative (Frabutt et al., 2006). In addition to collecting pre–post intervention crime data in the Daniel Brooks neighborhood to measure program effectiveness, the research team developed an interview protocol to assess residents' perceptions of community safety and quality of life in the Daniel Brooks neighborhood. Semistructured interviews were conducted with nine neighborhood residents before and after the neighborhood notification. Before inception of the initiative, virtually all respondents believed that there was too much drug and alcohol use in Daniel Brooks. They indicated repeatedly that drug use and drug trafficking were significant challenges for the neighborhood, and they also noted that drug deals similarly occurred out of homes and on the open-air streets. One resident even "saw guys out on the playground selling drugs." These observations were strongly corroborated by police surveillance, intelligence gathering, and undercover drug operations in the Daniel Brooks area, which had identified several drug houses.

Residents were re-interviewed following the notification of neighborhood drug dealers. Responses indicated reductions in criminal activity and improvements in quality of life: approximately one-third of residents reported that there continued to be too much crime in the neighborhood and two-thirds of respondents reported that drug use continued to be a problem for their community. Six out of nine (67 percent) respondents reported that their lives had improved since the notification session and, although most respondents disagreed that people watch out for each other within the community, more respondents reported trusting the people in their neighborhood subsequent to the inception of the initiative.

The consistent application of a partnership-driven, action research approach to crime issues has contributed to a paradigm shift in how community safety is conceptualized in the District. In 2007, the High Point Police Department was awarded Harvard University's Ash Institute for Democratic Governance and Innovations in American Government Award, which the chief of police dedicated to their community contingent, the High Point Community Against Violence. This citizen-led entity has been working in concert to support focused deterrence efforts in the city for over ten years. Further, to institutionalize the PSN strategic framework approaches to crime reduction, the High Point Police Department was reorganized with the goals of making sure that each officer has a role to play in focused deterrence strategies and of routinely and effectively "doing business" according to their focused deterrence model. Specifically, this reorganization (1) synergizes the efforts of all divisions to work smarter toward identifying the nexus between violent crime and guns, gangs, drugs, and locales, (2) institutionalizes data-driven processes (e.g., case reviews and responses to violent acts), and (3) involves street-level investigators in an overarching deterrence and prevention framework.

In another recent example, the High Point Police Department identified group dynamics as the drivers of spikes in armed robberies. Their response to this pattern involved several strategies including the delivery of a tailored notification message to leaders of these groups. The department continues to identify the current root problem through research and data analysis and respond with focused deterrence strategies.

REFLECTIONS ON KEY INGREDIENTS FOR SUCCESSFUL RESEARCH PARTNERSHIPS

Communication

Establishing clear, open, and readily accessible lines of communication is key to any university–community partnership and the PSN effort has been no exception (Ebata, 1996; Frabutt, 2003; Mattesich and Monsey, 1992). A few mechanisms were built into the action research process in the Middle District to foster optimal communication. First, there was frequent contact (e-mail, face-to-face, and phone) with the PSN Coordinator (an Assistant U.S. Attorney). These conversations could range from bigger picture issues (e.g., is it time to expand PSN to another city/area in our District?) to more immediate and practical issues (e.g., what percentage of homicides in Winston-Salem last year involved firearms?). Second, the Middle District has used a monthly, and more recently quarterly, meeting format to discuss PSN activities across the District. The research partner has a reserved time slot on each agenda to discuss ongoing and upcoming efforts. Much of the bi-directional discussion of new research directions (e.g., presentation of the research plan for the next quarter) and application of findings occur during these meetings. Through that feedback loop, relevant research and evaluation were seamlessly integrated into our violence reduction efforts as a whole.

Research is Valued and Supported

The inclusion of federal support for research partners and crime analysts from the initiation of PSN delivered a strong message about the value, need, and usefulness of strategic, action-oriented research. Despite that emphasis from the federal level, some PSN sites have experienced challenges in positioning the research component as a central part of gun violence reduction efforts. In the Middle Disrict, one essential element of our productivity and focus is a clear message—expressed from various levels—that the research partner efforts are valued and supported. Obviously one of the most important elements of that dynamic has been the direct support and engagement of the Middle District U.S. Attorney (Honorable Anna Mills Wagoner) and the Assistant U.S. Attorney and PSN Coordinator (Robert A. J. Lang). In advisory team meetings, planning sessions, and simple informal encounters, they have upheld the vision of a problem-solving approach, a vision that embraces and builds on the efforts of an engaged research partner. Beyond support from the U.S. Attorney's Office, community-level support from local task forces and violence reduction groups has been palpable. For example, communities especially value the multi-site (and sometimes regional and national) perspective that the research partner can provide. The research partner is well positioned to convey cross-site best practices and other experiences (both positive and negative). The vantage point of the research partner captures an overview of strategies and programs across multiple sites. That knowledge can be shared with sites—both existing and emerging—so that strategies can be customized, adapted, or developed anew to address the local crime problem (Lang et al., 2004).

Further, the objective positioning of the university research partner has been of critical importance in PSN partnership development, particularly in countywide sites. With multiple police departments and sheriff's departments working together and sharing their data, the outside partner can diffuse territorialism if it exists and can also assist departments with improving their data collection, analysis, and related efforts without "shaming" or exposing the weaknesses of any one department in these process areas. The outside researcher voice also brings credibility to the data analysis and reporting that is palatable for all participating law enforcement agencies. A supporting message delivered by the U.S. Attorney's Office is that the data and the driving violent dynamic "is what it is," and agencies must acknowledge what the problems are and commit to seeking resolutions with their community partners.

Multiple Outlets and Formats for Dissemination

Producing high-quality and timely research products represents only part of the equation for a successful research partnership. Another critical factor that contributes to success is the translation and dissemination of findings, observations, and conclusions through multiple outlets and formats. The research partner has used reporting methodologies such as brief reports, fact sheets, and oral presentations of key data. Reporting time frames have been negotiated as part of the collaborative process so that research and data are provided in a manner that is both timely and of optimal usefulness to the PSN task force and/or each target city's PSN task force. For example, research reports may be summaries of data that our local team have collected and analyzed, such as a qualitative analysis of the Zero Armed Perpetrators Program (Harvey, 2005b). Alternatively, the research team produces multiple research briefs and data summaries of relevant and current articles from fields such as criminology, adolescent development, and prevention science. These have ranged from an analysis of statewide gang trends (Hayes, 2005) to the factors that lead to effective after-school programming (Gottfredson et al., 2004). A citation is provided for each reviewed publication so that the reader will be able to retrieve the original document for further examination. Fact sheets and research briefs are dispersed through a Middle District listserve, posted on our Center's website, have appeared in the U.S. Attorney's Office newsletter, and are passed out in hard copy form

in local violent crime task force meetings. In addition to fact sheets and research briefs, the research partner has also distributed a PSN Resource Coordinator database to each target city to assist in standardized data collection and management. The database was available online and instructions for its downloading and use were electronically mailed to each Resource Coordinator. The research team worked on a personal basis with each Coordinator to ensure their ability to utilize this tool.

Breadth versus Depth

One major challenge of the PSN research partnership has been finding the appropriate balance of extending finite, limited resources to a broad target area. It is challenging to decide where and how to focus (i.e., what projects and in which cities). Moreover, multiple target cities and intervention sites often translated into a full schedule of meetings—PSN advisory, local violence reduction groups, and community and law enforcement subcommittees. Attendance at these is sometimes critical to maintaining a District-wide overview.

The PSN advisory team meeting and the individual meetings with the PSN Coordinator have been the appropriate forum to develop and prioritize the research plan. Essentially, this was a research triage of sorts: Durham really needs to be engaged in the crime incident review process over the next two months, then try to focus on the roll-out of the street-drug initiative in Winston-Salem, and after that observe and describe the juvenile notification in Salisbury. From a research point of view, breadth of coverage should not come to replace depth of research insight (Lang et al., 2004). The best course was to select research questions, identify data sets, and highlight findings that have the potential to inform policy and practice not only in the selected site but also in other target sites as well. For example, the research team devoted research resources to the process evaluation of High Point and Winston-Salem's street-drug strategy, with the hope that the model will ultimately be applicable for other cities.

CONCLUSION

Learning to apply problem-solving methods to violence reduction has been a varied process within each target city. In fact, it is probably more accurate to say that learning to apply problem-solving methods has been a developmental process: some cities are far along in grasping the concept and others are at earlier stages of understanding. From the research partner perspective, the goal is to assess and meet them where they are and try to them move them further along the continuum.

NOTE

1 The Center for Youth, Family, and Community Partnerships builds the capacity of families, service providers, researchers, teachers, and communities to ensure the health and well-being of children, bridging research, policy, and practice. The primary purpose of the Center is to partner with key stakeholders from the community and the University to carry out basic, applied, and action research; infuse community perspectives into university research and teaching; translate research into effective programs and practice; and facilitate quality programs, practices, and policies that yield positive outcomes for children and their families.

CHAPTER 11

The Participation of Academics in the Criminal Justice Working Group Process

Anthony A. Braga and Marianne Hinkle

In recent years, the demand for the participation of academic researchers in criminal justice working groups has increased as practitioners have recognized the importance of strategic information products in developing effective crime prevention interventions. Academics can be very helpful to criminal justice practitioners by conducting research on urban crime problems to better focus limited enforcement, intervention, and prevention resources on high-risk offenders, victims, and places. Strategic crime prevention initiatives based on research insights have been associated with a 60 percent reduction in youth homicide in Boston (Braga et al., 2001) and a 40 percent reduction in total homicide in Indianapolis (McGarrell and Chermak, 2003b). These success stories have made academic researchers an important part of new crime prevention initiatives. For example, the U.S. Department of Justice-sponsored Project Safe Neighborhoods initiative provides each of the 93 U.S. Attorneys' Districts[1] in the United States with funds to hire academic research partners to help understand and address serious gun violence problems in local jurisdictions.

These new crime prevention initiatives will move some academics out of the "ivory tower" and into a collaborative working group setting for the first time. Some academic research partners will be experienced in collaborating with criminal justice practitioners in working group settings. Many will

not. Unfortunately, past partnerships between academics and criminal justice practitioners have been characterized by role conflicts, such as researchers reporting the "bad news" that an evaluated program was not effective in preventing crime. For academic researchers, success or failure matters less than their commitment to the development of knowledge on what does or does not work in preventing crime (Weisburd, 1994). For criminal justice practitioners, this news could be interpreted as their personal failure, and the skepticism of academics may be viewed as irritating (Weisburd, 1994). Traditional research and evaluation roles played by academics, often involving data collection and analysis *after* programs have been developed, can also be viewed by practitioners as not particularly helpful in their efforts to do a better job in preventing crime. In this new wave of collaborations, the academic researcher is a partner who works with the group toward an end. The academic is not a critic who focuses on past mistakes and ineffective practices or a miracle worker who will solve crime problems by developing magic bullets.

This chapter is based on our practical experiences working in criminal justice working group settings. Over the past ten years, we have worked together on a series of strategic crime prevention initiatives, including Boston's Operation Ceasefire program and, currently, as partners in Project Safe Neighborhoods in the District of Massachusetts. The first part of this chapter presents ten observations on being an effective research partner made by Marianne Hinkle at a 2003 U.S. National Institute of Justice action research workshop. The second part of the chapter presents three discussion points intended to clarify the performance of an academic in a criminal justice working group made by Anthony Braga at the same workshop. Although we share similar views on how academics should function within a criminal justice working group and our insights overlap on certain key points, our thoughts developed from very different knowledge bases and concerns. Nonetheless, our perspectives are complementary and, taken together, can serve as a basic set of guiding principles for prospective research partners who are seeking to collaborate with criminal justice practitioners in a working group setting.

A PRACTIONER'S PERSPECTIVE ON AN EFFECTIVE RESEARCH PARTNER

An effective academic research partner needs to be sensitive to a variety of issues that will evolve over the course of working group meetings. There are obviously certain issues that are more important during the early phases of a partnership than in the later phases and vice versa. In this discussion, ten observations on how to be an effective research partner to criminal justice practitioners are placed in the time period in which they seem to be most important.

When the Partnership is Starting

1 *Listen first, then talk.* The front-line practitioners that staff a criminal justice working group usually have important insights on the nature of crime problems and a solid understanding of the benefits and limitations of their existing responses to crime problems. It is important to let your partners speak about their experi-

ences and share their ideas before you start asking questions and making suggestions. You will learn much from simply letting them talk and you will be better positioned to conduct research that will be supported by the group. It is crucial to make practitioners feel that their experiences are respected (as they should be) and that they have a real stake in the working group (as they must).

2 *Start where we are, not where you are.* For many practitioners, being part of a working group that engages a problem-solving process is an entirely new experience. Line-level law enforcement officials do not often get the opportunity to think strategically about addressing crime problems. We usually are responding to crises and moving rapidly from incident to incident. Although some will be familiar with the problem-oriented policing philosophy, others will not. You will need to take the time to walk us through problem identification, problem analysis, response development, and impact assessment.

3 *Help us stop and think.* Law enforcement officials are very action oriented. We manage our time by reacting to incidents and we are used to doing this without sufficient time, personnel, or money to do things the way we would like to. Police have to respond to crimes, prosecutors have to plead and try cases. We rarely have the luxury of time to stop and think about the bigger picture that arises from these incidents. You will need to play an active role in slowing us down and changing our mindset from responding to incidents to dealing with problems.

4 *Understand our data phobia.* We will not be initially comfortable with data collection and analyses. Most practitioners have not had positive experiences using data. In fact, the data we have seen have either been irrelevant to the realities of our jobs or been used to criticize the work we are doing without providing us

with any real assistance to design methods to help us respond in a more effective fashion.

When the Partnership is Solidified

5 *Stay focused on the bottom line.* Law enforcement officials are accustomed to working in groups such as multi-jurisdictional task forces. The ultimate goals of these enterprises are usually to disrupt existing criminal networks or to better focus traditional tactics on emergent crime problems. The ends of these working groups are usually arrests and prosecutions. Our responsibilities have not traditionally included a focus on preventing crime by taking proactive steps. Therefore, we may fall back into an individual case focus while failing, from time to time, to see the larger picture. We may need to be gently and routinely reminded that our tactics need to produce a different set of results such as fewer homicides or reduced fear in the community. Researchers can help us focus on the bottom line of preventing crime instead of simply responding to crime.

6 *Think big, but also think small.* You should be encouraged to think creatively about ideal responses to crime problems and to help us do the same. It will take time to develop the capacities to better focus existing programs and to engage alternative approaches. As such, you will need to help us set interim goals to keep the group moving in the right direction. A series of small achievements will eventually lead to a large change in practice.

7 *Put something good in my hands.* Practitioners need to justify their ongoing participation in a working group and will need, at some point, to argue for additional resources or changes in existing practices. Our efforts will be much easier if we have timely research findings that can be used to back up our claims. Given this, you will need to provide us with easy-to-understand reports and policy briefs that document your research contributions to the working group.

8 *Find a buddy.* You should develop an informal, candid relationship with one of your practitioner partners. This person will help resolve existing and potential problems, help gain insights on personal and political relationships among individuals and agencies, and advise you on how your research is being used or not used by the rest of the group.

As the Partnership Winds Down

9 *Think about how to put yourself out of business.* The analytic frameworks and methodologies used to diagnose problems and develop responses should be passed on to your partners. While you are conducting your research, you should also be educating others and developing existing capacities within law enforcement organizations to continue the work once you have finished.

Always

10 *If we cannot trust you, you should go home.* Trust is essential. Many of the law enforcement personnel in the working group are putting their careers on the line because they think they can do their jobs better by engaging this process. We must be able to talk openly about any substantive issues that arise. If your goal is to simply expose flaws and criticize us rather than to help us deal with problems, we do not want to work with you. Also, if the implemented strategies are successful, please give credit where credit is due. Although the researcher will be the one authoring the reports and articles on the project, you must always remember and recognize that the people who make these

jointly conceived strategies work are the police officers who patrol at 3 A.M., the prosecutors who agree to be awakened for notifications several times during the night, and the community partners who risked their safety to work with us.

AN ACADEMIC'S PERSPECTIVE ON THE WORK OF A RESEARCH PARTNER

1. Know Your Role

The academic researcher brings the power of an outside eye, insights from criminological research, and the analytic ability to explore and test ideas with data. The academic is not functioning as a pseudo-investigator or law enforcement agent. The practitioners have a wealth of investigative knowledge and will not be looking to their academic partners to help apprehend offenders or solve open cases. Rather, the academics' key contribution is in the description of crime problems in a way that leads to the focusing of enforcement, intervention, and prevention resources on identifiable risks such as crime hot spots, high-activity offenders, and repeat victims. The framing of key ideas, research questions, and plausible interventions should be a collaborative process within the working group setting.

Researchers essentially provide "real-time social science" aimed at refining the inter-agency working group's understanding of crime problems, creating information products for both strategic and tactical use, testing—often in elementary, but important, fashion—prospective intervention ideas, and maintaining a focus on outcomes and the evaluation of performance. The research does not need to be very sophisticated methodologically. But the ability to pin down key issues—such as who is killing and being killed, the role played by gangs and gang conflicts, and the sources of illegal guns—keeps the working group moving on solid ground,

helps the participating agencies understand the logic of proposed interventions (and the illogic of at least some competing interventions), and helps justify the intervention to the public. Academics can also be helpful in focusing practitioners on the "bottom line" of crime prevention. Criminal justice practitioners tend to focus on their tactics (e.g., making quality investigations) without much broader consideration of how their actions affect crime levels (e.g., reduced homicides, gun assaults, and the like). Although holding offenders accountable and doing justice are important goals, the working group should stay focused on violence prevention. Examining crime trends and assessing the impact of implemented interventions can keep the working group moving forward on developing effective crime prevention practices.

An early experience in the Boston Gun Project's Operation Ceasefire working group provides an example of how an outside eye, armed with criminological knowledge of crime prevention mechanisms, can make a large difference in developing interventions. After creating an inventory of responses to gang violence in Boston, the practitioner members of the Operation Ceasefire working group did not fully realize the strategic importance of an earlier successful violence prevention campaign, known as Operation Scrap Iron, which was launched on a Cape Verdean gang on Wendover Street. In essence, the Scrap Iron intervention was an early application of the "pulling levers" focused deterrence strategy. From the perspective of outside observers, the research team recognized the significance of these seminal practices and worked with our practitioner partners to develop its routine application to outbreaks of violence in the city (Kennedy et al., 2001). Moreover, conveying the importance of the new approach from the line level to the top policy ranks in their respective organizations would have been difficult for the members of the working group. As outsiders, academics can help validate and explain the importance of new ideas. With our Boston partners, we helped articulate and advocate the developed strategy by making formal presentations with our line-level partners to the agency managers.

2. Listen and Value

Some of the best insights on crime problems come from line-level practitioners who deal with offenders and community on a daily basis. Practitioners who are close to crime problems often have important experiential knowledge on the nature of offending and interesting ideas on plausible interventions. Academic researchers need to structure this qualitative knowledge, incorporate these hypotheses into their problem analysis research, and examine these ideas by using available quantitative knowledge. In Boston, our practitioner partners had very clear views on the nature of youth violence. They believed that the violence was highly concentrated among a small number of gang-involved, high-activity offenders who were well known to the criminal justice system (Kennedy et al., 1996). We set up our research tasks to test these ideas and found that our practitioner partners were generally right about youth gun violence in Boston. The resulting research description, although not news to the members of the working group who were on the front lines, was important in documenting the basic facts so that interventions could be developed and tailored to the nature of the problem. The research documentation was also invaluable in spreading these ideas outside the working group and garnering support from the participating criminal justice organizations and community groups.

Close research on crime problems may also present important dimensions that were underestimated by or unknown to practitioners. For example, in Boston, practitioners strongly believed that youth often possessed semi-automatic pistols that were recently purchased in southern states along Interstate 95 (Virginia, North Carolina, South Carolina, Georgia, and Florida). Our analysis of Bureau of Alcohol, Tobacco, Firearms and Explosives (ATF) firearms trace data associated with recovered youth crime guns revealed that this view was correct. However, the trace analysis also revealed that youth were also very likely to possess semi-automatic pistols that were first purchased in Massachusetts. In fact, the percentage of youth guns that were first purchased in Massachusetts was larger than the sum of all youth guns first purchased in southern states. Although the practitioners in the working group knew that we did have a problem with instate illegal diversions of firearms from legitimate commerce, they did not realize that this problem was larger than the interstate trafficking problem. As a result of the trace analysis, the members of the working group started to focus on developing instate and interstate gun trafficking prevention strategies.

3. Guide Law Enforcement Efforts, Do Not Direct Them

Academics can shape law enforcement interventions in important ways, but should not be involved in selecting specific targets or investigating individuals. As a basic rule, none of the informational products produced by the academics should be specific enough to result in persons being arrested as a direct result of the data being presented. Indeed, funding from the National Institute of Justice (NIJ) specifically prohibits NIJ-funded researchers from engaging in direct law enforcement actions as part of their research agenda. Practitioners should draw their own conclusions about specific actions from the data presented. For example, one key information product in diagnosing gang violence problems is the creation of a sociogram of active and latent gang conflicts (see, e.g., Kennedy et al., 1997). Certain gangs will be much more central to conflict than other gangs. Some gangs will be actively engaged in violent disputes whereas other gangs will not be causing any violence problems at the moment. It is proper for the researcher to comment that law enforcement should focus their limited resources on the gangs that are most central to conflict and currently engaged in violence. The researcher should not recommend to the group that they should focus on Group A and Group B. The practitioners can appraise these situations for themselves and will happily make their own decisions on which groups will receive focused enforcement attention.

There will be other times when researchers will produce information products that could result in the investigation of specific individuals. For example, an analysis of ATF trace data could identify suspicious purchase and sales patterns by particular individuals at specific licensed gun dealers. It is important to present these patterns to the working group as a business matter that needs to be dealt with. However, the presentation should be masked in basic facts such as "ten licensed dealers generate 60 percent of the traces to our city" and any discussions of specific patterns in the data need to be masked with phony names instead of the real names of the individuals and businesses involved. The presentation should be accompanied by a complete and thorough description of the methods used to identify these interesting patterns so that the practitioners can replicate the process and make their own decisions about the law enforcement actions that they will take. In the long run, this type of arrangement is actually better than directly feeding your criminal justice partners with leads. As the old saying goes, "provide a man with a fish and he eats for a day, teach a man how to fish and he eats for a lifetime."

Academic researchers are sometimes hired directly by criminal justice agencies as consultants to work with their data with the expressed purpose of helping them to identify suspicious persons and behavioral patterns for closer law enforcement scrutiny. In these instances, the academic should work directly with a member of the organization who will serve as the actual analyst. The academic can do exploratory data mining and serve as a "data analysis coach" to the proper person who can launch an actual investigation. It is always best to teach a law enforcement agent how to analyze data and let them put together the investigation based on their own manipulations of the data. The academic should avoid engaging in activities that could result in a subpoena.

FINAL REMARKS TO ACADEMICS

The academic plays an important role in facilitating the criminal justice working group process. The personal rewards of engaging work that influences practice and prevents crime are substantial. Unfortunately, most universities place less emphasis on public service and more value on conducting sophisticated research studies that generate high-quality journal articles. For young scholars seeking tenure, the pressure to produce in a way that fits with well-established scholarly traditions may prevent some from engaging the criminal justice working group process. However, it is important to recognize that conducting problem-oriented research for a working group and conducting high-quality research that will stand up to peer review are not mutually exclusive enterprises. Basic problem analysis can be expanded to a more rigorous examination of larger criminological issues. Innovative crime prevention programs can be evaluated and, by virtue of academic participation in program development, research designs can be developed to examine important related issues such as crime displacement and diffusion of crime control benefits. Finally, the trust that is built between academics and the criminal justice practitioners they are serving can result in richer data being made available for new analyses.

The invitation to join in the working group process can thus be viewed as an important research opportunity that can forward one's career, rather than as a potential distraction.

NOTE

1 Mariana Islands and Guam were treated as task force.

CHAPTER 12

Collaborations between Police and Research/Academic Organizations: Some Prescriptions from the Field

Jack R. Greene

The only source of knowledge is experience.

Things should be made as simple as possible, but not any simpler.

(Albert Einstein)

INTRODUCTION

In contrasting these two quotes from Albert Einstein the complexity of research in police and other governmental agency settings is highlighted. On the one hand police executives value real-world experience that confirms their "ordinary knowledge" (Lindblom and Cohen, 1979) and validates institutional assumptions about what works. On the other hand academic researchers must describe with clarity how things work theoretically and empirically, a process rooted in abstraction, ambiguity, and complexity.

The trick, of course, is merging both perspectives so that the agency can abstract from its experience a better understanding of the impact of its policies, procedures, and actions on the community at large based on concepts and methods that have validity and scientific rigor. This requires not only the use of a full range of techniques for conducting social science research in field settings, but also the "sociological imagination" (Mills, 1959) for such inquiry. For, as Einstein also said, "If we knew what it was we were doing it would not be called research, would it?"

This chapter briefly considers action research as it is applied to the study of police policies, programs, and practices, as well as a range of considerations that facilitate and/or inhibit such research. The focus here is on the need for successful research collaboration between those in the police and those in academic worlds. Without such collaboration, assessments of police policies, programs, and practices will likely be quite shallow. The danger is that they will be detached from what the police actually do, and thus be void of explanations for, or prediction of, police actions.

OBSTACLES TO CONDUCTING ACTION RESEARCH IN POLICE AGENCIES

Agency-based research in policing is often complicated by several interacting issues. Some of these issues are related to police agencies, particularly the receptivity of the research setting, whereas others are connected to problems in the research community, particularly the ability of social science to inform policy. We will first consider setting problems, followed by those of science.

Historically and even currently police agencies have been skittish about being assessed, most especially when those external to the agency conduct such assessments. Police agency assessments have often come on the heels of a scandal or an accusation of improper police behavior (see Sherman, 1978; Walker, 1977), or they are seen as the result of "local politics." After all, police services are in their final analysis political services—where to deploy, where to prevent, and where to arrest—each having political implications. The fear of the police is that those studying them often overlook the political stakes inherently reflected in many academic analyses.

The police, seeing themselves as perpetually marked as both ineffective and inefficient, often view external assessments as politically motivated and most likely negative in outcome. The cycle of "scandal and reform" and the general link between police chief tenure and the election cycle is well known in police chief circles (see Andrews, 1985). So, in important ways, the police view external assessment from a skeptical and suspicious vantage point, reflecting the cultural attributes of police work (Skolnick, 1966).

Such a view of external assessment more often than not produces wariness on the part of many police executives to become involved in such efforts. In the absence of a level introspection and trust between police policy makers and academics who would provide assessment, such wariness appears to be well founded, at least to the police. The general wariness of police agencies to external assessment remains a major obstacle to their systematic review. Nonetheless, police agencies are also continually stressed to demonstrate their effectiveness. Local governments and the community at large have increased pressure on all governmental functions, including the police, to demonstrate their "value for money," that is, what they produce that positively impacts community quality of life—that the benefits justify the costs (Sunstein, 2002). The tension between the need to establish organizational and policy effectiveness and the "political" consequences of such inquiry no doubt keeps many police executives up at night.

A second factor often negatively affecting police agency/research partnerships rests on the notion that policing has not yet become evidence-based (see Sherman et. al., 1997; National Research Council, 2004); rather, much of police practice continues to rely on the craft norms of the occupation illustrated by anecdotal evidence. The police remain an institution considerably shaped by traditions and institutional myths (Crank and Langworthy, 1992), including the myths that they continue to perpetuate and those tightly held by the populace.

Difficulty in measuring outcomes directly related to police efforts is further complicated because it has often been analytically difficult to separate the effects of the police from those of other social institutions on matters of crime and public safety (see Alpert and Moore, 1993). Many institutions impact public safety. Public education, health, social services, and even environmental infrastructure contribute to or detract from public safety. Effectively determining the differential impacts of these other institutions makes assessment of the police difficult. Consequently, the difficulty in establishing research partnerships lies both in the non-empirical nature of policing, and in the real limits of social science to disentangle the special impacts of the police on the public, as distinct from other public and private agency impacts occurring in the same time and space.

A third limit to effective collaboration is related to police agencies often lacking the resources and focus to adequately muster effective assessments, although such capacities are improving. The old adage that police agencies keep "records not data" supports the notion that much of the information capability of the police is not analytically rooted; nor is it easily made into an analytic tool (for an assessment of police data and its use see Maguire and Uchida, 2000).

Although the police have dramatically increased their use of computer mapping and spatial analysis to improve tactical and strategic interventions (see Weisburd et al., 2003), linking other police information systems such as records management system (RMS) and computer-aided dispatch (CAD), as well as investigative and intelligence systems, remains problematic. Moreover, linking the impact on public safety of its co-producers (e.g., schools, families, communities, economic institutions, private security and the like) is also a tedious and not well-grounded set of conceptual, methodological, or analytic propositions.

Lacking the internal capacity for effective assessment and often suspicious about those external to the agency, police agencies have shied from building longer-term effective liaisons with knowledgeable externals who might support their analytic needs. Moreover, some police agencies have felt "burned" by external assessors who ultimately challenged the effectiveness, efficiency, or legality of police actions in public settings based on the analysis conducted. It might be concluded that at best the relationship between police agencies and external assessors is mixed; at worst it is contentious.

Impediments to effective police/research collaboration are not found solely within policing. The strain that often occurs between those in the academic community and those in the policing community relates to the authoritativeness and independence of each. Agencies seek an authoritative edge while maintaining control over the independence of the investigation, whereas investigators also seek authoritative independence (see Lindblom and Cohen, 1979). For example, police agencies might want to know about the effectiveness of a particular strategy, but might be less willing to let researchers impose "experimental conditions" on the assessment, as such practices invariably shift authority and independence from the agency to the researcher. Such strain in the role and oversight process for agency-based research has often precluded or terminated such relationships.

Conflicts in building collaborations can also be linked to both the over- and the under-reach of social science in providing timely and useful information to the policy-making process. Much of what masquerades as "policy research" can be questioned as to its scientific integrity, thus providing "misleading evidence to evidence-led policy" (see Sherman, 2003). Here the concern is with how social science inquiry has been brought to bear on questions of policy. In many instances the scientific credibility of such evidence has been "oversold," leading to frustration on the part of policy makers to either use or discard the information provided. Problems associated with questionable scientific evidence in justice policy include the level of rigor in the use of scientific methods, researcher bias, and the "heavy hand" of research funders (see Austin, 2003). Each contributes to a degradation of the research findings and adds some suspicion as to whether they can or should direct policy.

ACTION RESEARCH IN POLICE AGENCIES

In many ways action research in police organizations is predicated on gaining and maintaining access to the agency's formal records, personnel, and informal culture, while at the same time providing the agency with usable and timely information to assess policy or program outputs or effects. Access as used here refers to the acceptance of the research project under way and the researchers involved. In the absence of such access, research—even if conducted—will be largely disconnected from the agency, its personnel, practices, and policies. The reams of unexamined, discounted, and criticized "external reports" that often line the bookcases of police chiefs attest to the need for access in the broadest sense of the term and for a closer connection between researcher and police agency. Simply put, research needs to be imbedded in police agencies, not marginally aligned with these agencies, as is currently the case.

But access is not enough if action research is to be successful. To be effective, action research projects within police agencies require the development of a collaborative environment within which police policy and decision makers and researchers can interact. Such an environment ultimately shapes access to the agency, sets research objectives, refines instrumentation, and conditions and reviews research findings (Sherman, 1998). When such a process is in place the research is likely to be viewed as successful.

BUILDING EFFECTIVE RESEARCH COLLABORATIONS

Effective collaborations are an essential ingredient in furthering police action research projects. In general terms they are the result of five intersecting factors: (1) common or overlapping interest, (2) trust through ongoing and sustained relationships, (3) appreciation of the analytic and policy issues to be addressed, (4) timeliness in approach and execution and (5) transparency in the process and in reviewing the findings. Such conditions are necessary to sustain access to police agencies and to produce information that is scientifically credible and actionable by the agency.

Access to police agencies is first built on a common interest or concern that gives rise to the collaboration. Like human relationships, those that last longest are built on some initial, and then sustained, commonality. The relationships cannot be arranged, or forced, although at times they are. Such "arranged marriages" often fail the initial test of common ground. Moreover, such common ground is not often the product of "contractual obligation." That is to say, although it appears rational to assume that one could reduce the research process to writing,

thereby establishing the "common ground," rarely do such "prenuptials" actually work. Legislating relationships between researcher and agency is likely to produce a lot of effort and little effect.

In addition to some common understanding of the nature of a problem or its need for resolution, effective collaborations require that each party earn the trust of the other. Trust is a tricky issue, for it means not that each party is a willing participant to the misdeeds or errors of the other, but rather that within the confines of the relationship each party believes that the other will be straightforward and direct. Such trust opens the parties to several important dimensions of the collaboration.

First, trust provides a currency for the exchange and discussion of information. That is to say, trust provides a level of comfort in the sharing of information, some of which may be sensitive, but nonetheless necessary to understand the nature of the problem confronted. Agencies trust that the researcher will be sensitive to the political pressures that the agency faces, and researchers trust that the agency will provide accurate and appropriate information and access in the inquiry at hand.

This trust relationship can become asymmetric when, for example, the agency "controls" access, or when the researcher publishes the results of the study without proper agency discussion. And both the agency and the researcher can adopt roles that ultimately defeat the trust proposition, such as when the agency seeks to co-opt the researcher, or when the researcher "goes native." Neither of these roles supports the necessary dimension of trust in the collaboration.

When trust is established, access to agency records, interpretations, and contexts is more likely. Such access helps shape the collection of data and its analysis. Without such trust researchers may find it difficult to actually gain access to important information, finding their efforts marginalized within the agency. And, of course, marginalized access produces marginalized results.

Second, trust is continually affected by the nature of the relationship between the researcher and the agency over time. Again similar to human relationships, trust is initially earned through what is perceived to be positive interaction at first and then on an ongoing basis. It is when the "honeymoon" is over that the test of the collaboration becomes most apparent.

In fact, in the world of action research within police agencies, maintaining access (continuing to work within a trustful context) may be more difficult than establishing initial access (the premise of trust). This suggests that both the agency and the researcher continually review the nature and quality of their relationship with each other, particularly as it relates to trust.

One issue in establishing a context of trust is normative sponsorship for the problem to be addressed by the agency and the researcher. Whereas researchers may be interested in testing theory or refining methodology, agencies are interested in obtaining information that addresses their problems, typically their immediate problems. Although each perspective is not necessarily mutually exclusive, part of the relationship and trust building in action research collaborations is centered on establishing common sponsorship of the problem to be addressed, and often the methods by which information will be obtained. Once such trust is established the nature of the problem investigated or the methods used can typically be broadened and made more elaborate, both for the agency and for the researcher.

This is often difficult territory as it requires that the agency surrender some of its authority in defining the problem and in providing access to the researcher, while at the same time the researcher is challenged to design a strategy that is least obtrusive and most likely to produce intended results. In this sense the "authoritative independence" of those in the research community is challenged by agencies that have a stake in the definition of the problem and in the interpretation of the results.

Timeliness of the research process in agency-based action research is also an essential condition for maintaining agency access and for sustaining the relationship to a successful conclusion. Whereas researchers are often focused on long-term research questions, agencies are clearly constrained by the immediate. This, of course, creates a natural tension in the interactions of each with the other. Researchers need to be cognizant of the time constraints of the agency, while not succumbing to pressures for results that may not be fully analyzed. In establishing such relationships, agencies need to be brought through the research process as a participant, not solely as the object of the research. That is, when the agency has some participatory role in shaping the research and in conducting parts of the analysis, it is more likely that both the relationship and the results can be seen as useful to the agency. Such participation also helps to ensure that the agency is apprised of the question pursued, the analysis conducted, and the finding achieved. Moreover, when such agency participation occurs, the research can be said to be *of* not *at* the agency.

Finally, sustaining access and maintaining a productive relationship between agency and researcher is predicated on the transparency of the process. Setting schedules and timelines, shaping discussion of preliminary and final results, and access to information and personnel within the agency to achieve these ends must be visible elements of the collaboration. Both the agency and the researcher need to strive for the most transparency possible to assure each that the other is making an appropriate and timely contribution. Such transparency, of course, also reinforces (or fails to reinforce) trust in the collaboration.

STAGES IN RELATIONSHIP BUILDING

Building a coalition in support of agency-based action research often proceeds through several developmental stages. These stages initiate and ultimately affirm the relationships within the coalition, thus helping to bind the participants together, or they fail to do so, and the coalition dissipates.

It should be remembered that a coalition, unlike a unitary form of social organization, depends not on a central authority system to bind participants together, but rather on the satisfaction of the vested self-interest of participants. Coalitions, then, are sustained to the extent that they contribute to the satisfaction of member needs. In the logic of collective action, coalitions are dynamic, with participants granting a limited sovereignty to the coalition in exchange for the gratification of each participant's needs (Olsen, 1965; Kramer et al., 1996). Without such gratification the coalition typically collapses or reforms with other participants.

Four stages of coalition building are briefly considered here: courting, nurturing the relationship, celebrating successes and discussing failures, and periodically renewing commitments. Each stages builds on its predecessor, and each is serially linked, although the last two stages become iterative.

Courting in coalitional relationships means establishing some common ground upon which the coalition can be built. From the perspective of the researcher this may mean developing relationships with key agency personnel, participating in forums that draw practitioners and researchers together, or seeking referral to the focal agency from significant others. From the perspective of the agency this may mean identifying area research support and inviting its participation in agency discussions. At this stage of the process the long-term goals and activities of the coalition are likely unclear, as are the individual motivations. Like dating in social life, each participant is "sizing up" its partners, determining if there is the "spark" of common ground.

Following the initial courtship, such research coalitions often need to nurture and broaden the relationship, often by creating some demonstration activities and/ or projects, or by broadening the discussion between researcher and agency. Typically such efforts further develop the relationship, establish the foundation of trust necessary for larger efforts, and set the stage for an effective longer-term collaboration. It is generally at this stage that the formal collaboration begins. Of course the experience and reputation of the researcher and the agency can accelerate these initial processes considerably.

Celebrating successes, discussing failures, and periodically reviewing commitments are activities that ultimately enlarge and sustain the collaboration (or fail to do so). Here the focus is on interim communications, value testing, challenging individual and organization assumptions, providing feedback (even negative feedback), and learning from the ongoing relationship. Each of these activities contributes to strengthening participation in the coalition, affirming the normative commitment of the participants. Of course, failing these activities, such coalitions often quickly dissolve.

These last two aspects of effective coalitions are related to the idea of engagement. When both the researcher and the agency are actively engaged in the process, continued support for the venture is likely to occur.

EVALUATING RELATIONSHIPS

Researchers and their agency partners are continually in the process of evaluating the relationships that give rise to the coalition. As previously suggested, coalitions are dynamic, needing to satisfy the overall aims of the coalition and those of the individual participants. The ongoing assessment of the relationship is a necessary condition for the stability and life course of the coalition.

Several evaluative questions are either implicit or explicit in this assessment. They include: Are both parties being satisfied? Is the communications process open? Is the relationship capable of adapting to changing circumstances? How long will (or can) this relationship endure? Answers to these questions ultimately shape the ongoing relationship or end it.

Again, as with most human relationships, feedback and communication are the means of growth, development, and maturation. Without such processes relationships become stilted, and ultimately collapse.

CONCLUDING COMMENTS AND FINAL PRESCRIPTIONS

Undertaking research within an agency setting is complex, particularly when those conducting the research are not of the organization. By "of the organization" is meant persons steeped in the organization's context, culture, structure, and communications. Those external to these agencies must first develop an appreciation for the subtleties of organizational life and the impact of these subtleties on the production functions of the enterprise. Understanding the manner and customs of the police in general, and those that occur within any particular agency, is a necessary condition for working effectively within the focal agency.

Having said this, police agencies are not unique. They behave like many other agencies in both the public and the private sectors.

Our understanding of organizational behavior abstracted from other settings can indeed be helpful in making assessments within police agencies. This is particularly important for policing that has neither the empirical nor the research traditions of other organizations (see Maguire and Uchida, 2000).

Oftentimes police executives are convinced that their problems are unique or more precisely the result of local environmental circumstances that differ from most others. Those in the research community can be an important source of interpretation of and communication with the larger police research/practitioner worlds, and provide assistance in "framing" the local questions of agencies into the larger body of knowledge about policing. At the same time this should not be taken as an excuse for dismissing differences in local communities that in fact shape policing locally.

The test of course is to bring some imagination to the process, encouraging experimentation and "trial and error" (as constrained as it may be) to police research efforts. Such trail and error, and learning that occurs from both success and failure, can ultimately improve the relationships between the research community and police executives. Moreover, such relationships are more likely to be successful in producing usable knowledge for the next generation of police leaders, while at the same time producing the next generation of field-based researchers. For, as Einstein so accurately noted, "Anyone who has never made a mistake has never tried anything new."

CHAPTER 13

The Challenge of Timeliness and Utility in Research and Evaluation

Wesley G. Skogan

There was a time, perhaps until the end of the 1980s, when researchers could conduct their work in police departments and depart with a cheery, "Hope you buy the book!" But now practitioners in the criminal justice field have grown too sophisticated to buy into this model of research or evaluation model. Today, they want to know what is in it for them, during their term of office. At my first presentation to the command staff of the Chicago Police Department describing plans to evaluate their community policing initiative, a savvy district commander rose and made his fears clear: we would get in his way and take up his time, and a book would appear five years later telling everyone what he did wrong. He did not think this was a good idea. We agreed, but other models of researcher–practitioner partnerships are a lot of work, and risky. There were advantages to wearing white lab coats and insisting that we had to keep "hands off."

Now it is necessary for evaluators to forge two-way relationships with their agency partners. Evaluators need access and cooperation, and the agencies will demand some payback for that. They have expectations about how research and evaluation can help them. What police administrators expect is information that is timely and useful for them. This paper reflects on my experience in trying to meet these twin expectations, in projects evaluating policing programs of all kinds, including activities of undercover narcotics squads and department-wide reorganizations to carry out community policing. My message is that these are very difficult expectations to meet. Our practitioner partners may need to develop a fuller understanding of the many important steps involved in conducting quality research, and how these intersect with the very important criteria that the findings be timely and useful.

Timeliness. Timeliness is a difficult issue in research. Researchers have a commitment to being data driven and broadly representative. We cannot do "evaluation by walking around," or conclude anything reliable from anecdotes and one or two ride-alongs. Researchers need a lot of time to work through a series of steps that make up almost any study.

1 First, we may have to raise money to support data collection. Perhaps a project can be carried out using existing data, but in that case an outside research team might not be needed either. If an agency cannot answer its questions with the data it has, interviewers, field observers, coders, and data entry staff may need to be hired. The proposals must include careful reviews of the research literature, clearly stated hypotheses to be tested, and descriptions of the data to be collected. If the issue is important to an agency because it is "home grown" and a real problem for them, the timetable for the research may not correspond to any

federal or state funding cycle. The agencies may have to weigh in and help with fundraising for research, often a new role for them. Although there are a few funding sources that are willing to support action research with a local focus, most funders want to support projects that address issues of national importance, and they want the issues and the answers for them to be cast with sufficient generality that the findings will be applicable in many places. Funding considerations, therefore, usually shape the nature of the research that can be undertaken.

2   It can take time to clarify the issues being investigated. In program evaluation, researchers have to figure out what the program really is, and monitor what it becomes. The program usually is not what the press release or the grant application said it was going to be, and plans never roll out as expected. Good projects remain a moving target for some time, as the participants learn while doing. But a useful final report will include a careful description of what was actually carried out in the field, so process monitoring has to be more or less continuous. A good evaluation will also look more deeply at the issues being addressed. A thorough assessment will look beyond the formal plan (the "manifest" strategy) to identify the "latent" issues that are also being addressed. These usually are rooted in the fundamental political and economic problems of the city, and are well understood—if unstated—by those who know what is going on. The first job of an evaluator is to clarify the real problems being addressed and the strategy being implemented (probably in more than one way) and to develop mechanisms for monitoring the implementation over time.

3   Researchers then need time to design instruments and develop research designs that will fairly evaluate the program as

they have construed it. They need to field the strongest designs possible, and ensure that data collection is extensive enough to detect effects of the magnitude that the program is likely to produce. The research design is how the entire project is set up to make valid inferences about what causes what or what the impact of a program was. Research designs range from randomized trials to "quasi-experimental interrupted time series" and statistical studies, and getting them right is one of the most important contributions of the researcher partner in a collaborative project. It can also take time and money to develop adequately large data sets, and this cannot be shortchanged. One way to commit murder through evaluation is to collect samples of outcome data that are too small to reliably document a realistic program effect, and then pronounce the program a failure because the results are "insignificant." At this point, human subjects issues must be addressed as well. University Institutional Review Boards must process, review, and formally approve any research involving human subjects before the work can begin.

4   The research team needs time to collect representative data from broad samples. All of those interviewers, field observers, coders, and data entry clerks need to be hired and trained. A police study probably will have to include people who start work at midnight, as hard as that can be. Citizen surveys have to reach hard-to-get people such as those working two jobs, and that takes many callbacks. In evaluations, the study design may call for the collection of pre-program baseline data, and this certainly will take a substantial amount of time, and many programmatic activities will have to wait until this is carried out. Crime and arrest data are usually very seasonal and so it can be difficult to gather sufficient data in less than

a year. One of the strongest non-experimental designs uses before-and-after time series, for both a project area and matched control groups, but the statistics for analyzing the data demand at least 60 months of data. Studies of particular populations, such as victims of domestic violence, often require a surprisingly long time period before enough subjects are assembled for the study. But the pressure is to come to conclusions quickly. Everyone wants results yesterday, and by the second day of a project people start asking "what your sense is."

5 Analysis of all of the data also takes time. It also takes time to come to measured and thoughtful conclusions. Data sets have many nooks and crannies that need to be investigated carefully. For example, only years after the results of a series of domestic violence experiments were released was it discovered that arrest deterred only better-off and employed men, and actually made things worse for their counterparts. Careful analysis considers and tests for alternative explanations for all of the key findings. It involves looking for complex interactions between various factors; the unexpected role that social class apparently plays in limiting the impact of arrest on domestic violence is an example of this. Finally, the researcher has the obligation to carefully consider the possibility that programs or treatments had unexpected *unwanted* consequences.

6 Many different kinds of reports may need to be prepared, in different formats for different audiences. Some stakeholders will need or expect verbal briefings. They may want to embargo the findings until a news conference can be organized. No one will want to be surprised by the release of findings; they all want to review the research and the findings, voice their disagreement over matters of fact and interpretation, and see any resulting

changes before anyone else sees the final product. All of this can be quite involved when there are multiple stakeholders in the project, including participating agencies, community groups, research funders, city council members, and other government agencies.

Academics also must make time for professional writing and publication. We work for universities that expect this as the product of research. In general, government reports do not impress university deans and departments. They want books published by university presses (which often take three years to produce) and articles in major peer-reviewed journals (ditto). They value abstraction and generality, as do the best academic journals. They currently favor things caused by "globalization." After I explained what I did to one of the most senior members of my academic department, he replied—looking down his nose—"isn't that a bit applied?"

So, how long should this all take? Three years, at a minimum, and in my experience many practitioners will not see that as timely.

What can be done to improve the timeliness of products from a research or evaluation project? Depending on the project, it may be possible to produce interim products. For example, an evaluator monitoring program implementation may be able to generate reports that keep it on target. However, it may just be that the research takes time. A domestic violence study, for example, must wait until enough qualified cases have been identified, and there may not be much that can be done to speed that process up.

Usefulness. Usefulness is another difficult criteria to meet. Part of the problem is that harried administrators usually want tactical information, material that they can use right away. This could include research-based recommendations about where or how to deploy their people next week, or identification of a list of specific high-risk potential offenders. In evaluations they might want to know where the program is not going well, and who is not doing their job. But the value-added contribution of researchers is more likely to be their ability to provide strategic information and analysis. This could include an identification of chronic crime and disorder hot spots, coupled with an analysis of how the routine activities of victims attract offenders to a particular location rather than somewhere else. In an evaluation this could include the identification of factors supporting and retarding change. Convincing harried administrators that strategic information is what they need can be one of the educational outcomes of a research collaboration.

Collaborators need eventually to work toward a shared understanding of what is both doable (don't forget the timeliness issues) and useful. One model is a "strategic feedback" approach to communicating evaluation findings. The focus is on issues, not personalities. Strategic feedback addresses questions such as what works; in what kinds of places does it work; and what are the managerial and supervisor issues involved in making it work. Strategic analysis identifies external forces that are impacting the process, and structural features of the organization that are helping or hindering things.

A related strategy is to focus on identifying good practices and the factors that foster them. Focusing on strategic issues and identifying good practices, rather than on tactical questions, can take some of the researcher's heat off the members of the organization who are doing the work. The researchers in a collaboration have to factor in their reading of what "bad news" model is operative in the organization, and in the city. If the bad news model is "terminate with extreme prejudice," the positive or critical focus of the feedback and the level of specificity in their report has to take this into account. It has been my experience that, the minute a head rolls down the steps of City Hall because of a revelation by a researcher, their ability to have frank conversations with the people in the department who do the work shuts down overnight. I have regularly briefed one mayor and at the first two meetings he pounded his conference table at every mention of bad news, demanding to know who was responsible for the shortcomings our research was describing. He learned that we were not going to name names and started to focus on our charts and graphs.

I have found that the briefing process should be "bottom up." My research team and I typically present our most preliminary findings at meetings with unit managers and their aides. We give them in advance a draft report section covering the issues that they are responsible for, and there has never been any difficulty in getting them to read and reflect on those carefully. They typically are very vigorous in correcting our facts, challenging our interpretations, and even in turning out new data. Later reports are much better for this process. It usually turns out that they are comfortable knowing that their bosses will be hearing what we have to say, once they have heard it first and have had concrete input into the process.

The research collaborators may also be committed to presenting their findings to the public. In particular, foundation funders may insist on public reports and presentations at their forums. Community policing evaluations usually have to find ways to effectively address the public, because the community groups and activists who get involved are themselves interested and demanding stakeholders. They are also "gatekeepers," because they control access to their own members and activities.

SECTION 4

Where Do We Go from Here?

This section completes the volume with discussions of the key lessons about effectiveness taken from the implementation of elements of the New Criminal Justice. The book finishes with a discussion of how the ideas behind the New Criminal Justice may be useful in thinking about education in the field of criminal justice.

The overall evaluation of Project Safe Neighborhoods provides suggestions for what works when it comes to crime reduction. McGarrell points out the value of problem-solving approaches, especially those with strong leaders, focused interventions, and integrated research partners. Specific strategies such as enhanced prosecution screening, incident reviews, and offender notification meetings have been useful. What have become known as pulling levers strategies have repeatedly shown benefits. In the years since the original Boston project, a substantial body of knowledge has been developed regarding best practices for addressing violence and gun crimes in particular. Of course the answers are not all in. Sustainability can be difficult and the importance of differences across sites is clear. Perhaps the most important lesson is that we continue to accumulate knowledge and understanding about crime reduction. Today, lack of knowledge is no longer a justification for inaction.

In a postscript Klofas raises the question of how these new lessons may be useful in education about criminal justice. He suggests that a myriad of interesting questions and complex circumstances, and a rich foundation of information, indicate that the practice of criminal justice has outpaced the teaching of the subject. Complaints about criminal justice education, especially its introduction, are familiar: there has been little concern with theory, an inattention to questions of justice, and marginal integration with criminology. A focus on the elements of the New Criminal Justice may enrich our pedagogy. It could focus attention on variation in local criminal justice rather than on common characteristics. It could further build a set of theories of criminal justice and provide new understandings of organizations. It might, Klofas argues, prompt a re-examination that has occurred in other fields and resulted in adoption of a problem-based approach to education which might mirror the activities of the field of criminal justice itself.

DISCUSSION QUESTIONS

1 In his review of interventions McGarrell describes the elements of a problem-solving process and some of the common interventions to flow from that process in jurisdictions around the country. As you think back to your earliest exposure to criminal justice, how is the problem-solving approach consistent or inconsistent with your early understanding of how criminal justice works? What new actors are present and what powers do they bring? How does the approach to crime differ from the system outlined in the President's Commission report?

2 The central thesis of McGarrell's summary arguably has to do with problem-solving approaches being taken in criminal justice today. What does he mean by problem solving? Is there evidence of differences in problem-solving approaches being taken across local criminal justice systems? The problems he focuses on relate to crime reduction. Could the approach apply to other problems? What other problems or aspects of the crime problem could these methods be applied to?

3 Do you agree with Klofas that early education in criminal justice is often overspecified and that criminal justice is often treated as more unified and less diverse than is the reality? What would it mean to focus on variation rather than common features across criminal justice? What would a problem-solving approach to criminal justice education look like? What would occur in courses and classes and do you think that this would be more or less useful than the linear review of the system as it is portrayed in most criminal justice textbooks today?

CHAPTER 14

Accumulating Lessons from Project Safe Neighborhoods

Edmund F. McGarrell

KEY FINDINGS, RESEARCH, AND POLICY CONSIDERATIONS

This chapter includes discussion of key findings as well as considerations for future research and policy based on the experiences of the 93 Project Safe Neighborhoods (PSN) task forces. The findings are organized by general observations on the components of successful implementation, the role of research and integration of research, and PSN strategy development. This is followed by a summary of the research findings on the impact of PSN on violent crime. Several theoretical and future research issues are considered and several policy implications are presented.

IMPORTANCE OF LEADERSHIP

Throughout this project the research team had the opportunity to interact with officials in every PSN task force, to visit over 36 districts, and to develop a series of strategic and site-specific case studies that involved interviews with numerous PSN officials. A consistent finding was that, in districts where PSN was being implemented in a serious and meaningful fashion, and where there was evidence that gun crime was being addressed in new ways following the implementation of PSN, the leadership of the U.S. Attorney and the U.S. Attorney's Office was critical. Many described the "power" of the Office to bring together other local, state, and federal law enforcement and criminal justice partners, as well as other elements of local government, social services, and neighborhood groups. Others described the importance of the U.S. Attorney making PSN a major priority of the Office and the reduction in violent crime a key goal.

There was also evidence of variation across the U.S. Attorneys in terms of the extent to which they made, or were able to successfully articulate and make actionable, PSN a major priority. This was evident in the variation in the patterns of PSN implementation and particularly in the variation in federal prosecution levels for firearms charges across the PSN districts. The finding that federal prosecution increased nationally by over 60 percent after the implementation of PSN suggested that the majority of U.S. Attorneys did make PSN and increased gun crime prosecution a priority. However, the national data minimize the wide variability across U.S. Attorneys' Offices. As described in Chapter 4, the top ten districts experienced an increase of 200 percent or more. Fifty of the districts observed increases of 60 percent or more. In sharp contrast, the bottom ten districts ranged from no change to a 38 percent decline in firearms charge filings. When viewed from the perspective of the level of federal prosecution of gun crime per capita, similar findings of wide variation emerged. The top 12 districts had a prosecution rate of

10.0 or more per 100,000 population. The bottom 13 districts had rates under 2.0 per 100,000 population. This was less than half the national average and five times lower than the top group of districts.

In districts with significant increases in federal prosecution the U.S. Attorney's Office typically took a number of steps. The first was to convey the priority within the office. Many established relationships with the local prosecutor and often used PSN funds to cross-designate local prosecutors as Special Assistant U.S. Attorneys who would prosecute gun cases in federal court. The development of joint case-screening processes with the local prosecutor, local law enforcement, and Bureau of Alcohol, Tobacco, Firearms and Explosives (ATF) was a similar step. Coordination with ATF on prioritization of gun cases for federal prosecution and communicating to local law enforcement the increased emphasis on federal prosecution of gun cases were also observed in districts where PSN was a clear priority.

Certainly there were justifiable reasons for some districts having a lower level of federal prosecution than other districts. Lower levels of violent crime and differences in penalties for gun crime under state law were two factors. Thus, for example, the District of Massachusetts had a lower per capita prosecution rate for gun crimes than the national average. One explanation was that the state of Massachusetts had comparatively strong penalties for gun crime. Further, the level of prosecution increased in the District of Massachusetts (+106 percent) above the national average, thus suggesting that PSN was a priority within the U.S. Attorney's Office. Without compelling evidence to the contrary, however, it is difficult to believe that PSN was made a major priority in the 11 districts that had no increase or a decline in federal prosecution of gun cases.

In addition to the leadership of the U.S. Attorney, districts with a high level of PSN implementation often developed what appeared to be a "distributed leadership" model. Within the U.S. Attorney's Office this frequently meant reliance on a team that included the PSN Coordinator (typically an Assistant U.S. Attorney) and the Law Enforcement Coordinator (LEC). In these districts, leadership was often found in the formal leaders of other partnering agencies including the local chief of police or sheriff, federal law enforcement,[1] probation and parole, the department of corrections, and local municipal or county government. In many task forces such leadership was provided by other partners including the schools, social services, Weed and Seed coalitions, neighborhood leaders, the faith community, and other community organizations. Additionally, effective task forces typically included leaders from throughout these organizations who represented the day-to-day line-level officials who were critical to changing the way that business was done with respect to gun crime. In a number of task forces, the research partner played an important leadership role.

IMPORTANCE OF FOCUSED INTERVENTIONS

One of the reasons for the inclusion of strategic planning and the integration of research in PSN was to support focused interventions. The promising programs upon which PSN was based all included a focused deterrence logic model whereby enforcement resources were aimed at the people, places, and contexts believed to be producing high rates of gun crime and violence. This was reinforced by a National Academies of Science review of research evidence on the effectiveness of policing strategies in reducing crime which found that, the more focused the intervention, the more impact on crime (National Research Council, 2004). The emphasis on focusing resources was included as a point of emphasis in the strategic problem-solving training provided to all PSN districts.

The concept of focusing resources was a

source of tension for many U.S. Attorneys. Specifically, many if not all U.S. Attorneys were understandably committed to serving their entire district. The emphasis on focusing on target cities or even target neighborhoods or police districts was often perceived as being in conflict with the goal of serving the entire district. For some PSN task forces, this was seemingly irreconcilable and the entire district remained the formal target area. For other districts, distinctions were made between components of the PSN strategy that could be delivered district wide (e.g., the media campaign; commitment to local law enforcement to review priority gun cases for federal prosecution) and those that could be delivered in a key target area (e.g., street-level gun enforcement teams; offender notification meetings; neighborhood redevelopment). The importance of developing a focus on key target areas was suggested in the case studies as well as the cross-city analyses of the impact of PSN on violent crime.

THE ROLE OF RESEARCH AND RESEARCH INTEGRATION

PSN also represented a federal commitment of resources to support law enforcement–researcher partnerships as an ingredient in the PSN task forces. This was an outgrowth of several factors. First, the inclusion of research partners was a key element of Boston Cease-fire (Gun Project) as well as the Strategic Approaches to Community Safety Initiative. Second, the research partners were considered instrumental in assisting the task forces in conducting problem analyses to develop the type of focused interventions described above. Third, PSN included an emphasis on accountability. It was hoped that the research partners would help gather performance measures and assess the impact of the local PSN programs.

The evidence suggested that, like other components of PSN, the inclusion of research partners produced mixed results across the 93 PSN task forces. Although difficult to measure systematically, it appeared that in about one-fifth of the districts there was very little evidence of the integration of research. In some cases this appeared to be the product of a lack of interest on the part of the U.S. Attorney or the PSN task force officials. Research partners were not included as members of the task force and minimal interaction occurred. In other instances this appeared to be based on the failure of the research partner to be part of the task force and/or to produce research findings considered relevant and of value to the task force. During the course of the PSN program the research team received calls of frustration from U.S. Attorneys and PSN Coordinators who complained that they were not getting anything of value from their research partner. At the same time, calls from research partners were received expressing frustration at not being included in the task force and not having the opportunity to understand task force goals and priorities for research. In these districts with no or limited success in the integration of research, the problems seemed to stem from combinations of the following:

- lack of interest in, or understanding of the value of, research on the part of the U.S. Attorney and/or the PSN task force
- lack of understanding or interest in the active research partner role on the part of the researcher (in contrast to a more detached research role)
- data availability problems that made delivery of timely and valuable analyses difficult.

On the other hand, there was evidence of research integration in the vast majority of PSN task forces. This was most apparent in the research partners providing data-driven analyses of the local gun crime problem. A compelling piece of evidence of the perceived value of research was the finding that over half of the PSN task forces provided discretionary funds to continue the work of their research partners after the initial grant award had expired. Another encouraging observation, from the perspective of police–research partnerships, was the emergence of long-term research partnerships that have seemingly emerged from PSN. Examples included the relationships in the Western District of Tennessee with the University of Memphis, the Northern District of Ohio with Kent State University, the District of Nebraska with the University of Nebraska at Omaha, and the Western District of New York with Rochester Institute of Technology. The Middle District of North Carolina established long-term relationships with teams of researchers at the University of North Carolina Greensboro and Winston-Salem State University, and the Eastern District of Wisconsin had similar relationships with a network of researchers from a number of institutions. The state of Massachusetts adopted the research partner model as a core element of the Shannon Project, a gang violence reduction initiative (Massachusetts Executive Office of Public Safety and Security, n.d.).

The importance of research integration was also suggested in the analyses of PSN implementation. Research involvement was positively related to two other key components of PSN: formal partnerships and level of federal prosecution (Zimmermann, 2006). That is, PSN districts that reported higher levels of research integration (by both PSN Coordinators and the research partner) also had a larger number of PSN partners and higher levels of prosecution. Two interpretations are plausible. The first is that the same districts that were most committed to PSN (thus having more partners and higher levels of prosecution) were also committed to integrating research. The second is that valuable research helped solidify partnerships and may have assisted in the focusing of resources on the gun crime problem, thereby increasing levels of federal prosecution. The data do not allow us to disentangle causal order.

Similar findings emerged in terms of the role of information infrastructure and PSN implementation. An absence of information infrastructure was associated with lower levels of PSN implementation (Zimmermann, 2006). This may indicate that, when the information infrastructure could not support research integration, the other PSN components of partnerships and federal prosecution also tended to suffer.

THE EMERGENCE OF GUN CRIME INTERVENTION STRATEGIES

As noted in previous chapters a variety of strategies were employed by PSN task forces. The most common were increased federal prosecution; joint federal–local prosecution case screening; directed police patrol; chronic violent offender programs; street-level firearms enforcement teams; offender notification meetings; re-entry programs; and firearms supply-side interventions. The most common prevention strategies included neighborhood development; education; and school-based prevention programs. It was impossible to distinguish the impact of specific strategies on trends in violent crime. The case studies suggested support for a Project Exile-style emphasis on increased federal prosecution of gun crime coupled with a communication strategy that sought to increase the perceived risk of prosecution of illegal gun possession and use. Additional case studies provided support for a strategic problem-solving, pulling levers set of strategies that used research-based problem analysis to direct resources at the key contexts driving violence and then used the threat of federal prosecution, direct communication to groups of at-risk individuals (offender notification meetings), and additional levers (probation/parole supervision, warrant service, street-level enforcement) to similarly increase the perceived risk of illegal gun possession and use. Although the research approach did not allow disentangling of the components of these strategies, interviews and observations suggested that a number of PSN task forces were able to combine multiple components into an overall strategy emphasizing focused deterrence.

INTEGRATING STRATEGIES IN PROJECT SAFE NEIGHBORHOODS

Although one of the central principles of PSN is establishing an inclusive and coordinated approach to reducing gun violence, when these approaches become collaborative rather than simply coordinated they appear more likely to be successful. For years, creating a task force had been a popular strategy in criminal justice to address crime problems. Such task forces typically involved sharing personnel and other resources in a combined effort to address crime. The collaborative model, however, suggested that not only were resources shared, communications improved, and operations coordinated, but also that decision making was shared across traditional agency boundaries. Often when this level of integration was attained there were considerable benefits beyond simple cooperation.

Perhaps the best example of this occurred in the area of case review. Almost every PSN district had a formal process for determining the most appropriate prosecution venue for gun cases. In some situations, this was conducted through referrals on an individual case basis from local prosecutors, whereas in other jurisdictions a formal meeting was held in which all gun cases were discussed. Although there is certainly no single best way of conducting this process, in many districts the formal discussion of cases often led to an exchange of information and intelligence. Such information was useful not only in determining prosecution venue but also in developing intelligence, generating informants, and identifying individuals who may be suitable for attention through a most violent offender initiative.

In addition, in many districts the case review discussion reflected a broad consideration of a variety of factors about the case and included viewpoints from not only federal prosecutors but also law enforcement as well as community prosecutors. With this range of input, decisions were often made reflecting the value of the case to the community and the role that the defendant played in gun violence or gangs rather than a strict calculation of sentencing vulnerability. This collective and shared decision-making process often led to a greater focus on the gang and gun violence problem beyond making individual case decisions.

Another commonly used component of many PSN initiatives was an incident review process. In these initiatives, information was reviewed from specific cases that were representative of gun violence incidents for the purpose of developing a more comprehensive picture of gang activity and gun violence in the jurisdiction and target areas. Although one objective of this activity was to assemble what was known about specific incidents from a variety of law enforcement sources, this information was also quite valuable for other PSN project components. In particular, information that was obtained through this process could be directly used in formulating most violent offender programs as well as in developing information that could be used to structure offender notification meetings.

An additional intervention that developed during the PSN program was the Drug Market Initiative. In this strategy, communities worked with law enforcement agencies to stop drug distribution and other structured criminal activities in the neighborhood. This initiative was pioneered in the Middle District of North Carolina in High Point and has now spread to many other jurisdictions. This strategy also demonstrated the value of integrating various PSN components. Although offender notification was central to this approach, successful implementation of this model often included incident reviews to obtain a larger picture of the drug market in the neighborhood and to identify the hierarchy of individuals in groups and gangs involved in drug distribution. In addition, the case-screening process helped distinguish drug offenders with chronic records and/or histories of violence, who would be prosecuted, from lower-level dealers, who would be included in an offender notification meeting and offered a second chance. The key point is that the integration of strategies appeared to focus enforcement resources as well as support the collaborative network involved in PSN through the sharing of information.

MOVING TOWARD EVIDENCE-BASED PRACTICE TO REDUCE GUN CRIME

The findings from the series of site-specific PSN case studies, when combined with a complementary series of studies that began with the Boston Gun Project, suggest that focused, deterrence-based interventions hold considerable promise for reducing levels of violent gun crime. These interventions can be summarized as falling into three categories: directed police patrol, Project Exile-style strategies, and strategic problem-solving/pulling levers strategies.

Directed Police Patrol

Directed police patrol with a focus on gun crime and illegal gun possession was one of the more popular strategies reported by U.S. Attorneys and PSN Coordinators in their reports to the Attorney General (58 percent reported utilizing it in 2005). It does not appear that directed patrol, as a specific strategy in isolation from more general PSN strategies, was systematically evaluated in PSN. The support for directed patrol comes from a series of quasi-experiments conducted in Kansas City, Indianapolis, and Pittsburgh in the 1990s (Sherman and Rogan, 1995;

McGarrell et al., 2001; Cohen and Ludwig, 2003). In all three studies, directed police patrol aimed at gun crime hot spots was associated with significant declines in gun crime. Further, it appeared that, with appropriate management and supervision, the intensive patrols were conducted in a way that did not generate police–citizen conflict, a concern associated with such focused enforcement.

Project Exile

Project Exile seeks to increase the threat of punishment for illegal possession and use of firearms as a way of discouraging gun possession and carrying among high-risk individuals (prior felons, misdemeanants with domestic violence convictions, mentally ill, and youths). The strict provisions of federal law, including no right to bail, long sentences with minimal good time, and incarceration in the federal prison system, are considered key elements of the deterrence message. This message is then communicated through a variety of media outlets including billboards, posters in jails and lock-ups, and radio and television public service announcements. The model was originally developed in Richmond, Virginia. Rosenfeld and colleagues (Rosenfeld et al., 2005) found that Exile was associated with a significant decline in homicide, controlling for a number of other factors.

As already described, two PSN case studies evaluated the impact of Exile-style interventions. The first took place in Montgomery in the Middle District of Alabama (McGarrell et al., 2007b). Time series analysis was used to examine the trend in assaults with a firearm, armed robbery with a firearm, and homicides. The key reduction was in assaults with a firearm. Homicides also declined, but the decline did not attain statistical significance. There was no change in armed robbery. In examining these trends it is important to note that gun assaults were by far the most common violent gun crime in Montgomery at about 25 per month. In contrast, armed robberies and homicides occurred at the rate of approximately two to three per month. Thus, the strategy appeared to impact the most serious component of gun crime in Montgomery. Because of the absence of an appropriate control or comparison site, the trend in gun crime was compared with the trend in property crime, measured as motor vehicle thefts and overall property offenses. Neither changed during this time period, thus minimizing the likelihood that the decline in gun assaults was due to some other factor influencing crime in Montgomery.

The second evaluation of a PSN Exile strategy took place in Mobile in the Southern District of Alabama (Hipple et al., forthcoming a). Time series analyses were also utilized. Once again a logical control or comparison site was not available. In this case, the trend in property crime was included in the time series models to control for the effect of unmeasured factors affecting all crime in Mobile. The results indicated that total gun crime declined by about 26 incidents per month. Violent crime with a gun declined by about 16 incidents per month and armed robberies by about 11 per month. Each decline was statistically significant. Further, gunshot wound admissions to the local trauma center declined at the same time that the police data indicated a reduction in gun crime, thus strengthening the conclusion that gun crime was reduced.

Strategic Problem Solving/Pulling Levers

The strategic problem-solving/pulling levers strategy refers to a comprehensive intervention that traces to the Boston Gun Project. Detailed problem analysis, conducted by a collaboration of a multi-agency law enforcement team and researchers, is used to pinpoint the people, groups, and contexts associated with gun crime. The analysis then informs a set of pulling levers interventions that seek to convey a strong deterrence message to those most at risk for being involved in gun crime

as offenders and victims. This is considered most powerful when the deterrence message is communicated to groups of potential offenders in offender notification meetings. The goal is to use the social network to reinforce the deterrence message. The deterrence message is coupled with a message of social support, typically offered by social service providers and local residents.

At the time of the development of PSN, the evidence for the potential impact of this strategy was largely based on studies in Boston and Indianapolis. In Boston, the pulling levers intervention conducted in the mid-1990s was associated with more than a 60 percent decline in youth homicide (Kennedy, 1997; Braga et al. 2001; Piehl et al., 2003). Following a very similar approach, the pulling levers intervention in Indianapolis was associated with a 34 percent reduction in homicides (McGarrell and Chermak, 2003b; McGarrell et al., 2006; Corsaro and McGarrell, 2009). Since that time, a number of other studies have found evidence of an impact of the pulling levers strategy on homicide and gun crime. These include Tita and colleagues' quasi-experiment conducted in Los Angeles (Tita et al., 2003) as well as a series of PSN case studies.

Anthony Braga, one of the researchers involved in the Boston Gun Project, served as research partner in the Eastern District of California. Braga conducted a thorough problem analysis that informed a pulling levers intervention in Stockton. The evaluation indicated a significant decline in gun homicides in Stockton compared with other similar California cities (Braga, 2008).

PSN officials in Lowell, Massachusetts, employed a pulling levers strategy to address youth gang gun violence. The pre- and post-analysis indicated a significant reduction in gun assaults compared with trends in gun crime in other Massachusetts cities (McDevitt et al., 2006; Braga et al., 2008). Similar results were observed in Omaha (District of Nebraska). Time series analyses revealed a

20 percent decline in total firearms offenses during a period in which property crime was unchanged (Hipple et al., forthcoming b).

The Middle District of North Carolina implemented the strategic problem solving/ pulling levers model in five communities: Durham, Greensboro, High Point, Salisbury, and Winston-Salem. The PSN case study focused on Durham, Greensboro, and Winston-Salem.[2] Time series analyses were conducted of the trend in total gun crimes (homicides with a firearm, robberies with a firearm, and aggravated assaults with a firearm). All three cities experienced declines, with the reductions in Greensboro (13 fewer incidents per month) and Winston-Salem (9 fewer incidents per month) being statistically significant.

As described in Chapter 6, a case study was also conducted in St. Louis in the Eastern District of Missouri (Decker et al., 2007). The PSN intervention focused on several very high crime neighborhoods and its impact on gun crime was compared with the trend in several comparison neighborhoods as well as the trend for the city as a whole. Although there was a statistically significant decline in the PSN target areas, there were also declines in the comparison areas and the entire city. Thus, although it is possible that PSN had an impact across the city, it is impossible to attribute the decline to PSN.

An additional systematic evaluation was conducted by the PSN research partners in Chicago (Northern District of Illinois). Similar to St. Louis, the PSN program in Chicago focused on specific high violent crime neighborhoods in different parts of the city. The evaluation involved comparison of these PSN treatment neighborhoods with other similar neighborhoods. The results demonstrated that the PSN treatment neighborhoods experienced a statistically significant decline in gun crime relative to comparison neighborhoods (Papachristos et al., 2007).

This series of studies results in 11 tests of the strategic problem solving/pulling levers approach to reducing gun crime. In 9 of the 11, a statistically significant decline in gun crime was associated with the implementation of the strategic problem-solving intervention. The two exceptions were St. Louis and Durham.[3] Both experienced declines in gun crime; however, in the case of St. Louis the decline also occurred in the comparison sites, and in Durham the decline was not statistically significant.

SUMMARY

Since the findings from Boston and Kansas City in the mid-1990s (Kennedy, 1997; Sherman and Rogan, 1995), an accumulating body of evidence has emerged suggesting that focused deterrence interventions can have an impact on reducing gun crime at a local level. PSN built on this evidence and contributed to the research evidence. The series of studies are summarized in Figure 14.1.

CROSS-CITY COMPARISON

The promising results described above from the case studies were reinforced by the analyses of trends in violent crime in all U.S. cities with populations over 100,000. As noted previously, evaluating PSN was challenging because of the national coverage of the program. Thus, the strategy was to compare cities that were PSN target sites with non-target sites and to compare cities based on the dosage level of PSN implementation. The logic behind the comparisons was that if PSN had its intended impact on violent crime it should be most apparent in PSN target cities and as the dosage level increased.

The findings consistently provided support for the idea that meaningful implementation of PSN led to reductions in violent crime. As the three component dosage measures (partnerships, research integration, federal prosecution of gun crime) increased, PSN target cities experienced lower levels of violent crime, contrasting the 2000–1 pre-PSN level

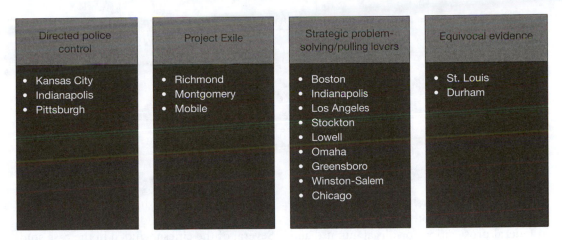

Figure 14.1 Studies suggestive of a focused deterrence impact on gun crime.

of crime with the trend in 2002–6. When the dosage measure was limited to the impact of increased federal prosecution, the findings again revealed that PSN target cities in high-dosage federal districts had the greatest decline in crime. Additionally, these cities resisted the uptick in violent crime witnessed across the country in 2005 and, although there was an increase in 2006, it was much less pronounced than in other cities. These results were consistent after controlling for other factors that have been shown to influence levels of violent crime (e.g., concentrated disadvantage, population density, levels of police staffing, incarceration trends) (see McGarrell et al., 2009 for details).

The results of these analyses are presented in Table 14.1. PSN target cities experienced over an 8 percent decline in violent crime whereas non-target cities experienced no change in violent crime (–0.25 percent). Non-target cities in high prosecution districts, and PSN target cities in low and medium prosecution districts were relatively similar with 3–5 percent declines. The most compelling evidence of a PSN effect is provided in the contrast between low-dosage, non-PSN target cities with high-dosage, PSN target cities. The low-dosage non-target cities experienced a 7.8 percent *increase* in violent crime during

this time period. A reasonable interpretation is that this is the anticipated changed in violent crime during the 2000–6 period without the PSN intervention. The high-dosage, PSN treatment sites experienced a 13.1 percent *decline* in violent crime during the same period. This suggested that cities that were the subject of an intensive PSN intervention based on a focused deterrence model witnessed a significant decline in violent crime in contrast to what would have been expected with no PSN intervention.

RESEARCH IMPLICATIONS

The key research finding was that the case studies and the cross-city analyses support the concept that focused deterrence strategies appear to have an impact on levels of violent crime. This point was reinforced when coupled with studies from the projects that served as a foundation for PSN. Having said this, future research could extend this study and the associated body of research in a number of ways.

With the exception of the directed patrol studies reviewed herein, the Project Exile model and the strategic problem-solving/pulling levers model share several components that were supported. Specifically,

Table 14.1 Summary of changes in violent crime in target and non-target cities, by level of federal prosecution

Level of federal prosecution	PSN target cities	Non-PSN target cities
Low	−5.3%	+7.8%
Medium	−3.1%	< −1.0%
High	−13.1%	−4.9%
Total[a]	−8.89%	−0.25%

Note

a   Total percentage change was calculated from the entire target/non-target city data.

both include partnerships led by the U.S. Attorney's Office, both include an increase in federal prosecution for illegal gun use and possession, and both include strategies to communicate the deterrence threat to at-risk populations. The strategic problem-solving/ pulling levers model put additional emphasis on research integration, inclusion of multiple strategies, and offender notification meetings as a tool for communicating to groups of at-risk individuals. Both models appear very promising in reducing violent crime. Future research would benefit from careful research designs that would allow for more systematic comparisons of these overall strategies as well as specific components of the strategies.

Similarly, this body of research provides much stronger evidence of the impact at a community level than it does of the impact at the individual level.[4] Very little systematic research has been published on the impact of these types of strategies on individuals subject to the interventions. From a theoretical standpoint, current research does not clarify whether the observed impact is due to incapacitation of chronic violent offenders, deterrence of illegal gun carrying and use, shifts in network norms and behavior among groups involved in gun crime, changes in the perceived legitimacy of the law, or some combination of these forces.

Additionally, research is needed to address the sustainability of these types of multi-agency interventions. Boston and Indianapolis, whose pulling levers interventions served as models for PSN, both suffered

increased levels of homicide and violent crime during the decade that began in 2000. Several of the cities included in the case studies later experienced increases in homicide. The violent crime trends reviewed in Chapter 7 reflected an increase in violent crime after 2004. Several interpretations are plausible.

It could be that the impact of increased federal prosecution, the communication strategies, and the pulling levers interventions fades over time. That is, there is a short-term impact of these largely enforcement strategies but it is not sustained. This explanation is largely focused on the logic of the intervention model. Critics of the intervention would likely argue that it is insufficient in the absence of longer-term strategies to invest in human capital and community economic and physical development. Some critics would go a step further and warn that the short-term enforcement may ultimately be self-defeating by working against human and social capital.

A second interpretation is that the theory behind the intervention is sound but that it is difficult to sustain these multiple agency coalitions and focused interventions over time. Decay can occur as personnel turnover results in losses of leadership, new task force members join who are unfamiliar with the logic model, or enforcement activities become routinized rather than strategically focused on the people, networks, places, and contexts currently driving violence. Follow-up studies of PSN task forces that have remained active and focused over a long period of time would be very helpful in understanding the sustainability of coalitions.

A third interpretation is that the rebound in violent crime experienced in many cities in 2005–6 was caused by broader economic, social, and political factors (e.g., Police Executive Research Forum, 2006) and that the increase in crime would have been worse in the absence of PSN. Support for this argument would point to the delay in the rebound and the much more modest increase in violent crime when comparing PSN target cities in high prosecution districts with other cities, particularly non-target cities in low prosecution districts.

At this point available research does not provide an answer to these three interpretations. More research is needed to advance understanding of the long-term impact of these types of interventions and about the sustainability of research-driven, multi-agency coalitions.

POLICY CONSIDERATIONS

The valuable experience of being involved in the national PSN initiative resulted in several policy considerations. First, the call for more research should not be taken as a reason to delay action. The human toll of violent gun crime and the deleterious impact of gun violence on families and communities demand action. The body of evidence that has emerged since the mid-1990s on focused deterrence strategies suggests that multiple agency coalitions, working with community partners, can have a significant impact on violent crime at the local level. The current PSN research suggests that the leadership of the U.S. Attorney's Office and the use or threat of federal prosecution are important tools for the focused deterrence approach.

Second, the limitations of existing crime information systems became apparent in PSN. To the credit of the Department of Justice, PSN included an emphasis on accountability through performance measures and outcome measures, and it included funding for

research partners to assist in gathering performance measures and assessing outcomes. Unfortunately, the limits of existing crime information systems precluded effective implementation of these goals. The national crime reporting system, Uniform Crime Reporting (UCR), does not include measures of gun crime. Incident-based reporting systems can generate measures of gun crime but are not available in many jurisdictions and are thus of limited value for cross-city comparisons and national estimates of gun crime. The National Crime Victimization Survey provides national estimates of violent crime but not at the local level. Given the advances in information technology, development of an improved national reporting system, at least for the nation's largest cities that generate a disproportionate amount of violent gun crime, would be a significant advance and is critical for supporting future assessment of the impact of federal violence reduction interventions.

The goal of seeking to reduce gun crime nationally is certainly laudable. Given the wide variation in the community-level risk of gun crime victimization, resource constraints, and the evidence-based practice of highly focused interventions, a tiered approach to national violence reduction programs may be advisable. Needs assessment of the capacity to implement multi-agency focused interventions could be coupled with risk assessment to prioritize funding for program intervention. This approach could improve future evaluation of impact as well as increase capacity for implementation.

From a research and evaluation standpoint, if resources to support high-dosage interventions are limited then a larger pool of sites could be identified for potential implementation. Random allocation or other systematic approaches (e.g., matching by propensity) could be used to select treatment and comparison sites, thus greatly strengthening the ability to assess impact.

Additionally, for sites considered low on

information infrastructure and with little experience with multi-agency collaboration, the results of this study suggest that efforts to build capacity on these dimensions could help support future implementation effectiveness (Zimmermann, 2006).

Ultimately PSN has advanced knowledge and provided support for practice in several key ways. First, it built upon and extends evidence-based practice that emerged in the mid-1990s. There are highly promising interventions that appear to offer officials sound strategies to reduce gun crime at the local level. Although there is still much to be learned about successful interventions, lack of knowledge should no longer serve as an excuse for inaction in addressing gun crime. Second, it lent support to the power of the Office of the U.S. Attorney to lead local, state, and federal coalitions in addressing crime control and prevention priorities. Third, it fostered law enforcement–researcher partnerships that, although not always successful, were associated with more successful implementation of program goals.

NOTES

1 Most commonly this was ATF but in a number of task forces DEA, FBI, the Marshals Service, and other federal agencies were important task force members.

2 Salisbury was included in the analysis; however, its smaller population produces very low base rates of gun crime and low statistical power to assess impact. High Point was not included because it is currently part of a separate National Institute of Justice evaluation.

3 St. Louis was also distinct from the other sites in the list of "strategic problem-solving/pulling levers" sites in that the PSN task force did not utilize offender notification meetings as a tool for communicating the focused deterrence message to groups of high-risk individuals. The task force did, however, rely on other mechanisms to communicate the threat of federal prosecution and local officials reported that the word on the street was to avoid gun charges, which would mean being "walked across the street" from local to federal court.

4 Examples of studies finding non-significant impacts of offender notification meetings at the individual level include Chermak (2007) and McGarrell et al. (2003). This is not to question the effectiveness of offender notification meetings but rather to note that their established impact is more evident at the neighborhood than the individual level.

CHAPTER 15

Postscript: Teaching the New Criminal Justice

John M. Klofas

INTRODUCTION

How do you explain the great attraction of the study of crime and criminal justice? It is often the subject of the most popular books, television shows, and movies. In all of those venues, reality almost always trumps fiction. The true crime drama, trial court coverage, and prison documentary seem destined to garner large audiences. By all measures the subject is interesting and important.

What is it, though, about criminal justice that qualifies it as interesting and important? Perhaps we are drawn in by our seemingly infinite capacity to do evil as well as good. Maybe it is our belief in redemption that motivates us. Or is it the simultaneous attraction and repulsion of calling for our pound of flesh? Maybe it is the struggle for order while never sacrificing justice; or the struggle for justice that forces us to question the basis for order. Perhaps it is simply our capacity to build, reform, and rebuild complex systems to address our changeable and often contradictory impulses.

There is something, however, that many of us with some experience in the field might agree often fails to reflect the gripping characteristics of our subject matter. It is, unfortunately, the tools that most often introduce our students to serious study in the field—its introductory textbooks and, perhaps occasionally, the courses they support. Among the introductory tomes one

finds a near perfect similarity in description of a seemingly lifeless, frozen in time, if not fossilized criminal justice system. After some introductory material and before some chapters that just don't seem to fit anywhere else, the novice student is led, at the tempo of a Souza march, through a description of case processing. Little difference separates most of these volumes (see Withrow et al., 2004) and, although they all struggle to look interesting, with colorful presentations and often fascinating photographs and charts, these often seem to be mostly window dressing covering a dull corpse of what should be a vibrant, complex, living, and evolving organism that seeks to solve some of society's most vexing problems.

Our pedagogy does not require such oversimplification. In fact, most professors struggle to overcome the dullness of their introductory text by supplementing readings and lecturing on some of the many truly interesting aspects of the field—whether they are the dilemmas of eyewitness testimony, the meaning of the fourth amendment when there is no intention of using evidence in a trial, or the disparity between what we know of demographic patterns of drug use and demographic patterns of arrest for drug use. What seems most interesting is what defies the often overly determined textbook presentations. What in textbooks may be only hinted at as outliers, anomalies, the unusual, and the exception often seem far more central in the classroom. Lecture topics such as federal versus state crimes and rules of evidence, drug courts, pretrial treatment programs, civil penalties against gangs, and the imprisonment of the elderly and infirmed illustrate the variety in criminal justice and suggest the incompleteness, and the frequent lack of nuance, in texts that instead emphasize common features and central tendency in case processing.

In this chapter we will consider how the New Criminal Justice with its emphasis on local communities, partnerships, and action research can influence teaching and learning in the field and how it might provide opportunities to rethink and redesign the tools used to provide access to the relevant body of knowledge.

CRIMINAL JUSTICE THEORY AND THE NEW CRIMINAL JUSTICE

The 1969 President's Commission left an inevitable and indelible mark on criminal justice education. Its wide-ranging analysis of the field has been enormously influential, but perhaps no part of its work has been as influential as its model of the criminal justice system. It is reprinted in nearly every introductory text and its outline of how cases are processed—the sequence running from police through courts and corrections—forms the core of the contents of nearly every book. That model does accomplish an important task by reflecting the dynamic character of criminal case processing. It is well accepted and well demonstrated in introductory tests that changes in one part of the system will reverberate in other parts. It has also been argued recently that more advanced approaches to general systems theory can be informative (Bernard et al., 2005). All of this highlights the important contributions of the Commission to understanding efficiency and effectiveness in the system.

Scholars in the field today, however, continue to be critical of the overall failure to advance the development of theories of criminal justice; theories that are separate and apart from criminological theories (see, e.g., Kraska, 2006; Clear 2001; Crank, 2003). The parameters of such theories are described by Duffee and Allan (2007) as:

> explanations of the variations in responses to crime . . . Criminal justice theory seeks to explain and examine variations in, and the causes of, aspects of government social control systems, which select the criminal sanction over other forms of social control and share the nature of the criminal sanction to be employed.

Introductory material remains especially vulnerable to criticism over the lack of attention to more general questions of theory (see Willis, 1983; Henderson and Boostrom, 1989). A broad theory or set of theories of criminal justice itself has not been widely embraced; however, significant work has been carried out and, at the very least, certain key theoretical concepts are widely accepted as relevant to understanding the field.

A useful framework for discussion of criminal justice theory is provided by Bernard and Engel (2001) and embraced by several others (Snipes and Maguire, 2007; Kraska, 2006). They argue that such theories can be classified by the dependent variables they consider and they describe three broad categories: theories addressing individual behavior of criminal justice agents, those focused on organizational behavior, and those dealing with the aggregate behavior of the criminal justice system and its components as a whole.

The authors refer to a range of organizational behavior and management theories and cite the work of Feeley (1973) specifically to illustrate models of organizational influence. They also refer to David Duffee, who suggests that criminal justice be examined in a theoretical framework "in which it is assumed that criminal justice operations are determined by community political and social structure"

(1980, p. 137). It is an argument illustrated by his later work with Edward Maguire (Duffee and Maguire, 2007).

An emphasis on locality and local functioning is central to what this volume has described as the New Criminal Justice. That focus highlights one source of variability across criminal justice systems and facilitates a community-level analysis. Attention is directed to such areas as differences in choice of police and prosecution strategies, differences in rates of use of force, arrests, conviction, the extent and nature of criminal sentences, the presence or absence of significant innovation, and a host of other variables. The body of scholarship on community provides access to relevant theory and hypotheses that can be used to help explain these sorts of variables. This explanation can draw on research on a wide variety of community characteristics including differences in the way that community functions are carried out (Warren, 1978), or the role of local elites and the distribution of political power (Hagan, 1989), or a range of other community-related attributes.

JUSTICE AND THE NEW CRIMINAL JUSTICE

One, perhaps unexpected, criticism of introductory criminal justice texts and classes has been that even the seemingly fundamental concept of justice gets little attention (Owen et al., 2006). Along similar lines Castellano and Gould argue that to the extent we emphasize description and management we may risk missing the forest for the trees. Their point is "the criminal justice system must be about justice—about just processes, just outcomes and the just use of state power" (2007).

It seems striking that discourse in criminal justice and the supporting material can provide so much detail on how cases are processed in criminal justice and so little on the most basic goals of those processes. That is not to say that component goals are not addressed. Certainly operational-level purposes such as order maintenance and solving crime are well covered; as are goals of adjudication that may include proper convictions and moving cases forward. And of course sentencing discussions inevitably must address the legislative and judicial goals of that process. The broader meanings of justice associated with the system itself, however, seem far more neglected.

One remedy for this problem may be to consider differences in the way that justice is understood and operationalized when other sources of variation are explored. Again, the study of variability across practice, rather than central tendency, may be useful. The New Criminal Justice directs attention to variation in case processing and criminal justice systems across localities. It also suggests the relevance of differences in networks of relevant organizations, and differences in the way that research is used at the local level. For example, local variation calls attention to questions of how different concepts of justice may manifest themselves across communities. Are there communities, or times in the life of communities, in which utilitarian goals rise to prominence over others? If so, how are those goals reflected in the organization of criminal justice services and the processing of cases? The same questions may be asked of other justice goals such as interest in equality and fairness or retribution or rehabilitation. Likewise, there is the question of whether communities operating under different views of justice also engage different partners or the same partners differently. And too, even with that, the questions would remain as to the direction of the causal relationship between approaches to justice and participating organizations. Finally, attention must be paid to how the use of data, such as criminal intelligence data or program outcome or recidivism data, influences local approaches to justice. Will, for example, evidence of efficacy of treatment interventions affect local justice goals, which are then reflected in the structure of local systems and/or the processing of cases?

Bernard and Engel (2001) argue approvingly that one of the distinguishing features of theories of criminal justice is that they are most often implicitly or explicitly prescriptive. A shared "standard of legitimacy" exists, they argue, in a dynamic interactive relationship with the reality of criminal justice as it is revealed in research. Thus, theories of criminal justice can incorporate standards that allow them to build in critical concepts such as those of justice, fairness, and humanness. The New Criminal Justice, through its attention to variation across communities, and its concern with the use of research, encourages exploration of that "standard of legitimacy" and the ways that it can be achieved. That is, the New Criminal Justice helps investigate the prescriptive question of how some local factors may be arranged to achieve some desirable condition or goal related to criminal justice or crime.

INDIVIDUAL BEHAVIOR IN CRIMINAL JUSTICE ORGANIZATIONS

There is no question that criminal justice texts and classes address the problem of individual behavior in criminal justice organizations. Indeed, it is often some of the richest and most engaging material presented. Relevant topics include corruption at all levels of criminal justice, graft, the use of excessive force, brutality, even the malfeasance that may lead to conviction of the innocent. These and similar topics are often described in considerable detail and illustrated with all-too-common real-world examples. Efforts to explain these instances using theory, however, are often quite limited. In recent years these scandals have often been examined by invoking concepts of morality and ethical conduct (see Pollock, 1993; Dreisbach, 2008).

Some scholars have argued that one orientation for theories of criminal justice can be found in organizational analyses and theory (Bernard and Engel, 2001). The New Criminal Justice complements that perspective by focusing on the nature of organizational arrangements in local criminal justice. Thus, the abundant work carried out in the areas of organizational goals and processes as well as that on the nature of inter-organizational relations becomes relevant to even rudimentary efforts to understand individuals within criminal justice organizations. Studies of misbehavior can thus be informed by consideration of this organizational background.

The study of organizational goals has had significant impact on understanding individual behavior in organizations. Goal conflict can produce a range of responses, from selective emphasis on one set of directives to immobilization and perversion of broad public goals. Sykes (1958) pointed out how conflict between punishment and reform can produce a form of benign custodianship in prison, which seems consistent with neither goal. In their classic work, March and Simon (1958) have shown that complex goals result in a Pareto-optimal solution, which provides only minimally acceptable levels of achievement of all important but competing goals. In his analysis of street-level bureaucracies such as the police, Lipsky (1980) has included officers as policy makers because of the broad discretion they have and he has attributed their policy choices to a broad range of organizational factors. Even studies of corruption have identified a category of behavior known as "official deviance," which refers to illegal actions taken by officials that are clearly oriented toward the needs and goals of the organization (Lee and Visano, 1981). The "Dirty Harry Problem" (Klockars, 1980) provides one illustration in which the illegal use of force is promoted by the view that morality can be subservient to organizational interests and goals. In the classroom, then, the New Criminal Justice directs attention to problems of individual behavior and helps move easily beyond the descriptive stage by providing access to theory to help explain the phenomenon.

The New Criminal Justice not only suggests a focus on organizational influences but also goes still further to suggest consideration of the nature of inter-organizational links and their impact on behavior. The model indicates that once loosely coupled organizations continue to grow closer and come to share goals and goal-related problems. The new partnerships thus can influence a wide range of behavior that results from the combination of resources, goals, and organizational constraints.

CRIMINOLOGY AND THE NEW CRIMINAL JUSTICE

The relationship between criminology, the study of causes of crime, and criminal justice, the study of societal responses to crime, has sometimes been awkward. There have been efforts to distinguish the fields by their commitment to scientific principle or by their intellectual traditions (Gibbons and Blake, 1977). Those favoring criminology tend to argue a superior intellectual foundation. Those favoring criminal justice counter with considerations of relevance (see Hale, 1998; Zalman, 1981). Early influences in the development of the field continue to reverberate (see Morn, 1995). Protagonists on both sides often seem to favor pejorative characterizations of their would-be intellectual cousins. The truce represented in academic departments, courses, and textbooks seems uneasy.

As a practical matter the separation of these fields today seems counterproductive at best. In general, it seems an unsound argument to suggest that those genuinely concerned with how to impact crime could be unconcerned with its causes. Likewise the greatest relevance of understanding crime's causes would be in the application of that knowledge for the purpose of reducing crime. In that sense the mainstream of criminology and the interests of criminal justice do ultimately come together.

One place where one perspective on the state of the relationship between these two topics is on exhibition is in the outline of most introductory criminal justice texts. For the most part the tables of contents feature an early chapter dedicated to a wide-ranging review of criminological theory. In some cases the topic is returned to late in the book when delinquency is discussed, usually within a chapter on juvenile justice.

To most who study from those texts this apparent effort to demonstrate the importance of theory must only serve to diminish it. The encyclopedic chapter, disemboweled from the core of the volume, in fact diminishes both criminology and criminal justice. It suggests both that the causes of crime can adequately be treated in less than 10 percent of the pages of the text, and that the same subject is irrelevant to the other 90 percent of pages in the book.

Recent developments in criminological theory argue strongly against this segregation. Today a broad range of theories of crime causation have clear and direct implications for practice. The most obvious example may be found in the broad category of theories involving rational choice. This set of theories addresses a range of important factors, among them the impact of sanctions, including informal sanctions such as shaming (Braithwaite, 1989). It includes environmental theories, such as routine activities theory (Cohen and Felson, 1979; Felson, 1998), that have direct implications for manipulation of characteristics of social and physical environments. A host of "situational crime prevention" strategies (Clark, 1997) have emerged from this category of theory.

Just as criminological theory can inform practice, concern with practice has led to significant advances in theory. Broken windows theory (Wilson and Kelling, 1982; Kelling and Coles, 1996), for example, is clearly a theory of crime causation but one that emerged from an interest in police-led crime reduction strategies. Similarly David

Kennedy has led the development of theories of focused deterrence (1997) based primarily on his work with "Ceasefire," a crime reduction strategy. All of these developments have clearly strengthened the intellectual and practical bond between criminological theory and criminal justice. Perhaps the strongest collective statement of the importance of this connection has been assembled by Scott Decker and Hugh Barlow (2009) in the book *Criminology and Public Policy: From Theory to Practice*. The volume is a significant collection of essays by established criminologists who address the specific policy implications of a range of criminological theories.

The cumulative evidence of mutual relevance, and the application of theory to real-world problems as illustrated by Decker and Barlow, should signal a direction for education in the field. There is a critical role for theory in applied criminal justice. With its focus on crime reduction the New Criminal Justice also invites the application of criminological knowledge to understanding criminal justice. Theories explaining criminal behavior are relevant to every step of the criminal process. Understanding causation is relevant to consideration of such things as patterns of crime, criminogenic environments, the careers of criminals, and the impact of interventions ranging from the transfer of cases to problem-solving courts, to the use of long prison sentences for incapacitation. Sentencing choices, the practice of probation, adjustment during and after incarceration all can be better understood with reference to criminological theory. It is no longer sound educational practice to keep these fields apart.

SYSTEMS ANALYSIS

Considering the details of the New Criminal Justice can suggest still another concept of pedagogical value. Systems analysis is a general term for which there are a variety of meanings in the literature. It is related to but not the equivalent of systems theory. Simi-

larly, it is related to but is not the same as the process used to study and manage computer systems. Systems analysis, for our purpose, refers to that strain of thinking that emerged following World War II from the recognition that biological phenomena could not be explained by the "analytic, mechanistic, one way casual paradigm of classical science" (von Bertalanffy, 1968, p. xxi).

Systems analysis, or cybernetics as it became known in the scholarship of Gregory Bateson (1972), suggests that even organizations can be studied as complex systems that interact with their environments with nonlinear, that is, complicated, cause and effect relationships. Bateson was interested in such issues as information flow and feedback, control and self-stabilizing characteristics of organisms and their environments.

The importance of this for the study of criminal justice is that it directs attention to the structures of criminal justice as they lay imbedded in their physical, social, and political environments. In other words, looking at local criminal justice as an integrated whole is substituted for the dissection of the criminal justice system into disengaged component parts arranged in a largely linear fashion. For example, invoking systems analysis, one would not study police powers in the abstract but would instead examine the powers exercised by the police in context. That may include the types and levels of local crime, broad community differences, historical period, community relations, the local power structure, court oversight, and other influences. The goal would be to consider why some departments might exercise police powers differently than others over the same or different time periods. Systems analysis could also help explore variation in local incarceration rates. Why do some communities use jail incarceration extensively whereas others do not? What types of things may account for the local development of problem-solving courts or sophisticated networks of pretrial or post-conviction alternatives? The point is, cybernetics opens the analysis to consider not only the cases that may be passed on from one organization to another in criminal justice but also a range of other factors that may help explain what might otherwise be seen as non-uniformity, outliers, or exceptions.

It is, however, not just variation at a given point in time that is of interest under the New Criminal Justice, but variation over time, or change, as well. The use of systems analysis can help understand change and stability in criminal justice. The analysis will help place criminal justice organizations in a complex environment of local and national influences, partner agencies, and a broad range of other relevant environmental factors that act on them and with them. Systems analysis then allows us to study how criminal justice organizations change in response to those factors. Considering several other key concepts will help understand this process.

The New Criminal Justice suggests some other concepts that may be useful in systems analysis. One idea that will help students understand contemporary criminal justice is research. That, of course, includes a focus on research in its traditional sense: understanding the state of knowledge in the area being studied and whether some specific practice is consistent or not consistent with available research. But another perspective on research will also be valuable. Students should understand how criminal justice organizations produce and consume research. At the theoretical level the issue gets at Bateson's original interest in recursive feedback mechanisms that control organizations. Put in more practical terms, students should learn how criminal justice organizations may adopt or resist new information and the consequences of those choices.

Attention to another set of key concepts may also be a consequence of adopting a systems analysis approach in the classroom. As this volume should make clear, the inter-related processes of problem solving (McGarrell and Chermak, 2003a) and inter-

vention (Bynum, 2001) play significant roles in criminal justice today. Attention to these issues will force students to investigate how problems in criminal justice are identified and how different organizations respond to them. For example, their analysis would bring them to investigate the forces that led to the widespread adoption of anti-violence strategies or the growth in drug courts or, for that matter, the continued popularity of gun buy-back programs or the anti-drug program DARE despite unsupportive research.

At first glance the adoption of systems analysis in the criminal justice classroom may seem an unnecessary complication. But the same misgivings that led to its development in the field of biological sciences apply in this field. The classical paradigm of cause and effect in science proved inadequate in explaining multivariable processes in the natural world. Complex systems require complex models. "The systems true character is lost from view when its distinguishable components are investigated independently of one another" (Bale, 1995, p. 31). Systems are more than simply the sum of their parts. That, arguably, is a principle that can be useful in exploring criminal justice.

CONCLUSION

It may be true that understanding complex subjects requires some form of simplification. It might follow that the more novice the student the greater the simplifications must be. In criminal justice the effort to introduce the field to new students seems fraught with overgeneralization and other forms of simplification. Many textbooks appear to adopt the untested assumption that there is a common or average type of criminal case that can be easily described as it traverses the ins and outs of criminal justice. But the truth is more complex. The vast majority of cases processed in criminal justice deal with minor offenses and most often there is no intention to carry them through to fully available sanction, and so questions of rights and proper procedure are complicated. For those serious cases in which the full weight of the system is brought to bear there are still nuanced differences and alternate paths to understand.

The choice of simplification may be little more than a pedagogical device but, even as that, it may overreach. In the quest to be understood, the first course and its accompanying text may oversimplify, trivialize, and perhaps ignore a vast pool of knowledge including an increasingly rich reserve of important research in the field.

It is argued here that the New Criminal Justice provides a more complex portrait of criminal justice—one in which local communities stress their own values and priorities, in which organizations pool their resources, and in which changing knowledge and information can inform practice. The result is a complex set of approaches to criminal justice that can vary tremendously over time and place. The manifest differences are not attributable to error but instead they encourage students to consider theories that might explain how differences emerge and what their consequences are. The New Criminal Justice encourages students to locate justice as a core concept and to consider how communities define and pursue just outcomes and how successful they are in that pursuit. Under this perspective an emphasis on crime reduction means that students are also encouraged to link the understanding of the causes of crime with societal responses to crime and to appreciate how all aspects of criminal justice can benefit from the application of criminological theory. Finally, it is argued that there are benefits in analyses that seek to understand local criminal justice as integrated and inseparable from its environment, as opposed to studying its detached individual components. It is suggested that whole problems, complicated decision processes, and the forces behind change and intervention can be examined and understood whereas their dissection into small components would obscure their meaning.

It may sound as though these pages are suggesting the need for painful introspection or worse. One might even be tempted to conclude that, even if desirable, satisfying the suggested criteria for changing education would be an unrealistic and impossible task. But ours would not be the first field to be concerned that minutiae can come to dominate, or that became worried that they may have confused their own argot with meaningful concepts, or that wondered, more generally, whether the forest has gone missing for the trees.

One area in which serious efforts at educational reform have taken place has been medical education (Epstein, 2004; Dolmans et al., 2005). Doctors appear to have been the first to act on their wholesale discontent with the emphasis of their own education on facts and formulae. Beginning in the 1960s they began to adopt problem-based learning approaches that emphasized contextual learning, apprenticeships, and clinical experience. The approach has received positive evaluations which showed that doctors gained competency in addressing problems and responding to increases in information and that they suffered no detriment with regard to factual knowledge (Major and Palmer, 2001). Since then problem-based learning has expanded to many fields, and numerous national education organizations and advisory groups have called for the expansion of problem-based learning into undergraduate curricula. In 1998, the Boyer Report, *Reinventing Undergraduate Education: A Blueprint for America's Research Universities*, recommended a broad-based adoption of problem-based approaches. A few years later it was reported that faculty in over 300 colleges and universities were using the method. In those institutions problem-based learning is widely used as the instructional approach in complete classes and for whole subject curricula (Sternberg, 2008; Allen et al. 2008).

Problem-based learning refers to a range of pedagogical approaches that engage students in learning through their participation in addressing a research problem. Mastery of facts, vocabulary, theory, and other topics is incidental to the problem-solving exercise. Small groups of students work together on a project, which begins with discussion of what starts as a broad problem area. For introductory criminal justice such a problem might be something as broad as "gun violence" or "police use of force" or "probation effectiveness." The group then converts the broad problem into a number of researchable problems, sorts those problems, and selects the one to work on. Problem-solving work can take weeks to complete terms and can result in a number of products leading up to a final report. A team, for example, could settle on a research problem to examine how police can prevent gun homicides. That would require them to study police strategies, training, legal rights, patterns in criminal homicide, and gun law and regulation. A group studying drug crime would need to study the evidence on patterns of drug use, the nature and distribution of drug-related crimes, the efficacy and practicality of drug treatment, and perhaps even the problem of replacement of drug sellers in the community. In the process of solving problems students are exposed to many of the ideas that would form the primary content of the introductory textbook.

It has been argued that the local nature of criminal justice, the collaboration of agencies, and the use of research and information have transformed criminal justice in this modern era. Attention to those elements can provide tools that are useful in examining criminal justice today and particularly education in the field. That examination seems likely to result in some degree of dissatisfaction with present approaches to teaching. The field is simply far more interesting and important than our pedagogy now seems to support. Thinking about the New Criminal Justice, and considering the lessons of other fields, may help us build in new opportunities for our students to think more comprehensively, more theoretically, and more creatively about the enterprise that we invite them into.

REFERENCES

Allen, D. E., Duch, B. J., Groh, S. E., Watson, G. B., and White, H. B. (2008). "Scaling Up Research-Based Education for Undergraduates: Problem-Based Learning. Reinvigorating the Undergraduate Experience." Retrieved August 2008 from http:/www.cur.org/publications/aire_raire/delaware.asp.

Alpert, G. P. and Moore, M. H. (1993). *Performance Measures for the Criminal Justice System*. Washington, DC: U.S. Department of Justice, BPS-Princeton University Study Group.

Andrews, A. H., Jr. (1985). "Structuring the Political Independence of the Police Chief." In W. A. Geller (Ed.), *Police Leadership in America*. New York: Praeger. pp. 5–19.

Austin, J. (2003). "Why Criminology is Irrelevant." *Criminology and Public Policy*, (3), 557–64.

Balcazar, F. E., Taylor, R. R., Kielhofner, G. W., Tamley, K., Benziger, T., Carlin, N., and Johnson, S. (2004). "Participatory Action Research: General Principles and a Study with a Chronic Health Condition." In L. A. Jason, C. B. Keys, Y. Suarez-Balcazar, R. R. Taylor, and M. I. Davis (Eds.), *Participatory Community Research: Theories and Methods in Action*. Washington, DC: American Psychological Association. pp. 17–35.

Bale, L. S. (1995). "Gregory Bateson, Cybernetics, and the Social/Behavioral Sciences." *Cybernetics and Human Knowing*, 3 (1), 27–45.

Bateson, G. (1972). *Steps to an Ecology of Mind*. San Francisco, CA: Chandler.

Berman, G. and Feinblatt, J. (2001). "Problem Solving Courts." *Law and Policy*, 23, 125–40.

Bernard, T. and Engel, R. S. (2001). "Conceptualizing Criminal Justice Theory." *Justice Quarterly*, 18 (1), 1–30.

Bernard, T., Paoline, E. A., and Pare, P. P. (2005). "General Systems Theory and Criminal Justice." *Journal of Criminal Justice*, 38, 203–11.

von Bertalanffy, L. (1968). *General Systems Theory*. New York: George Braziller.

Blumstein, A. (1994). "The Task Force on Science and Technology." In J. Conley (Ed.), *The 1967 President's Crime Commission Report: Its Impact 25 Years Later*. Cincinnati: Anderson. pp. 145–58.

Boyer Commission on Educating Undergraduates in the Research University. (1998). *Reinventing Undergraduate Education: A Blueprint for America's Research Universities*. New York: Carnegie Foundation for the Advancement of Teaching.

Boyer, E. L. (1990). *Scholarship Reconsidered: Priorities of the Professorate*. Princeton, NJ: Carnegie Foundation for the Advancement of Teaching.

Braga, A. A. (2008). "Pulling Levers Focused Deterrence Strategies and the Prevention of Gun Homicide." *Journal of Criminal Justice*, 36, 332–43.

Braga, A. A. and Weisburd, D. (2007). "Police Innovation and Crime Prevention: Lessons Learned from Police Research over the Past 20 Years." Unpublished manuscript presented at National Institute of Justice Policing Research Workshop: Planning for the Future, Washington, DC.

Braga, A. A., Kennedy, D. M., Waring E. J., and Piehl, A. M. (2001). "Problem-Oriented Policing, Deterrence, and Youth Violence: An Evaluation of Boston's Operation Ceasefire." *Journal of Research in Crime & Delinquency*, 38 (3), 195–225.

Braga, A. A., Pierce, G. L., McDevitt, J., Bond, B. J., and Cronin, S. (2008). "The Strategic Prevention of Gun Violence among Gang-Involved Offenders." *Justice Quarterly*, 25 (1), 132–62.

Braithwaite, J. (1989). *Crime, Shame and Reintegration*. Cambridge, UK: Cambridge University Press.

Bynum, T. S. (2001). *Using Analysis for Problem-Solving: A Guidebook for Law Enforcement*. Washington, DC: U.S. Department of Justice Office of Community Oriented Policing Services.

Bynum, T. and Decker, S. (2006). *Chronic Offender Lists: Case Study 4. Project Safe Neighborhoods Strategic Interventions*. Washington, DC: Office of Justice Programs.

Bureau of Justice Assistance. (2002). "Proposal Guide for Project Safe Neighborhoods Research Partner/Crime Analyst Grant." Retrieved February 20, 2006, from http://www.ojp.usdoj.gov/BJA/psngrants/psn18.html.

Castellano, T. C. and Gould, J. B. (2007). "Neglect of Justice in Criminal Justice Theory: Causes, Consequences, and Alternatives." In D. Duffee and E. R. McGuire (Eds.), *Criminal Justice Theory: Explaining the Nature and Behavior of Criminal Justice*. New York: Routledge. pp. 71–92.

Chermak, S. (2007). *Reducing Violent Crime and Firearms Violence: The Indianapolis Lever-Pulling Experiment (Final Report)*. U.S. Department of Justice: National Institute of Justice (Grant # 2003-IJ-CX-1038).

Clark, R. (1997). *Situational Crime Prevention: Successful Case Studies*. Albany, NY: Harrow and Heston.

Clear, T. (2001). "Has Academic Criminal Justice Come of Age?" *Justice Quarterly*, 18 (4), 709–27.

Clear, T. and Karp, D. (1999). *The Community Justice Ideal: Preventing Crime and Achieving Justice*. Boulder, CO: Westview.

Cohen, J. and Ludwig, J. (2003). "Policing Crime Guns." In J. Ludwig and P. J. Cook (Eds.), *Evaluating Gun Policy: Effects on Crime and Violence*. Washington, DC: Brookings Institution Press. pp. 217–50.

Cohen, L. E. and Felson, M. (1979). "Social Change and Crime Rate Trends: A Routine Activity Approach." *American Sociological Review*, 44, 588–608.

Cohen, M. D., March, H., and Olsen, J. P. (1972). "A Garbage Can Model of Organizational Choice." *Administrative Science Quarterly*, 17, 1–25.

Coleman, V., Holton W. C., Jr., Olson, K., Robinson, S. C. and Stewart, J. (1999, October). "Using Knowledge and Teamwork to Reduce Crime." *National Institute of Justice Journal*, 16–23.

Combs, N. A. (2007). *Guilty Pleas in International Law: Constructing a Restorative Justice Approach*. Stanford, CA: Stanford University Press.

Conley, J. (1994). "Introduction." In J. Conley (Ed.), *The 1967 President's Crime Commission Report: Its Impact 25 Years Later*. Cincinnati, OH: Anderson. pp. ix–xiv.

Cook, P. and Ludwig, J. (2000). *Gun Violence: The Real Costs*. New York: Oxford University Press.

Cope, N. (2004). "Intelligence Led Policing or Policing Led Intelligence." *British Journal of Criminology*, 44, 188–203.

Cornwall, A. and Jewkes, R. (1995). "What is Participatory Research?" *Social Science and Medicine*, 41, 1667–76.

Corsaro, N. and McGarrell, E. F. (2009). "Testing a Promising Homicide Reduction Strategy: Re-assessing the Impact of the Indianapolis 'Pulling Levers' Intervention." *Journal of Experimental Criminology*, 5, 63–82.

Corsaro, N., Brunson, R. K., and McGarrell, E. F. (2009). "Problem-Oriented Policing and Open-Air Drug Markets: Examining the Rockford 'Pulling Levers' Deterrence Strategy." *Crime & Delinquency*, 55, 1–23.

Crank, J. (2003). *Imagining Justice*. Cincinnati: Anderson.

Crank, J. P. and Langworthy, R. H. (1992). "An Institutional Perspective of Policing." *Journal of Criminal Law and Criminology*, 83 (2), 338–63.

Crawford, A. (1997). *The Local Governance of Crime: Appeals to Community and Partnerships*. Oxford: Oxford University Press.

Cronin, T. E., Cronin, T. Z., and Milakovich, M. (1981). *US v. Crime in the Streets*. Bloomington, IN: Indiana University Press.

Cullen, F. and Gilbert, K. (1982). *Reaffirming Rehabilitation*. Cincinnati, OH: Anderson.

Cureton, S. R., Frabutt, J. M., and Gathings, M. J. (2004). *Project Safe Neighborhoods: Preliminary Review of Homicides in Greensboro, North Carolina (January 2003–May 2004)*. Greensboro, NC: Center for Youth, Family, and Community Partnerships, University of North Carolina at Greensboro.

Dalton, E. (2003). "Lessons in Preventing Homicide: Project Safe Neighborhoods Report." Retrieved August 15, 2007, from: http://cj.msu/Eoutreach/psn/erins_report_jan_2004.pdf.

Davis, M. S. (2006). "Crimes Mala in Se: An Equity-Based Definition." *Criminal Justice Policy Review*, 17, 270–89.

Decker, S. and Barlow, H. (2009). *Criminology and Public Policy: From Theory to Practice*. Philadelphia: Temple University Press.

Decker, S. and McDevitt, J. (2006). *Gun Prosecution Case Screening: Case Study 1. Project Safe Neighborhoods Strategic Interventions*. Washington, DC: U.S. Department of Justice, Office of Justice Programs.

Decker, S. H., Huebner, B. M., Watkins, A., Green, L., Bynum, T., and McGarrell, E. F. (2007). *Project Safe Neighborhoods: Strategic Interventions: Eastern District of Missouri, Case Study 7*. Washington, DC: U.S. Department of Justice, Office of Justice Programs.

Di Luca, K. (2007). *Findings from the Alamance County Incident Review*. Greensboro, NC: Center for Youth, Family, and Community Partnerships, University of North Carolina at Greensboro.

Di Luca, K. and Sellers, D. (2008). *Orange County Crime Incident Review Update*. Presentation to the Orange County Community Threat Group. Greensboro, NC: Center for Youth, Family, and Community Partnerships, University of North Carolina at Greensboro.

Dolmans, D. H., de Grave, W., Wolfhagen, I. H., and van der Vleuten, C. P. (2005). "Problem-Based Learning: Future Challenges for Educational Practice and Research." *Medical Education*, 39, 732–41.

Dreisbach, C. (2008). *Ethics in Criminal Justice*. New York: McGraw-Hill.

Duffee, D. (1980). *Explaining Criminal Justice: Community Theory and Criminal Justice Reform*. Cambridge, MA: Oelgeschlager.

Duffee, D. (1990). *Explaining Criminal Justice: Community Theory and Criminal Justice Reform*. Prospect Heights, IL: Waveland Press.

Duffee, D. and Allan, E. (2007). "Criminal Justice, Criminology and Criminal Justice Theory." In D. Duffee and E. R. Maguire (Eds.), *Criminal Justice Theory: Explaining the Nature and Behavior of Criminal Justice*. New York: Routledge. pp. 1–22.

Duffee, D and Maguire, E. R. (Eds.) (2007). *Criminal Justice Theory: Explaining the Nature and Behavior of Criminal Justice*. New York: Routledge.

Ebata, A. T. (1996). "Making University–Community Collaborations Work: Challenges for Institutions and Individuals." *Journal of Research on Adolescence*, 6 (1), 71–9.

Eisenstein, J., Flemming, R., and Nardulli, P. (1988). *The Contours of Justice: Communities and Their Courts*. Boston, MA: Little Brown.

Ekblom, P. (1998). *Getting the Best out of Crime Analysis*. Crime Prevention Unit: Paper 10. London: Home Office.

Ekland-Olson, S. and Martin, S. (1988). "Organizational Compliance with Court Ordered Reform." *Law and Society Review*, 22, 359–84.

Ellis, E., Fortune, J., and Peters, G. (2007). "Partnership Problems: Analysis and Re-design." *Crime Prevention and Community Safety: An International Journal*, 9 (1), 34–51.

Epstein, R. (2004). "Learning from Problems of Problem-Based Learning." *BMC Medical Education*, 4 (1). Retrieved August 2008 from http://biomedial central.com/1472-6920/4/1.

Feeley, M. (1973). "Two Models of the Criminal Justice System: An Organizational Perspective." *Law and Society Review*, 7, 407–25.

Feeley, M. (1979). *The Process is the Punishment: Handling Cases in a Lower Criminal Justice Court*. New York: Sage.

Feinblatt, J., Berman, G., and Sviridoff, M. (1998). *Neighborhood Justice: Lessons from the Midtown Community Court*. New York: Center for Court Innovation.

Felson, M. (1998). *Crime and Everyday Life*, 2nd edition. Thousand Oaks, CA: Pine Forge.

Forst, M. L. (1977). "To What Extent Should the Criminal Justice System be a 'System?'" *Crime & Delinquency*, 23, 403–16.

Frabutt, J. M. (2003). "Catholic Higher Education as a Context for University–Community Partnerships." In T. C. Hunt, E. A. Joseph, R. J. Nuzzi, and J. O. Geiger (Eds.), *Handbook of Research on Catholic Higher Education*. Greenwich, CT: Information Age Publishing. pp. 325–44.

Frabutt, J. M., Easterling, D. V., and MacKinnon-Lewis, C. (2001). *A Preliminary Evaluation of the High Point Notification Program*. Greensboro, NC: Center for the Study of Social Issues, University of North Carolina at Greensboro.

Frabutt, J. M., Gathings, M. J., Hunt, E. D., and Loggins, T. J. (2004). *High Point West End Initiative: Project Description, Log, and Preliminary Impact Analysis*. University of North Carolina at Greensboro: Center for Youth, Family and Community Partnerships.

Frabutt, J. M. Gathings, M. J., Jackson, D. T., and Buford, A. P. (2006). *High Point Daniel Brooks Initiative: Project Description and Preliminary Impact Analysis*. University of North Carolina at Greensboro: Center for Youth, Family and Community Partnerships.

Freed, D. J. (1969). "The Nonsystem of Criminal Justice." In J. S. Campbell, J. R. Sahid, and D. P. Stang (Eds.), *Law and Order Reconsidered: A National Staff Report to the Commission on the Causes and Prevention of Violence*. Washington, DC: U.S. Government Printing Office. pp. 265–84.

Fyfe, J. (1997). "Good Policing." In S. Stojkovic, J. Klofas, and D. Kalinich (Eds.), *The Administration and Management of Criminal Justice Organizations*. Prospect Heights, IL: Waveland. pp. 113–33.

Gaines, L., Worrall, J., and Southerland, M. (2003). *Police Administration*, 2nd edition. Boston, MA: McGraw-Hill.

Gathings, M. J. and Frabutt, J. M. (2005). *Evaluation of the Durham Police Department's S.T.A.R.S. Notification Program*. Greensboro, NC: Center for Youth, Family, and Community Partnerships, University of North Carolina at Greensboro.

Gathings, M. J. and Frabutt, J. M. (2006). *Standing the Test of Time: An Examination of the S.T.A.R.S. Notification Program's Efficacy over Time*. Greensboro, NC: Center for Youth, Family, and Community Partnerships, University of North Carolina at Greensboro.

Gibbons, D. C. and Blake, G. F. (1977). "Perspectives in Criminology and Criminal Justice: The Implications for Higher Education Programs." *Criminal Justice Review*, 2 (1), 23–40.

Goldstein, H. (1990). *Problem-Oriented Policing*. New York: McGraw-Hill.

Gottfredson, D. C., Gerstenblith, S. A., Soule, D. A., Womer, S. C., and Lu, S. (2004). "Do after School Programs Reduce Delinquency?" *Prevention Science* 5 (4), 253–66.

Greene, J. (2004). "Community Policing and Police Organizations." In W. Skogan (Ed.), *Community Policing: Can It Work?* Belmont, CA: Wadsworth. pp. 30–54.

Hagan, J. (1989). "Why is There so Little Criminal Justice Theory? Neglected Macro and Micro Links between Organization and Power." *Journal of Research in Crime & Delinquency*, 26 (2), 116–35.

Hale, D. (1998). "Criminal Justice Education: Traditions in Transition." *Justice Quarterly*, 15 (3), 385–94.

Hall, A., Henry, A., Perlstein, J., and Smith, W. (1985). *Alleviating Jail Crowding: A Systems Perspective*. Washington, DC: National Institute of Justice.

Hall, M. (2007, July 24). "State-Run Sites Not Effective against Terror." *USA Today*, p. 1.

Hartley, R. D., Maddan, S., and Spohn, C. C. (2007). "Prosecutorial Discretion: An Examination of Substantial Assistance Departures in Federal Crack-Cocaine and Powder-Cocaine Cases." *Justice Quarterly*, 24 (3), 383–407.

Harvey, L. K. (2005a). *The New Hope Initiative: A Collaborative Approach to Closing an Open-Air Drug Market and a Blueprint for Other Communities*. Winston-Salem, NC: Center for Community Safety, Winston-Salem State University.

Harvey, L. K. (2005b). *Qualitative Evaluation of Zero Armed Perpetrators (ZAP): A Summary Report*. Winston-Salem, NC: Center for Community Safety, Winston-Salem State University.

Harvey, L. and Frabutt, J. M. (2004). *Summary of Homicide Review in Winston-Salem, North Carolina: Project Safe Neighborhoods*. Winston-Salem, NC: Center for Community Safety, Winston-Salem State University.

Havelock, R. (1979). *Planning for Innovation through Dissemination and Utilization of Knowledge*. Ann Arbor, MI: Institute of Social Research.

Hayes, H. and Daly, K. (2003). "Youth Justice Conferencing and Reoffending." *Justice Quarterly*, 20 (4), 725–64.

Hayes, R. (2005, Spring). *Gangs in North Carolina: A Comparative Analysis between 1999 and 2004*. Raleigh, NC: SystemStats: North Carolina Criminal Justice Analysis Center.

Henderson, J. and Boostrom, R. L. (1989). "Criminal Justice Theory: Anarchy Reigns." *Journal of Contemporary Criminal Justice*, 5 (1), 29–39.

Hipple, N. K., O'Shea, T., McGarrell, E. F., and Corsaro, N. (forthcoming a). *Project Safe Neighborhoods: Strategic Interventions: Southern District of Alabama, Case Study*. Washington, DC: U.S. Department of Justice, Office of Justice Programs.

Hipple, N. K., Perez, H. A., McGarrell, E. F., Corsaro, N., and Robinson, T. H (forthcoming b). *Project Safe Neighborhoods: Strategic Interventions: District of Nebraska, Case Study*. Washington, DC: U.S. Department of Justice, Office of Justice Programs.

Hipple, N. K., Frabutt, J. M., Corsaro, N., McGarrell, E. F., and Gathings, M. J. (forthcoming c). *Project Safe Neighborhoods: Strategic Interventions: Middle District of North Carolina, Case Study*. Washington, DC: U.S. Department of Justice, Office of Justice Programs.

Hudzik, J. and Cordner, G. (1983). *Planning in Criminal Justice Organizations and Systems*. New York: McMillan.

Irwin, J. (1985). *The Jail: Managing the Underclass in American Society*. Berkeley, CA: University of California Press.

Israel, B. A., Schultz, A. J., Parker, E. A., and Becker, A. B. (2001). "Community-Based Participatory Research: Policy Recommendations for Promoting a Partnership Approach in Health Research." *Education for Health*, 14, 182–97.

Israel, B. A., Schultz, A. J., Parker, E. A., Becker, A. B., Allen, A. J., and Guzman, J. R. (2003). "Critical Issues in Developing and Following Community Based Participatory Research Principles." In M. Minkler and N. Wallerstein (Eds.), *Community-Based Research for Health*. San Francisco, CA: Jossey-Bass. pp. 53–76.

Karp, D. and Clear, T. (Eds.) (2002). *What is Community Justice: Case Studies of Restorative Justice and Community Supervision*. Thousand Oaks, CA: Sage.

Katzenbach, N. (1967). "Foreword." *The Challenge of Crime in a Free Society*. Washington, DC: U.S. Government Printing Office.

Kaufmann, A. and Gupta, M. (1991). *Introduction to Fuzzy Arithmetic Theory and Application*. New York: Van Nostrand Reinhold.

Kelling, G. and Coles, C. (1996). *Fixing Broken Windows: Restoring Order and Reducing Crime in Our Communities*. New York: Touchstone.

Kellogg Commission on the Future of State and Land-Grant Universities. (1999). *Returning to Our Roots: Executive Summaries*. Washington, DC: National Association of State Universities and Land-Grant Colleges.

Kennedy, D. (1997). "Pulling Levers: Chronic Offenders, High Crime Settings, and a Theory of Prevention." *Valparaiso University Law Review*, 31 (2), 449–84.

Kennedy, D. (1998). "Pulling Levers: Getting Deterrence Right." *National Institute of Justice Journal*, 248, 2–8.

Kennedy, D. (2009). "Drugs, Race and Common Ground: Reflections on the High Point Intervention." *NIJ Journal*, 262, 12–17.

Kennedy, D. and Braga, A. A. (1998). "Homicide in Minneapolis: Research for Problem Solving." *Homicide Studies*, 2, 263–90.

Kennedy, D., Piehl, A., and Braga, A. (1996). "Youth Violence in Boston: Gun Markets, Serious Youth Offenders, and a Use-Reduction Strategy." *Law and Contemporary Problems*, 59, 147–96.

Kennedy, D., Braga, A., and Piehl, A. (1997). "The (Un)known Universe: Mapping Gangs and Gang Violence in Boston." In D. Weisburd and J. T. McEwen (Eds.), *Crime Mapping and Crime Prevention*. New York: Criminal Justice Press. pp. 219–62.

Kennedy, D. A., Braga, A. A., and Piehl, A. M. (2001). *Research Report, Reducing Gun Violence: The Boston Gun Project's Operation Ceasefire*. Washington, DC: National Institute of Justice.

Klir, G. J. and Yuan, B. (1995). *Fuzzy Sets and Fuzzy Logic: Theory and Applications*. Saddle River, NJ: Prentice Hall.

Klockars, C. (1980). "The Dirty Harry Problem." *Annals of the American Academy of Political and Social Science*, 452, 33–47.

Klofas, J. (1990). "The Jail and the Community." *Justice Quarterly*, 7, 69–102.

Klofas, J. and Delaney, C. (2002). "Crime Incident Reviews in the Local Criminal Justice System." Presented by Rochester Police Department in association with Department of Criminal Justice, Rochester Institute of Technology.

Klofas, J. and Hipple, N.K. (2006). *Criminal Incident Reviews: Case Study 3. Project Safe Neighborhoods Strategic Interventions*. Washington, DC: Office of Justice Programs.

Kramer, R. M, Brewer, M. B., and Hanna, B. A. (1996). "Collective Trust and Collective Action: Decisions to Trust a Social Decision." In R. M. Kramer and T. R. Tyler (Eds.), *Trust in Organizations: Frontiers of Theory and Research*. Thousand Oaks, CA: Sage Publications. pp. 357–89.

Kraska, P. (2006). "Criminal Justice Theory: Toward Legitimacy and an Infrastructure." *Justice Quarterly*, 2, 167–85.

Kuhn, T. (1970). *The Structure of Scientific Revolutions*. Chicago, IL: University of Chicago Press.

Lang, R. A. J., Canary, L., Cloud, J. M., Frabutt, J. M., Haynes, S. D., and Whisler, B. (2004, June). "Expanding Project Safe Neighborhoods into New Sites: A Research Partner Perspective on the Multi-site Approach." Panel discussant, Project Safe Neighborhoods National Conference, Kansas City, MO.

Lee, J. H. and Visano, L. H. (1981). "Official Deviance in the Legal System." In H. L. Ross (Ed.), *Law and Deviance*. Beverly Hills, CA: Sage. pp. 215–50.

Lerner, M. J. (1965). "Evaluation of Performance as a Function of Performer's Reward and Attractiveness." *Journal of Personality and Social Psychology*, 1, 355–60.

Lerner, R. M. and Simon, L. A. K. (1998). "The New American Outreach University." In R. M. Lerner and L. A. K. Simon (Eds.), *Michigan State University Series on Children, Youth, and Families: University–Community Collaborations for the Twenty-First Century—Outreach Scholarship for Youth and Families*. New York: Garland Publishing. pp. 3–23.

Lewin, K. (1948). "Action Research and Minority Problems." In K. Lewin (Ed.), *Resolving Social Conflicts: Selected Papers in Group Dynamics*. New York: Harper & Row. pp. 5–100.

Lindblom, C. E. and Cohen, D. K. (1979). *Usable Knowledge: Social Science and Social Problem Solving*. New Haven, CT: Yale University Press.

Lipsky, M. (1980). *Street-Level Bureaucracy*. New York: Russell Sage Foundation.

McDevitt, J., Decker, S., Hipple, N. K., and McGarrell, E. F. (2006). *Offender Notification Meetings: Case Study 2. Project Safe Neighborhoods Strategic Interventions*. Washington, DC: Office of Justice Programs.

McDevitt, J., Braga, A. A., Cronin, S., McGarrell, E. F., and Bynum, T. S. (2007). *Project Safe Neighborhoods: Strategic Interventions: Lowell, District of Massachusetts, Case Study 6*. Washington, DC: U.S. Department of Justice, Office of Justice Programs.

McGarrell, E. F. and Chermak, S. (2003a). "Problem Solving to Reduce Gang and Drug Related Violence in Indianapolis." In S. H. Decker (Ed.) *Policing Gangs and Youth Violence*. Newbury Park, CA: Wadsworth. pp. 77–101.

McGarrell, E. F. and Chermak, S. (2003b). *Strategic Approaches to Reducing Firearms Violence: Final Report on the Indianapolis Violence Reduction Partnership*. Final report submitted to the U.S. National Institute of Justice. East Lansing, MI: School of Criminal Justice, Michigan State University.

McGarrell, E. F., Chermak, S., Weiss, A., and Wilson, J. (2001). "Reducing Firearms Violence through Directed Police Patrol." *Criminology and Public Policy* 1 (1), 119–48.

McGarrell, E. F., Hipple, N., and Banks, D. (2003) "Community Meetings as a Tool in Inmate Re-entry." *Justice Research and Policy*, 5 (2), 1–28.

McGarrell, E., Chermak, S., Wilson, J., and Corsaro, N. (2006). "Reducing Homicide through a Lever Pulling Strategy." *Justice Quarterly*, 23, 214–29.

McGarrell E., Freilich J., and Chermak, S. (2007a). "Intelligence-Led Policing as a Framework for Responding to Terrorism." *Journal of Contemporary Criminal Justice*, 23, 142–58.

McGarrell, E. F., Hipple, N. K., Corsaro, N., Pappanastos, E., Stevens, E., and Albritton, J. (2007b). *Project Safe Neighborhoods Middle District of Alabama: Case Study 5*. Washington, DC: U.S. Department of Justice, Office of Justice Programs.

McGarrell, E. F., Hipple, N. K., Corsaro, N., Bynum, T. S., Perez, H., Zimmermann, C. A., and Garmo, M. (2009). *Project Safe Neighborhoods: A National Program to Reduce Gun Crime*. Washington, DC: Final Report submitted to the National Institute of Justice.

Mackinem, M. B. and Higgins, P. (2007). "Tell Me about the Test: The Construction of Truth and Lies in Drug Court." *Journal of Contemporary Ethnography*, 36 (3), 223–51.

MacKinnon-Lewis, C. and Frabutt, J. M. (2001). "A Bridge to Healthier Families and Children: The Collaborative Process of a University–Community Partnership." *Journal of Higher Education Outreach and Engagement*, 6 (3), 65–76.

Maguire, E. R. and Uchida, C. D. (2000). "Measurement and Explanation in the Comparative Study of American Police Organizations." In D. Duffee (Ed.), *Measurement and Analysis of Crime and Justice, Criminal Justice 2000, Vol. 4*. Washington, DC: National Institute of Justice. pp. 491–558.

Major, C. H. and Palmer, B. (2001). "Assessing the Effectiveness of Problem-Based Learning in Higher Education: Lessons from Literature." *Academic Exchange Quarterly*, 5 (1), 1–5.

March, J. G. and Simon, H. A. (1958). *Organizations*. New York: Wiley.

Massachusetts Executive Office of Public Safety and Security. (n.d.). "Senator Charles E. Shannon, Jr. Community Safety Initiative." Retrieved December 29, 2008, from http://www.mass.gov/?pageID=eopssubtopic&L=5&L0=Home&L1=Funding+%26+Training+Opportunities&L2=Justice+%26+Prevention&L3=Grant+Programs&L4=Senator+Charles+E.+Shannon%2c+Jr.+Community+Safety+Initiative&sid=Eeops.

Mastrofski, S. (2006). "Community Policing: A Skeptical View." In D. Weisburd and A. A. Braga (Eds.), *Police Innovation: Contrasting Perspectives*. New York: Cambridge University Press. pp. 44–73.

Mattessich, P. W. and Monsey, B. R. (1992). *Collaboration: What Makes It Work? A Review of Research Literature on Factors Influencing Successful Collaboration*. St. Paul, MN: Amherst H. Wilder Foundation.

Mazerolle, L., Soole, S., and Rombouts, S. (2007). "Drug Law Enforcement: A Review of the Evaluation Literature." *Police Quarterly*, 10, 115–53.

Miller, T. R. and Cohen, M. A. (1997). "Costs of Gunshot and Cut/Stab Wounds in the United States, with some Canadian Comparisons." *Accident Analysis and Prevention*, 29, 329–41.

Mills, C. W. (1959). *The Sociological Imagination*. New York: Oxford University Press.

Minkler, M. and Wallerstein, N. (2003). "Introduction to Community-Based Participatory Research." In M. Minkler and N. Wallerstein (Eds.), *Community-Based Research for Health*. San Francisco, CA: Jossey-Bass. pp. 3–26.

Morn, F. (1990). "Prostitution, Police and City Culture in a Small Midwestern City: A History, 1900–1960." *Journal of Crime and Justice*, 13 (2), 149–73.

Morn, F. (1995). *Academic Politics and the History of Criminal Justice Education*. Westport, CT: Greenwood Press.

Murphy, D. and Worrall, J. L. (2007). "The Threat of Mission Distortion in Police–Probation Partnerships." *Policing: An International Journal of Police Strategies & Management*, 30 (1), 132–49.

Nardulli, P., Eisenstein, J., and Flemming, R. (1988). *The Tenor of Justice: Criminal Courts and the Guilty Plea Process*. Urbana, IL: Illinois University Press.

National Commission on Terrorist Attacks upon the United States. (2004). *The 911 Commission Report*. New York: Norton.

National Institute of Justice. (2007). Annual Research Conference. Washington, DC.

National Research Council. (2004). *Fairness and Effectiveness in Policing: The Evidence*. Committee to Review Research on Police Policy and Practices. W. Skogan and K. Frydl (Eds.). Committee on Law and Justice, Division of Behavioral and Social Science Education. Washington, DC: The National Academies Press.

Neubauer, D. (2004). *America's Courts and the Criminal Justice System*. Belmont, CA: Wadsworth.

Office of Human Subjects Research Protections. (2004). http://www.hhs.gov/ohrp/.

Olsen, M. (1965). *The Logic of Collective Action*. New Haven, CT: Yale University Press.

Owen, S. S., Fradela, H.. Burke, T., and Joplin, J. (2006). "Conceptualizing Criminal Justice: Revising the Introductory Criminal Justice Course." *Journal of Criminal Justice Education*, 17 (1), 3–26.

Papachristos, A. V., Meares, T. L. and Fagan, J. (2007). "Attention Felons: Evaluating Project Safe Neighborhoods in Chicago." *Journal of Empirical Legal Studies*, 4, 223–72.

Pattavina, A. (2005) *Information Technology and the Criminal Justice System*. Thousand Oaks, CA: Sage.

Petersilia, J. (1999). "Parole and Prisoner Reentry in the United States." In *Crime and Justice: A Review of Research*, Vol. 26. Chicago, IL: University of Chicago Press. pp. 479–529.

Pettiway, L. (1995). "Copping Crack: The Travel Behavior of Crack Users." *Justice Quarterly*, 12, 499–524.

Piehl, A. M., Cooper, S. J., Braga, A. A., and Kennedy, D. M. (2003). "Testing for Structural Breaks in the Evaluation of Programs." *Review of Economics and Statistics*, 85, 550–8.

Pisciotta, A. (1994). "A Retrospective Look at the Task Force Report on Juvenile Delinquency and Youth Crime." In J. Conley (Ed.), *The 1967 President's Crime Commission Report: Its Impact 25 Years Later*. Cincinnati, OH: Anderson. pp. 81–100.

Police Executive Research Forum. (2006). *Chief Concerns: A Gathering Storm*. Washington, DC: Police Executive Research Forum.

Pollock, J. (1993). *Ethics in Crime and Justice: Dilemmas and Decisions*. Belmont, CA: Wadsworth.

President's Commission on Law Enforcement and Administration of Justice. (1967a). *The Challenge of Crime in a Free Society*. Washington, DC: U.S. Government Printing Office.

President's Commission on Law Enforcement and Administration of Justice. (1967b). *Task Force Report: Science and Technology*. Washington, DC: U.S. Government Printing Office.

Project Safe Neighborhoods. (2001). *Project Safe Neighborhoods: America's Network against Gun Violence: Implementation Guide for PSN Partners*. Washington, DC: U.S. Department of Justice.

Quijas, L. F., MacKinnon-Lewis, C., and Frabutt, J. M. (2001, November). "Youth Violence Prevention and Intervention: A Community-Based, Family-Centered Approach." Presented at Family Re-Union 10: Back to the Future, Accomplishments and Next Steps, Vanderbilt University, Nashville, TN.

Raphael, S. and Ludwig, J. (2003). "Prison Sentence Enhancements: The Case of Project Exile." In J. Ludwig and P. J. Cook (Eds.), *Evaluating Gun Policy: Effects on Crime and Violence*. Washington, DC: Brookings Institute Press. pp. 251–77.

Ratcliffe, J. (2002). "Intelligence–Led Policing and the Problems of Turning Rhetoric into Practice." *Policing and Society*, 12 (1), 53–66.

Ratcliffe, J. H. (2008). *Intelligence Led Policing*. Cullompton, Devon, UK: Willan Publishing.

Reiss, A. (1994). "An Evaluation and Assessment of the Impact of the Task Force Report: Crime and its Impact—an Assessment." In J. Conley (Ed.), *The 1967 President's Crime Commission Report: Its Impact 25 Years Later*. Cincinnati, OH: Anderson. pp. 1–20.

Renauer, B. B. (2007). "Understanding Variety in Urban Community Policing: An Institutional Theory Approach." In D. E. Duffee and E. R. Maguire (Eds.), *Criminal Justice Theory: Explaining the Nature and Behavior of Criminal Justice*. New York: Routledge. pp. 121–50.

Rengert, G. (1996). *The Geography of Illegal Drugs*. Boulder, CO: Westview Press.

Rengert, G. and Wasilchick, J. (1989). *Space, Time, and Crime: Ethnographic Insights into Residential Burglary*. Washington, DC: Final Report Submitted to National Institute of Justice.

Richman, D. (2001). "Project Exile and the Allocation of Federal Law Enforcement Authority." *Arizona Law Review*, 43, 369–411.

Ritter, N. (Ed.). (2007). "Al Blumstein: 40 Years of Contributions to Criminal Justice." *National Institute of Justice Journal*, 257, 14–18.

Roehl, J., Huitt, R., Wycoff, M. A., Pate, A., Rebovich, D., and Coyle, K. (1996, October). *National Process Evaluation of Operation Weed and Seed, Research in Brief*. Washington, DC: U.S. Department of Justice, National Institute of Justice.

Roehl, J. Rosenbaum, D., Costello, S., Coldren, J., Schuck, A., Kunard, L., and Forde, D. (2008). *Paving the Way for Project Safe Neighborhoods: SACSI in 10 U.S. Cities*. National Institute of Justice Research in Brief. Washington, DC: United States Department of Justice, Office of Justice Programs.

Rosenbaum, D. P. (Ed.). (1994). *The Challenge of Community Policing: Testing the Promises*. Newbury Park, CA: Sage Publications.

Rosenbaum, D. P. (2002). "Evaluating Multi-Agency Anti-Crime Partnerships: Theory, Design, and Measurement Issues." *Crime Prevention Studies*, 14, 171–225.

Rosenfeld, R., Fornango, R., and Baumer, E. (2005). "Did Ceasefire, Compstat, and Exile Reduce Homicide?" *Criminology and Public Policy*, 4, 419–50.

Ruback, R. B. and Bergstrom, M. H. (2006). "Economic Sanctions in Criminal Justice: Purposes, Effects, and Implications." *Criminal Justice and Behavior*, 33(2), 242–73.

Safe Streets. (2008). "CITY Coalition Brochure." Retrieved July 14, 2008, from http://www.safestreets. org/downloads/CITY-Coalition-Brochure-08.pdf.

Sampson, R. J., Raudenbush, S. W. and Earls, F. (1997). "Neighborhoods and Violent Crime: A Multilevel Study of Collective Efficacy." *Science*, 277, 918–23.

Schafer, M. (2004). "Jails and Judicial Review: Spatial Problems for Local Facilities." In S. Stojkovic, J. Klofas, and D. Kalinich (Eds.), *The Administration and Management of Criminal Justice Organizations*. Prospect Heights, IL: Waveland. pp. 442–56.

Sherman, L. W. (1978). *Scandal and Reform: Controlling Police Corruption*. Berkeley, CA: University of California Press.

Sherman, L. W. (1998). *Evidence Based Policing*. Washington DC: The Police Foundation.

Sherman, L. W. (2003, September). "Misleading Evidence and Evidence-Led Policy: Making Social Science More Experimental." *Annals of the Academy of Political and Social Science*, 589, 6–19.

Sherman, L. W., and Rogan, D. P. (1995). "Effects of Gun Seizure on Gun Violence: 'Hot Spots' Patrol in Kansas City." *Justice Quarterly* 12 (4), 673–93.

Sherman, L. W., Gottfredson, D., MacKenzie, D., Eck, J., Reuter, P., and Bushway, S. (1997). *Preventing Crime. What Works? What Doesn't? What's Promising?* Washington, DC: National Institute of Justice.

Sherman, L., Strang, H., and Woods, D. (2000). *Recidivism Patterns in the Canberra Reintegrative Shaming Experiments (RISE)*. Canberra, Australia: Centre for Restorative Justice, Australian National University.

Silverman, E. B. (1999). *NYPD Battles Crime: Innovative Strategies in Policing*. Boston, MA: Northeastern University Press.

Skogan, W. G. (2006). *Police and Community in Chicago: A Tale of Three Cities*. Oxford: Oxford University Press.

Skogan, W. G., Steiner, L., Hartnett, S., DuBois, J., Bennis, J., Rottinghaus, B., Kim, S. Y., Van, K., and Rosenbaum, D. (2003). *Community Policing in Chicago Years Eight and Nine*. Chicago, IL: Criminal Justice Information Authority

Skolnick, J. H. (1966). *Justice without Trial*. New York: John Wiley and Sons.

Small, S. A. (1995). "Enhancing Contexts of Adolescent Development: The Role of Community-Based Action Research." In D. S. Palermo and R. M. Lerner (Series Eds) and L. J. Crockett and A. C. Crouter (Vol. Eds), *The Penn State Series on Child and Adolescent Development: Vol. 5. Pathways through Adolescence: Individual Development in Relation to Social Contexts*. Mahwah, NJ: Lawrence Erlbaum. pp. 211–32.

Small, S. A. (1996). "Collaborative, Community-Based Research on Adolescents: Using Research for Community Change." *Journal of Research on Adolescence*, 6, 9–22.

Smith, D. A. and Visher, C. A. (1981). "Street Level Justice: Situational Determinants of Police Arrest Decisions." *Social Problems* 29 (2), 167–77.

Snipes, J. B. and Maguire, E. R. (2007). "Foundations of Criminal Justice Theory." In D. Duffee and E. R. Maguire (Eds.), *Criminal Justice Theory: Explaining the Nature and Behavior of Criminal Justice*. New York: Routledge. pp. 27–49.

Sobol, J. J. (1997). "Behavioral Characteristics and Level of Involvement for Victims of Homicide." *Homicide Studies*, 1 (4), 359–76.

Sternberg, R. J. (2008). "Interdisciplinary Problem-Based Learning: An Alternative to Traditional Majors and Minors." *Liberal Education*, 94 (1), 1–7.

Stojkovic, S., Kalinich, D., and Klofas, J. (2008). *Criminal Justice Organizations: Administration and Management*. Belmont, CA: Wadsworth.

Sudnow, D. (1965). "Normal Crimes: Sociological Features of the Penal Code in a Public Defender's Office." *Social Problems*, 12, 255–76.

Sumner, M. A., Hunt, E. A., and Frabutt, J. M. (2005, November). "The High Point Drug Market Intervention." In D. A. Kennedy (Chair), *Focused Deterrence and Drug Markets*. Paper presented at the 2005 American Society of Criminology Conference, The Interdisciplinary Roots and Branches of Criminology, Toronto, Canada.

Sunstein, C. R. (2002). *Risk and Reason: Safety, Law and the Environment*. Cambridge, UK: Cambridge University Press.

Sykes, G. (1958). *Society of Captives*. Princeton, NJ: Princeton University Press.

Tita, G. K., Riley, J., and Greenwood, P. (2003). "From Boston to Boyle Heights: The Process and Prospects of a 'Pulling Levers' Strategy in a Los Angeles Barrio." In S. H. Decker (Ed.), *Policing Gangs and Youth Violence*. Newbury Park, CA: Wadsworth. pp. 102–30.

Toch, H. and Grant, J. D. (1982). *Reforming Human Services: Change through Participation*. Beverly Hills, CA: Sage.

Tonry, M. (1997). "Building Better Policies on Better Knowledge." In L. Robinson (Ed.), *The Challenge of Crime in a Free Society: Looking Back, Looking Forward*. Washington, DC: Office of Justice Programs. pp. 93–124.

Turnbull, A. P., Friesen, B. J., and Ramirez, C. (1998). "Participatory Action Research as a Model for Conducting Family Research." *Journal of the Association for Persons with Severe Handicaps*, 23, 178–88.

Ulmer, J. (1997). *The Social Worlds of Sentencing: Court Communities under Sentencing Guidelines*. Albany, NY: SUNY Press.

United States Census Bureau. (2000). "United States Census 2000." Retrieved November 15, 2005, from http://www.census.gov/main/www/cen2000.html.

United States Department of Justice. (1998). *The Challenge of Crime in a Free Society: Looking Back, Looking Forward—Symposium on the 30th Anniversary of the President's Commission on Law Enforcement and Administration of Justice* (NCJ 170029). Washington, DC: U.S. Department of Justice, Office of Justice Programs. Retrieved November 23, 2009, from http://www.ncjrs.gov/pdffiles1/nij/170029.pdf.

United States Department of Justice. (2001). *Toolkit: Project Safe Neighborhoods—America's Network against Gun Violence*. Washington, DC: United States Department of Justice, Office of the Attorney General.

United States Department of Justice. (2007). *Ten Site PSN Comprehensive Anti-Gang Initiative*. Washington, DC: United States Department of Justice.

Viswanathan, M., Ammerman, A., Eng, E., Gartlehner, G., Lohr, K. N., Griffith, D., Rhodes, S., Samuel-Hodge, C., Maty, S., Lux, L., Webb, L., Sutton, S. F., Swinson, T., Jackman, A., and Whitener, L. (2004). *Community-Based Participatory Research: Assessing the Evidence*. Evidence Report/Technology Assessment No. 99. Prepared by RTI-University of North Carolina Evidence-Based Practice Center under Contract No. 290-02-0016. AHRQ Publication 04-E022-2. Rockville, MD: Agency for Healthcare Research and Quality.

Waegel, W. B. (1981). "Case Routinization in Police Work." *Social Problems*, 28, 263–75.

Walker, S. (1977). *A Critical History of Police Reform*. Lexington, MA: Lexington Books.

Walker, S. (1978). "Reexamining the President's Crime Commission." *Crime & Delinquency*, 24, 1–12.

Walker, S. (1988). *Sense and Nonsense about Crime*. Belmont, CA: Wadsworth.

Warren, R. (1972). *The Community in America*. Chicago, IL: Rand McNally.

Warren, R. (1978). *Community in America*, 3rd edition. Chicago, IL: Rand McNally.

Webb, V. and Katz, C. (2003). "Policing Gangs in an Era of Community Policing." In S. H. Decker (Ed.), *Policing Gangs and Youth Violence*. Belmont, CA: Thomson and Wadsworth Publishing. pp. 17–49.

Weisburd, D. (1994). "Evaluating Community Policing: Role Tensions between Practitioners and Evaluators." In D. Rosenbaum (Ed.), *The Challenge of Community Policing: Testing the Promises*. Thousand Oaks, CA: Sage Publications. pp. 278–84.

Weisburd, D. and Braga, A. A. (Eds.). (2006). *Police Innovation: Contrasting Perspectives*. Cambridge, MA: Cambridge University Press.

Weisburd, D., Mastrofski, S., McNally, A. A., Greenspan, R., and Willis, J. J. (2003). "Reforming Top Preserve: COMSTAT and Strategic Problem Solving in American Policing." *Criminology and Public Policy*, (3), 421–56.

Whitten, J. L. and Bentley, L. D. (2005). *Introduction to Systems Analysis and Design*. New York: McGraw-Hill.

Williams, E. (2007). Personal communication with Chicago Police Department Deputy Superintendent.

Willis, C. L. (1983). "Criminal Justice Theory: A Case of Trained Incapacity." *Journal of Criminal Justice*, 11 (5), 447–58.

Wilson, J. Q. and Kelling, G. L. (1982, March). "Broken Windows: The Police and Neighborhood Safety." *Atlantic Monthly*, 249 (3), 29–42.

Withrow, B., Weible, K., and Bonnett, J. (2004). "Aren't They All the Same? A Comparative Analysis of Introductory Criminal Justice Textbooks." *Journal of Criminal Justice*, 15 (1), 1–18.

Worden, A. P. (2007). "Courts and Communities: Toward a Theoretical Synthesis." In D. E. Duffee and E. R. Maguire (Eds.), *Criminal Justice Theory: Explaining the Nature and Behavior of Criminal Justice*. New York: Routledge. pp. 181–216.

Wright, K. (2004). "The Desirability of Goal Conflict within the Criminal Justice Systems." In S. Stojkovic, J. Klofas, and D. Kalinich (Eds.), *The Administration and Management of Criminal Justice Organizations*. Prospect Heights, IL: Waveland. pp. 457–77.

Zalman, M. (1981). *A Heuristic Model of Criminology and Criminal Justice*. Chicago, IL: Joint Committee on Criminal Justice Education and Standards.

Zimmermann, C. A. (2006). "Federal Incentives to Address Gun Violence: A Model of Success and Failure." Unpublished doctoral dissertation. Michigan State University, East Lansing, MI.

CONTRIBUTORS

Anthony Braga, Ph.D., is a Lecturer in Public Policy at Harvard University's John F. Kennedy School of Government and Senior Research Fellow in the Berkeley Center for Criminal Justice at the University of California, Berkeley. He currently serves as the Chief Policy Advisor to the Boston Police Commissioner. Braga's research focuses on developing problem-oriented policing strategies to prevent gang violence, disrupt illegal gun markets, and address violent crime hot spots. He has served as a consultant on these issues to police departments in numerous cities—including Los Angeles, New York, Minneapolis, and Baltimore—as well as the U.S. Department of Justice and the U.S. National Academy of Sciences. Braga was a Visiting Fellow at the U.S. National Institute of Justice and teaches in the Police Executive Research Forum's Senior Management Institute for Police. He received his MPA from Harvard University and Ph.D. in Criminal Justice from Rutgers University.

Timothy S. Bynum, Ph.D., is a Professor in the School of Criminal Justice at Michigan State University as well as the Director of the National Archive of Criminal Justice Data at the University of Michigan. He is the former Associate Director of the Institute of Public Policy and Social Research at Michigan State, where he directed the Evaluation Research Division. He is the co-director of an initiative to provide training, technical assistance, and research in support of Project Safe Neighborhoods. In addition, he is the co-director of the evaluation of DOJ's Comprehensive Anti-Gang Initiative. He is a former visiting fellow with the COPS Office, where he authored the monograph *Using Analysis for Problem Solving: A Guide for Law Enforcement*. His principal research interests are focused upon the evaluation of public policies and interventions in crime and justice. He has served on the evaluation team for a number of major national initiatives including Weed and Seed, the Federal Sentencing Guidelines, the Juvenile Accountability Block Grant Program, the Youth Firearms Violence Initiative, and the Gang Reduction Program.

Nicholas Corsaro, Ph.D., is an Assistant Professor in the Department of Criminology and Criminal Justice at Southern Illinois University–Carbondale. He received his Ph.D. from the School of Criminal Justice at Michigan State University in 2007. His research focuses on the implementation and evaluation of crime prevention strategies, pulling levers policing, and quantitative analytical techniques. He is the author of several scholarly articles, which most recently appear in *Crime & Delinquency*, *Journal of Experimental Criminology*, *Victims & Offenders*, and *Justice Quarterly*.

Kristen Di Luca earned her Master of Arts Degree in Sociology from UNC Greensboro in 2006 and her Bachelor of Arts Degree in Psychology from Humboldt State University in 1998. She currently serves as Assistant Director for the Center for Youth, Family, and Community Partnerships at the University of North Carolina at Greensboro. Kristen brings six years of experience working with communities across the Middle District of North Carolina in implementing focused deterrence gun and gang violence reduction strategies. She is a strong advocate for building sustainable, community-based approaches to violence reduction through implementation of comprehensive evidence-based prevention, intervention, and suppression strategies. Her current projects include evaluation of overt drug market interventions, Project Safe Neighborhoods comprehensive partnerships, gang violence reduction models, statewide community-based re-entry initiatives, and youth violence prevention efforts as well as supporting training and technical assistance across the state of North Carolina for sites implementing focused deterrence group violence reduction models.

James M. Frabutt, Ph.D., is a faculty member in the Mary Ann Remick Leadership Program in the Alliance for Catholic Education, and Concurrent Associate Professor of Psychology at the University of Notre Dame. He previously served as Deputy Director of the Center for Youth, Family, and Community Partnerships at the University of North Carolina at Greensboro. He has employed action-oriented, community-based research approaches to areas such as juvenile delinquency prevention, school-based mental health, teacher/administrator inquiry, racial disparities in the juvenile justice system, and community violence reduction. He currently serves as an Associate Editor of the *Journal of Community Engagement and Higher Education*.

Jack R. Greene, Ph.D., is Professor and former Dean of the College of Criminal Justice at Northeastern University in Boston, where he led academic and research programs focused on matters of criminology and justice policy. An expert on matters of police service delivery, community approaches to policing, crime prevention, and police management, Greene has written widely, as author/editor of five books, a two-volume *Encyclopedia of Police Science*, and over 100 research articles, book chapters, research reports, and policy papers on matters of policing in the United States and internationally. Dr. Greene is a Fellow of the Academy of Criminal Justice Sciences and has been a consultant to major police and governmental agencies throughout his career. He was also a Commissioner on the Commission for the Accreditation of Law Enforcement Agencies. He is currently co-editing *Criminologists on Terrorism* (Cambridge University Press) with colleagues Brian Forst and James Lynch, and is working on a book tentatively entitled *Re-Imagining Policing in the Millennium*.

Lynn K. Harvey, Ph.D., is Associate Professor of Sociology and Interim Chair of the Department of Behavioral Sciences and Social Work at Winston-Salem State University (WSSU) in Winston-Salem, North Carolina. He has been affiliated with WSSU's Center for Community Safety since its opening in January 2001, and he led the university's Justice Studies program through its first two years. Through the Center Dr. Harvey's work has focused on the evaluation of community-based initiatives and research on domestic violence.

Marianne Hinkle, JD, was a federal prosecutor at the time of the writing of Chapter 11.

Natalie Kroovand Hipple, Ph.D., is a Research Specialist at the School of Criminal Justice at Michigan State University. Hipple's research focuses on several federally funded projects including the Drug Market Initiative and the Comprehensive Anti-Gang Initiative. She is an instructor for the DHS-funded Intelligence Training Program and teaches for the online Master's in Law Enforcement Intelligence program. Additional areas of research include restorative justice, arrestee drug abuse monitoring, evaluation of criminal justice programs, inmate re-entry, crime analysis, and attitudes toward crime and justice. Hipple has published numerous articles and reports, the most recent in *Justice Quarterly* and *Policing: An International Journal of Police Strategies & Management*. Previously, she was the Director of the Crime Control Policy Center at Indianapolis-based Hudson Institute. Dr. Hipple has a Ph.D. in Criminal Justice from Indiana University.

John M. Klofas, Ph.D., is Professor of Criminal Justice, Chairperson of the Department of Criminal Justice at Rochester Institute of Technology, and Director of the Center for Public Safety Initiatives (CPSI). He received his Ph.D. in Criminal Justice from the University at Albany. He has worked closely with the Rochester Mayor, Rochester Police, and other local criminal justice agencies for over a decade. His research has involved communities and justice, management in criminal justice, and corrections. He is particularly interested in the application of action research in the field of criminal justice.

Edmund F. McGarrell, Ph.D., is Director and Professor of the School of Criminal Justice at Michigan State University. McGarrell has been the Principal Investigator of an initiative sponsored by the National Institute of Justice (NIJ) whereby the School of Criminal Justice served as the national research team for Project Safe Neighborhoods. Grants from NIJ and the Bureau of Justice Assistance (BJA) extend this research to an evaluation of gang violence reduction and drug market violence reduction initiatives. McGarrell has conducted several long-term research projects including an experiment on the use of restorative justice conferences as an alternative response to juvenile crime and a strategic problem-solving initiative to reduce homicide and firearms violence. He is a Fellow of the Academy of Experimental Criminology. Recent articles appear in the *British Journal of Criminology, Crime and Delinquency, Justice Quarterly, Journal of Experimental Criminology*, and *Policing*.

Lois Felson Mock is a retired Senior Social Scientist in the Office of Research and Evaluation at the National Institute of Justice, U.S. Department of Justice. She joined the Institute in 1972 and has been involved in criminal justice research for over 35 years, retiring in December 2007. Her areas of expertise have ranged from crime prevention and white collar and organized crime to firearms, violence, policing, and terrorism, and she has written numerous papers, articles, and reports on these topics throughout her career. She created and managed NIJ's extensive research program in firearms violence from its inception in 1980 until her retirement and she has been actively involved in policing research throughout these years, as well, more recently focusing on the police role in terrorism prevention and response. In addition, during the last decade, she has become an active participant in and promoter of "action research"—comprehensive strategic problem-solving programs in which researchers and practitioners work as partners to reduce crime and increase security in their communities. As part of this support, she served as a core federal team member, planning and coordinating the implementation of Project Safe Neighborhoods, a major Department of Justice initiative to reduce gun violence nationwide. Lois Mock has been an active member of the American Society of Criminology and the Academy of Criminal Justice Sciences during her career, as well as the Homicide Research Working Group and the International Association for the Study of

Organized Crime. She completed her undergraduate work at Oberlin College and her graduate work at the University of Michigan.

Heather Perez is an Outreach Specialist for Project Safe Neighborhoods, the Comprehensive Anti-Gang Initiative, and the Drug Market Intervention Training Initiative. Her duties and responsibilities include, but are not limited to, coding and tracking site activities and reports, providing training and technical assistance both on site and off, report writing, conducting telephone and face-to-face interviews, collecting and analyzing data, and conference and training planning and attendance. Before joining the research faculty at Michigan State University (MSU), School of Criminal Justice, Ms Perez has carried out consulting work for a wide variety of criminal justice agencies as well as working for the National Criminal Justice Reference Service (NCJRS) and the Institute for Law and Justice (ILJ). Ms. Perez is also a Lead Interviewer/Site Supervisor for the Arrestee Drug and Alcohol Monitoring (ADAM) project, formerly known as the Drug Use Forecasting (DUF) Project. With a Master's Degree in Criminal Justice from the University of Nebraska at Omaha (UNO), Ms. Perez has over 13 years' experience with evaluation research and design and has published in scholarly journals including the *International Journal of Comparative and Applied Criminal Justice*.

Jan Roehl, Ph.D., has conducted justice-related research for over 30 years, studying partnerships, community policing, drug courts, crime prevention, domestic violence, and dispute resolution. Dr. Roehl is currently participating in the third national evaluation of the Weed and Seed Program funded by the Department of Justice, and provides consulting services in grant writing and program evaluation to nonprofits and local units of government. She received her Ph.D. in Social Psychology at George Washington University in Washington, DC.

Dennis Rosenbaum, Ph.D. in Psychology, is Professor of Criminology, Law and Justice and Director of the Center for Research in Law and Justice at the University of Illinois at Chicago. Previously he served in the positions of Department Head and Dean. His areas of research expertise include police organizations, community policing, community crime prevention, school-based drug prevention, multi-agency partnerships, and program evaluation methods. Dr. Rosenbaum is a Fellow in the Academy of Experimental Criminology and represents the United States on the Scientific Committee of the International Center for the Prevention of Crime.

Wesley G. Skogan, Ph.D., is a Professor of Political Science and a Faculty Fellow at the Institute for Policy Research Northwestern University. Skogan's research has focused on victimization, fear of crime, the impact of crime on communities, public involvement in crime prevention, and policing. His books on Chicago police include *Police and Community in Chicago* (2006), *On the Beat: Police and Community Problem Solving* (1999), and *Community Policing, Chicago Style* (1997). In 2003 he edited *Community Policing: Can It Work?*, a collection of original essays on innovation in policing. His 1990 book, *Disorder and Decline*, won the 1991 Distinguished Scholar Award of the Section on Crime and Deviance of the American Sociological Association. Skogan has been a technical consultant for the Home Office Research Unit of Great Britain and a Senior Fellow of the Open Societies Institute. Earlier he spent two years at the NIJ, as a Visiting Fellow. He is a fellow of the American Society of Criminology. In the 2000s, he chaired a Committee on Police Policies and Practices for the National Research Council. He was a co-author of the committee report, which appeared as a book, *Fairness and the Effectiveness in Policing: The Evidence*, from the Academies Press in 2004.

INDEX